My Neighbor Seki **1**

Tonari no Seki-kun

Takuma
Morishige

Schedule

My
Neighbor
Seki

1

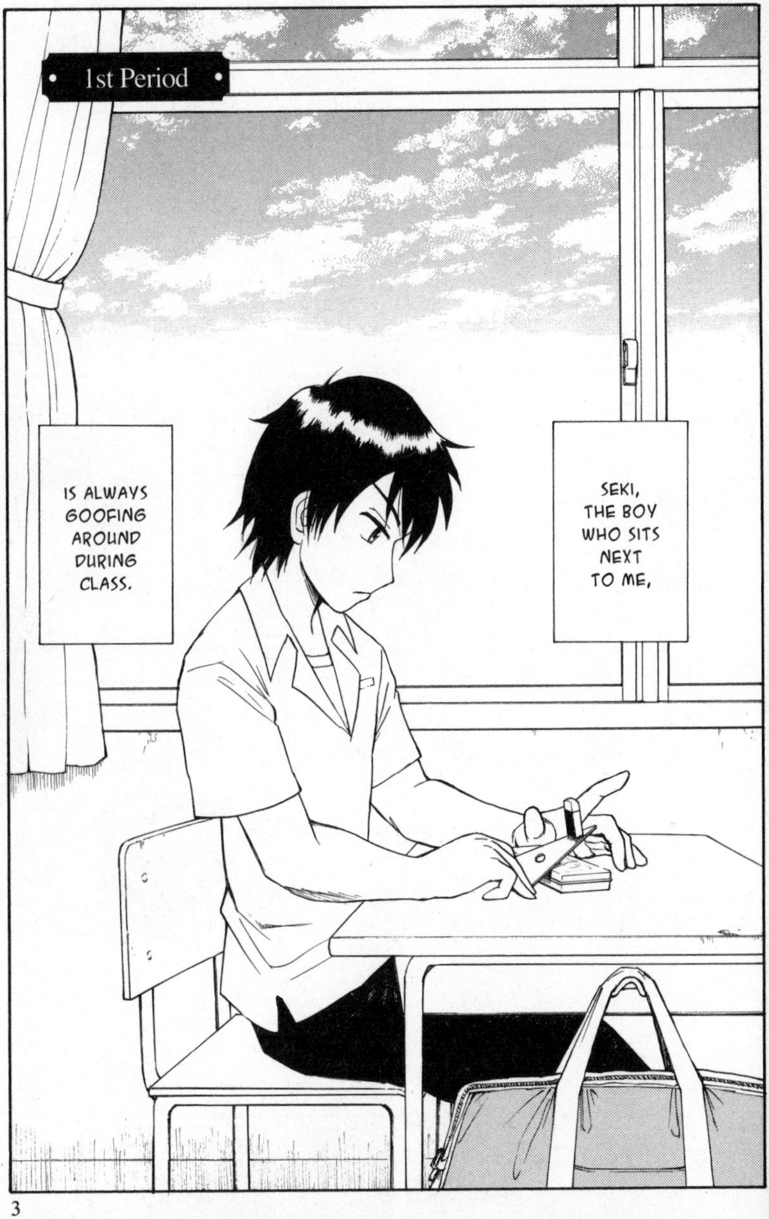
1st Period
SEKI, THE BOY WHO SITS NEXT TO ME,
IS ALWAYS GOOFING AROUND DURING CLASS.

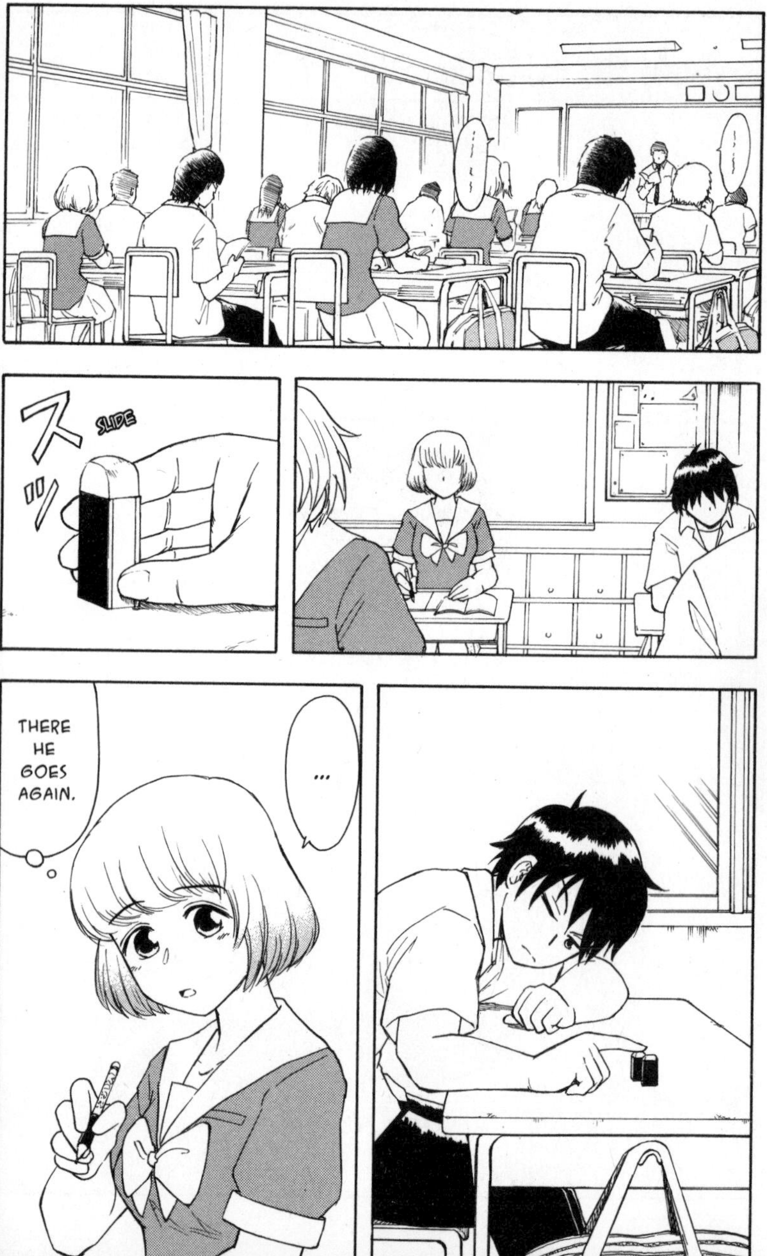
スッ
SLIDE
...
THERE HE GOES AGAIN.

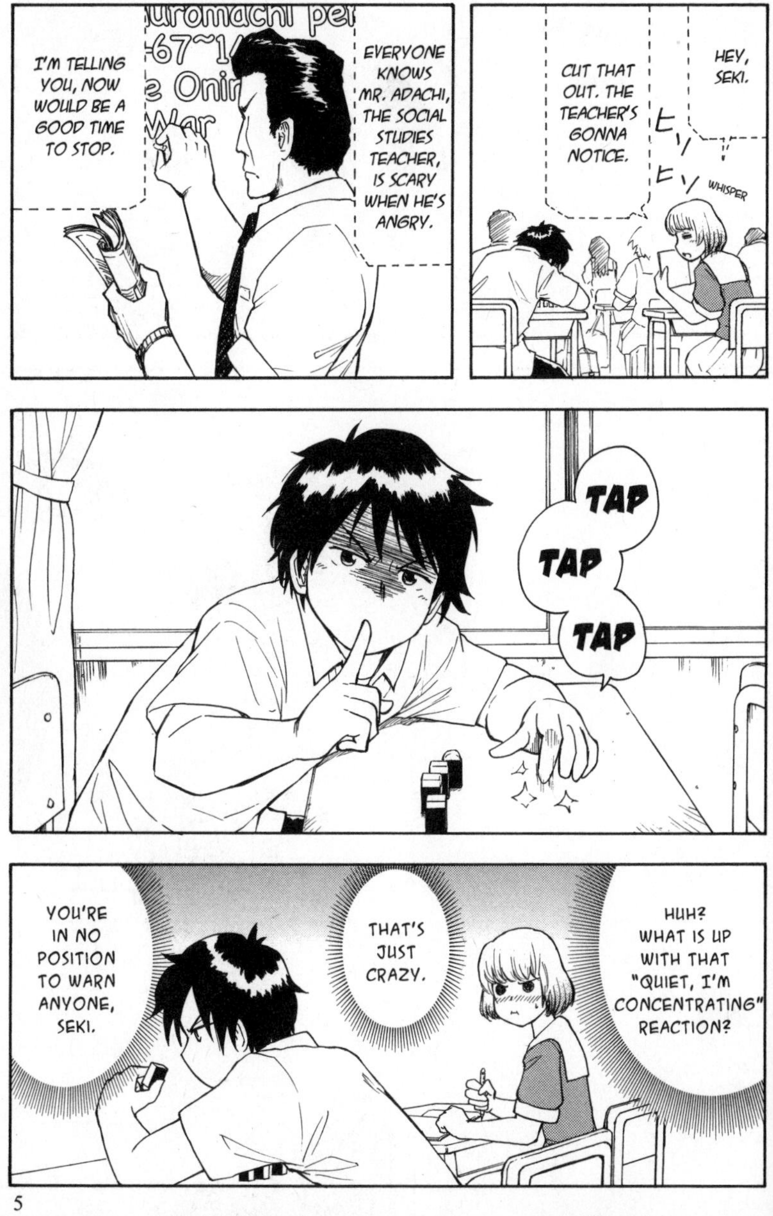
HEY, SEKI.
CUT THAT OUT. THE TEACHER'S GONNA NOTICE.
WHISPER
EVERYONE KNOWS MR. ADACHI, THE SOCIAL STUDIES TEACHER, IS SCARY WHEN HE'S ANGRY.
I'M TELLING YOU, NOW WOULD BE A GOOD TIME TO STOP.
TAP
TAP
TAP
HUH? WHAT IS UP WITH THAT "QUIET, I'M CONCENTRATING" REACTION?
THAT'S JUST CRAZY.
YOU'RE IN NO POSITION TO WARN ANYONE, SEKI.

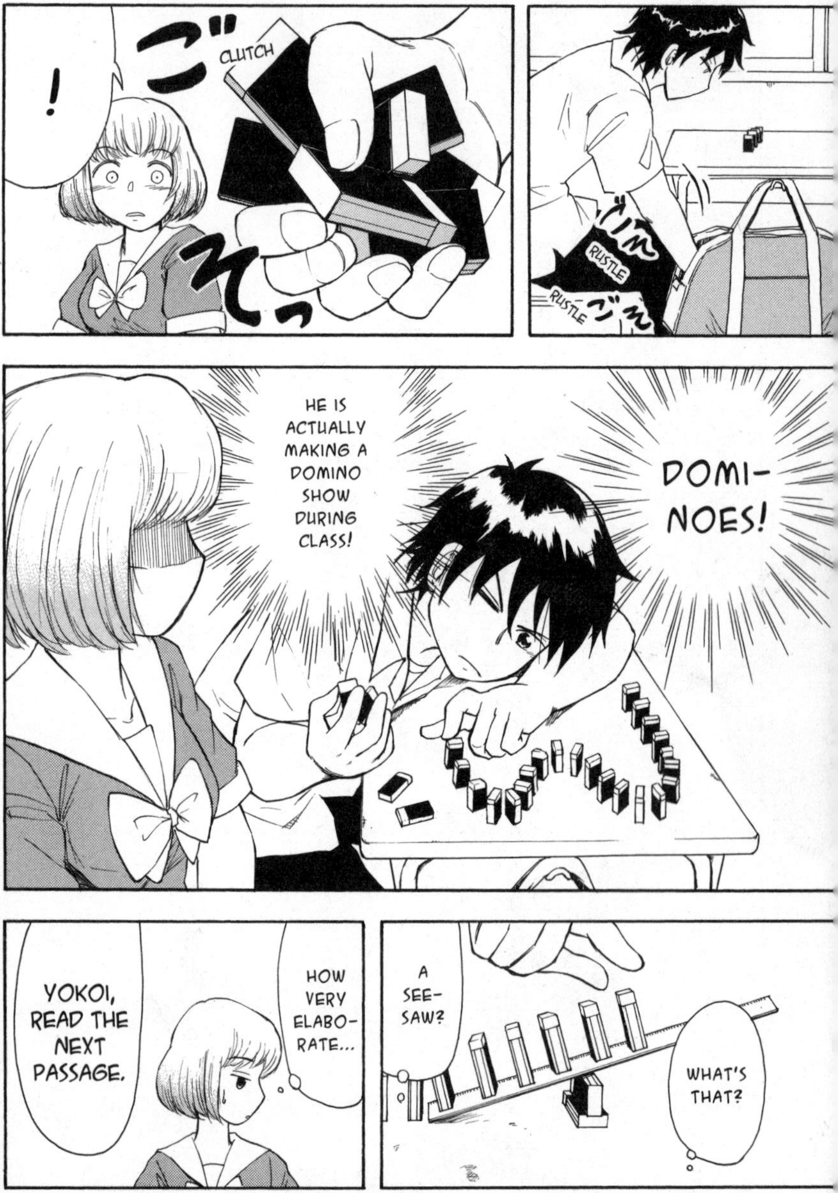
ごそ
RUSTLE
ごそ
RUSTLE
!
ご
CLUTCH
そっ
DOMI-NOES!
HE IS ACTUALLY MAKING A DOMINO SHOW DURING CLASS!
WHAT'S THAT?
A SEE-SAW?
HOW VERY ELABO-RATE...
YOKOI, READ THE NEXT PASSAGE.

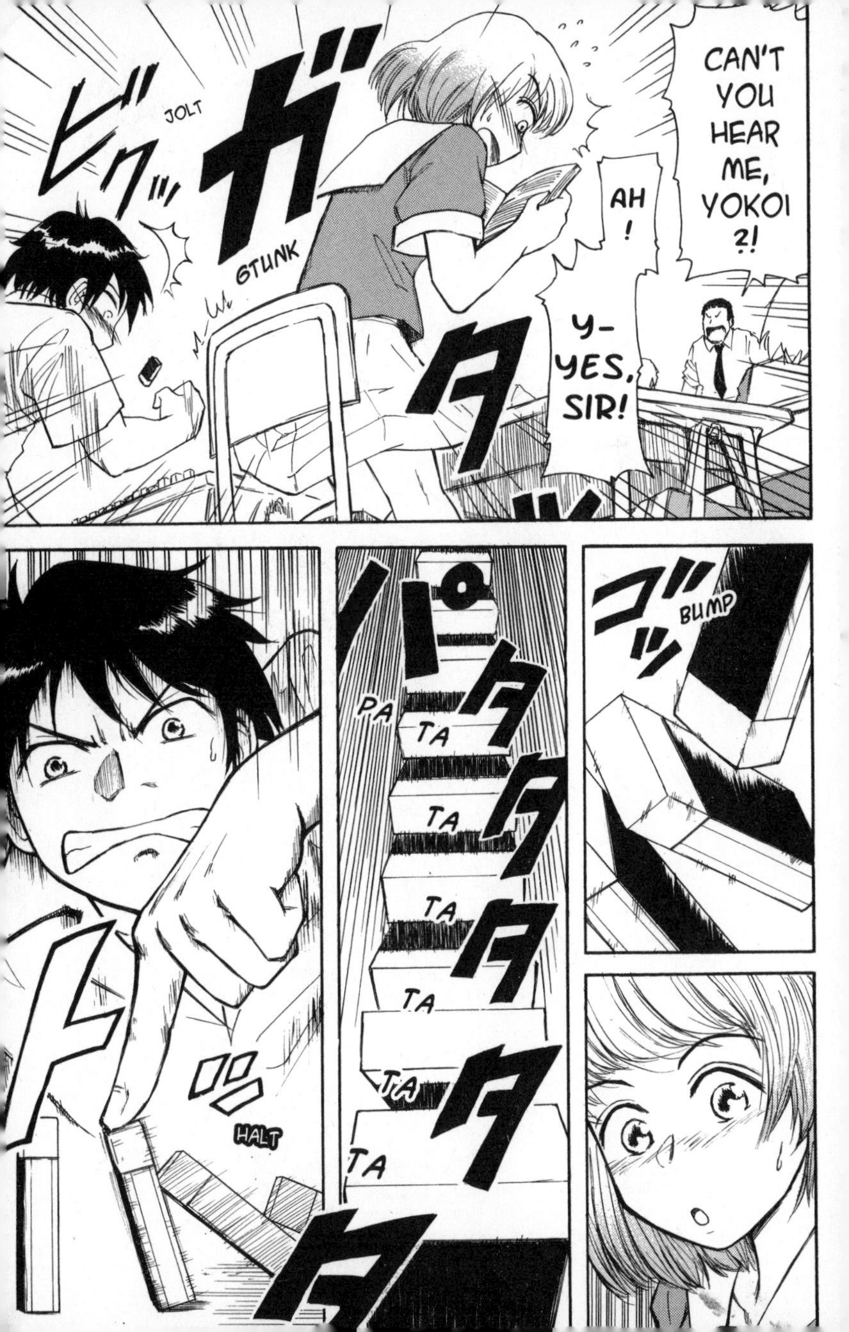
CAN'T YOU HEAR ME, YOKOI ?!
AH !
Y-YES, SIR!
GTUNK
JOLT
BUMP
PA TA TA TA TA TA TA
HALT

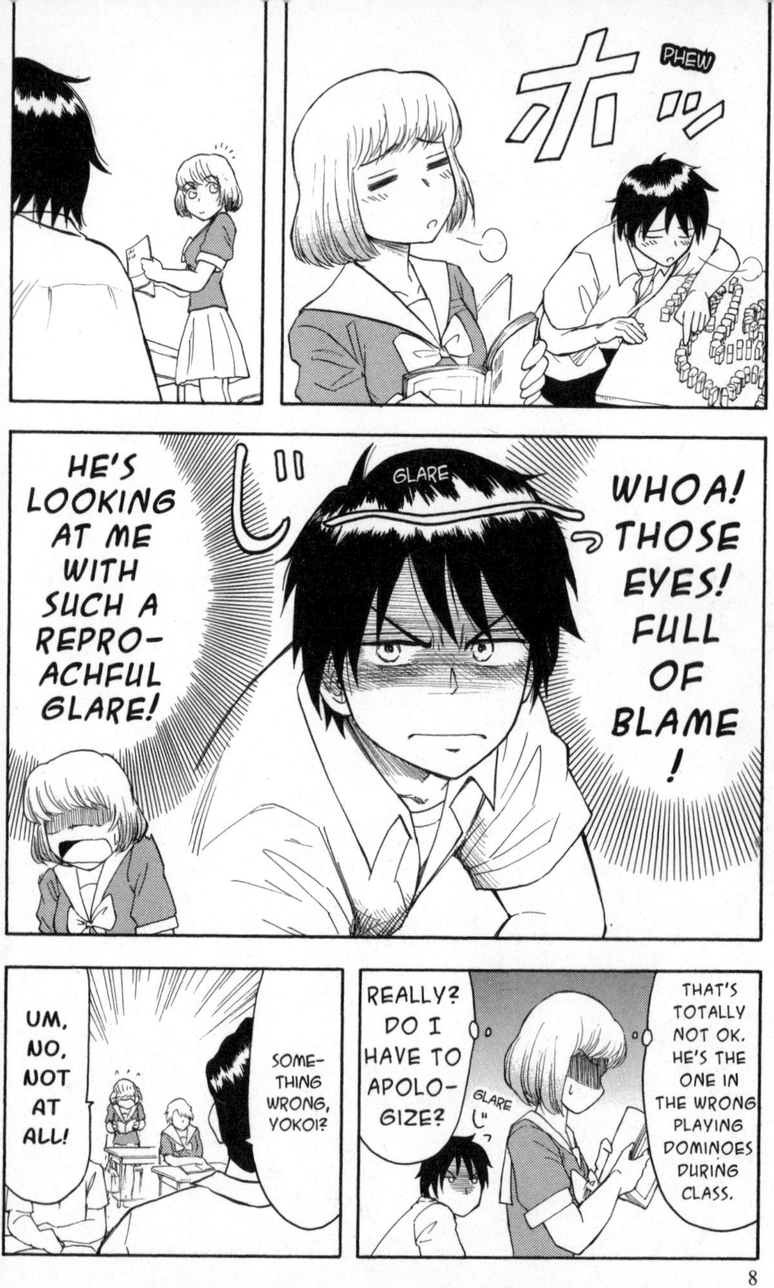
PHEW
ホッ
GLARE
WHOA! THOSE EYES! FULL OF BLAME!
HE'S LOOKING AT ME WITH SUCH A REPRO-ACHFUL GLARE!
THAT'S TOTALLY NOT OK. HE'S THE ONE IN THE WRONG PLAYING DOMINOES DURING CLASS.
REALLY? DO I HAVE TO APOLO-GIZE?
GLARE
SOME-THING WRONG, YOKOI!?
UM. NO. NOT AT ALL!

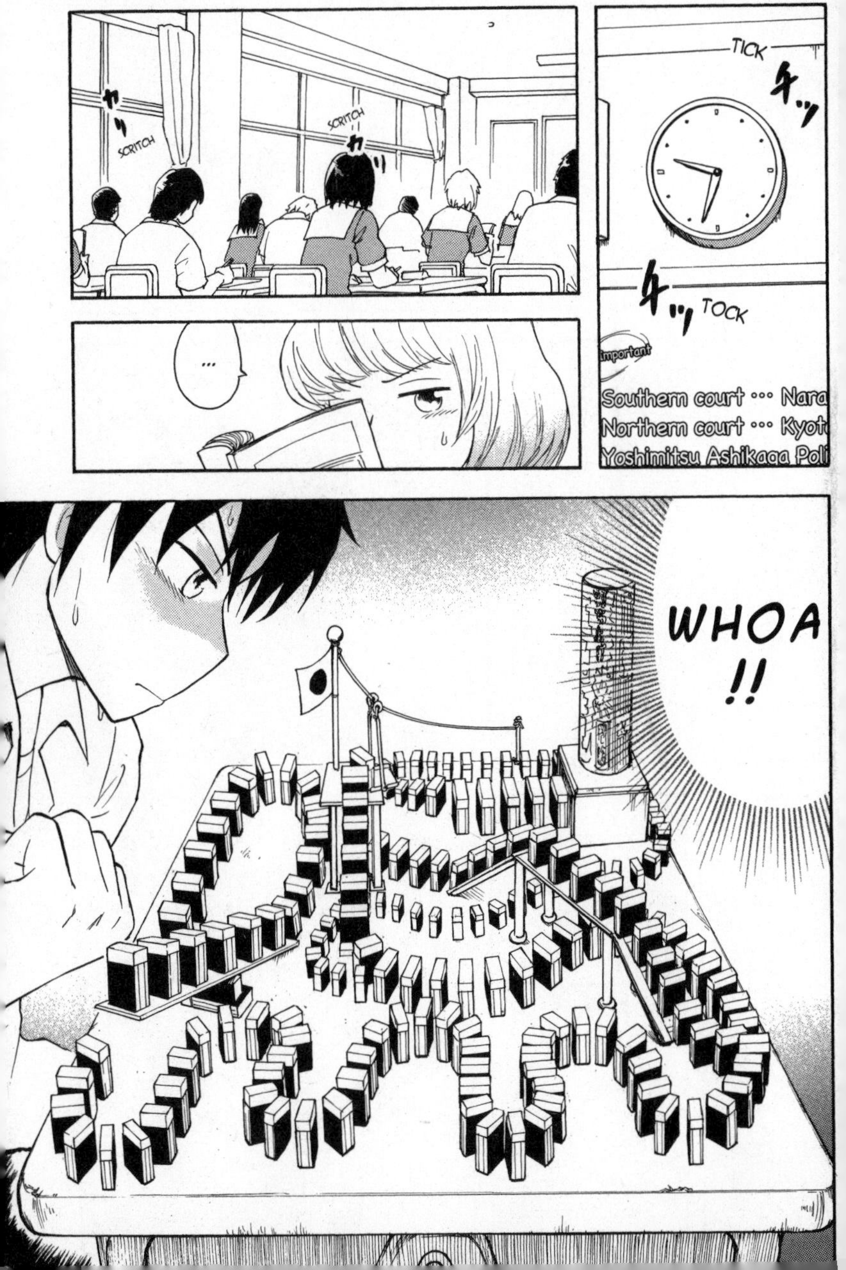
TICK
チッ
チッ
TOCK
Important
Southern court ··· Nara
Northern court ··· Kyot
Yoshimitsu Ashikaga Poli
カリ
SCRITCH
SCRITCH
カリ
...
WHOA !!

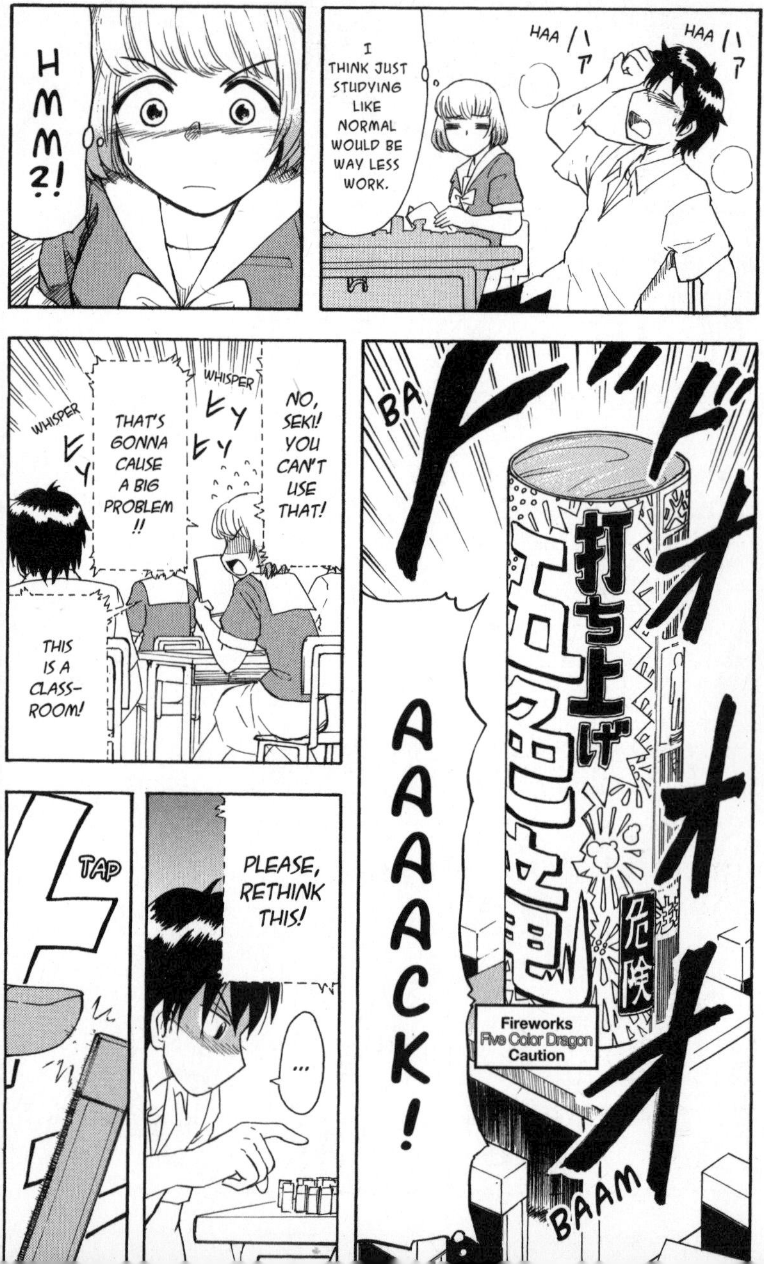
HAA ハア
HAA ハア
I THINK JUST STUDYING LIKE NORMAL WOULD BE WAY LESS WORK.
HMMM?!
BA
ドドオオオ
打ち上げ
五色竜
危険
Fireworks
Five Color Dragon
Caution
AAAACK!
BAAM
WHISPER ヒソ
NO, SEKI! YOU CAN'T USE THAT!
WHISPER ヒソ
THAT'S GONNA CAUSE A BIG PROBLEM!!
THIS IS A CLASS-ROOM!
PLEASE, RETHINK THIS!
...
TAP

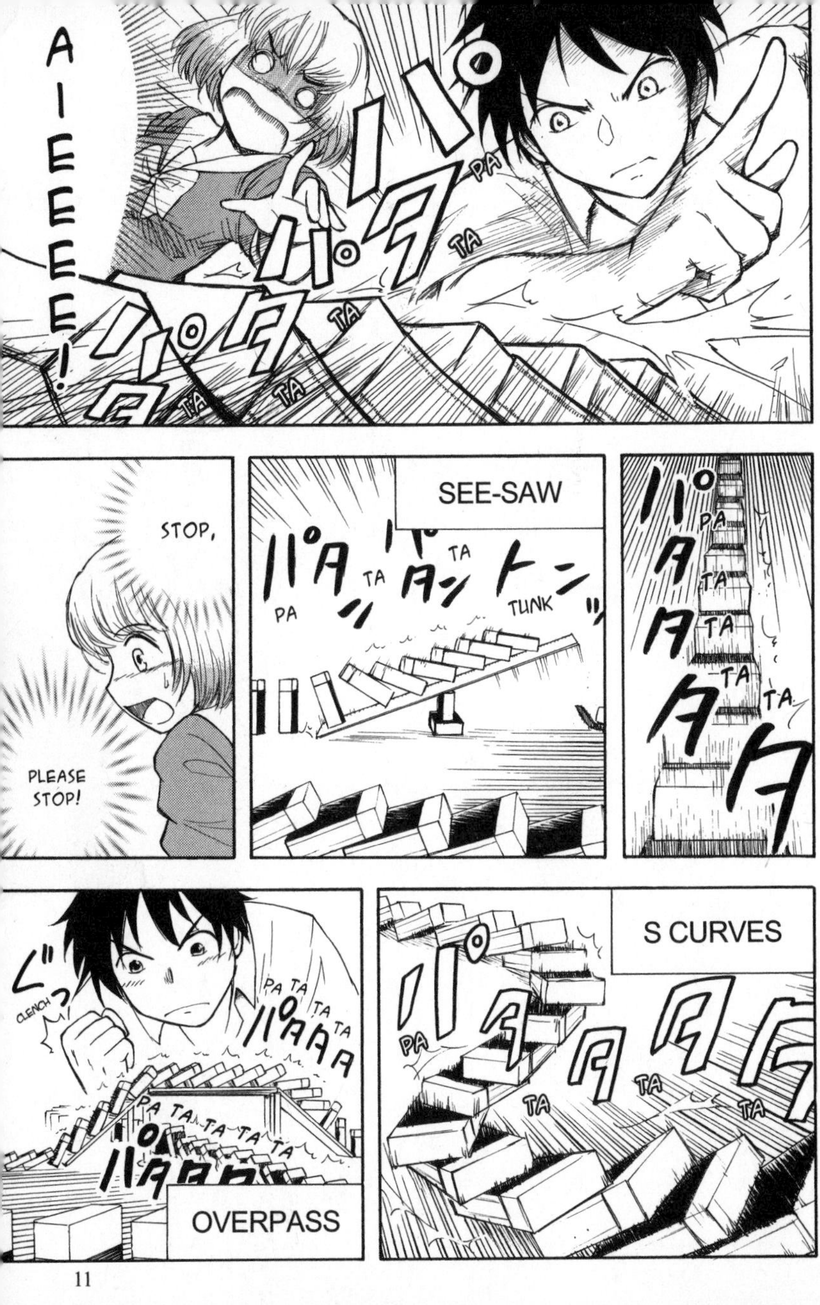
PA
TA
TA
TA
TA
AIEEEEE!
PA
TA
TA
TA
TA
SEE-SAW
TA
TA
PA
TUNK
STOP,
PLEASE STOP!
S CURVES
PA
TA
TA
TA
PA TA TA TA TA
CLENCH
PA TA TA TA TA
OVERPASS

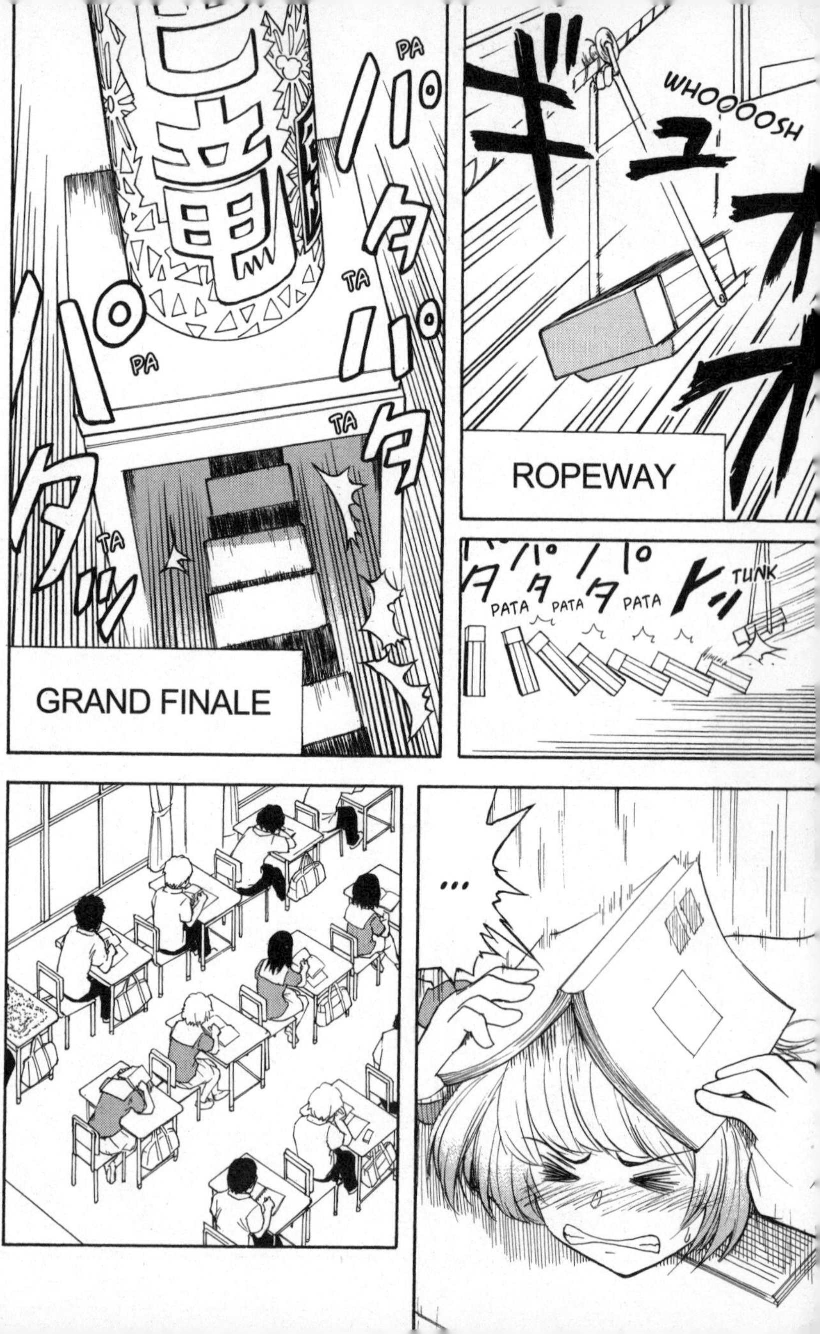
WHOOOOSH
ROPEWAY
PATA
PATA
PATA
TUNK
PA
TA
PA
TA
PA
TA
TA
GRAND FINALE
...

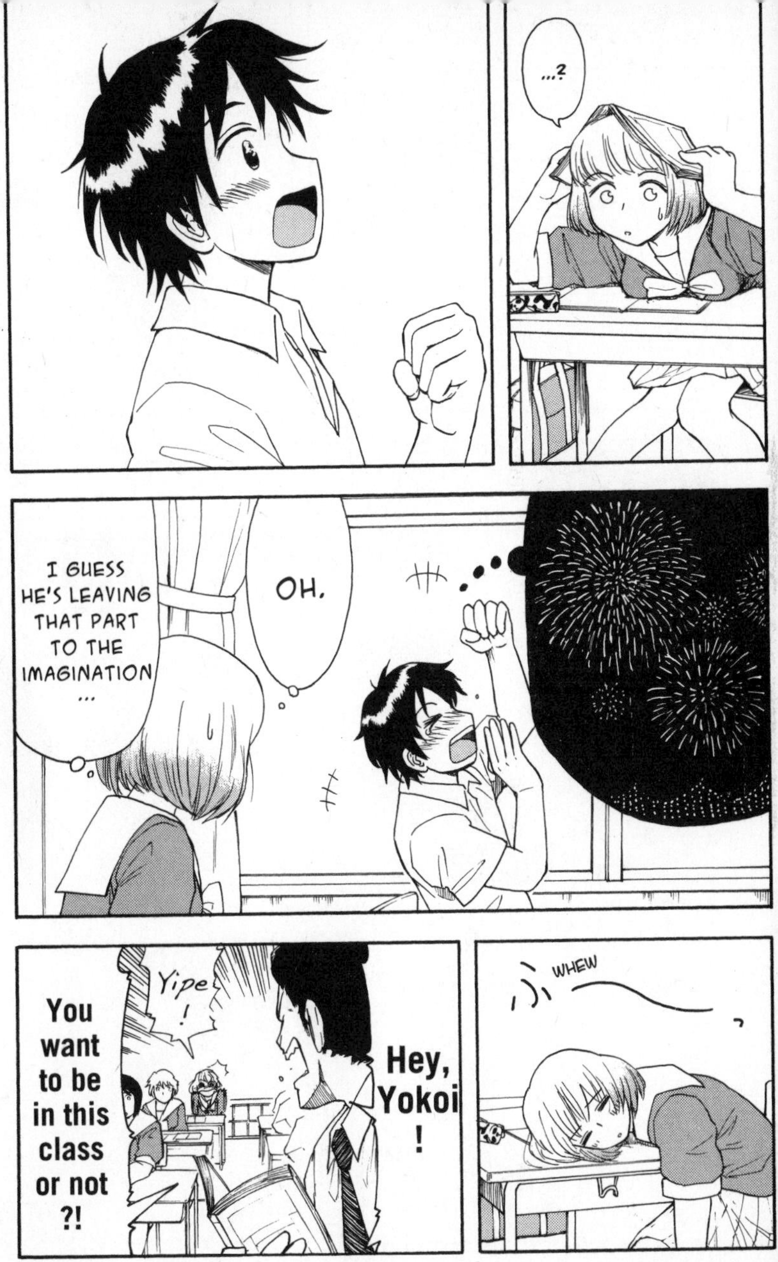
...?
OH.
I GUESS HE'S LEAVING THAT PART TO THE IMAGINATION ...
WHEW
Hey, Yokoi!
Yipe!
You want to be in this class or not?!

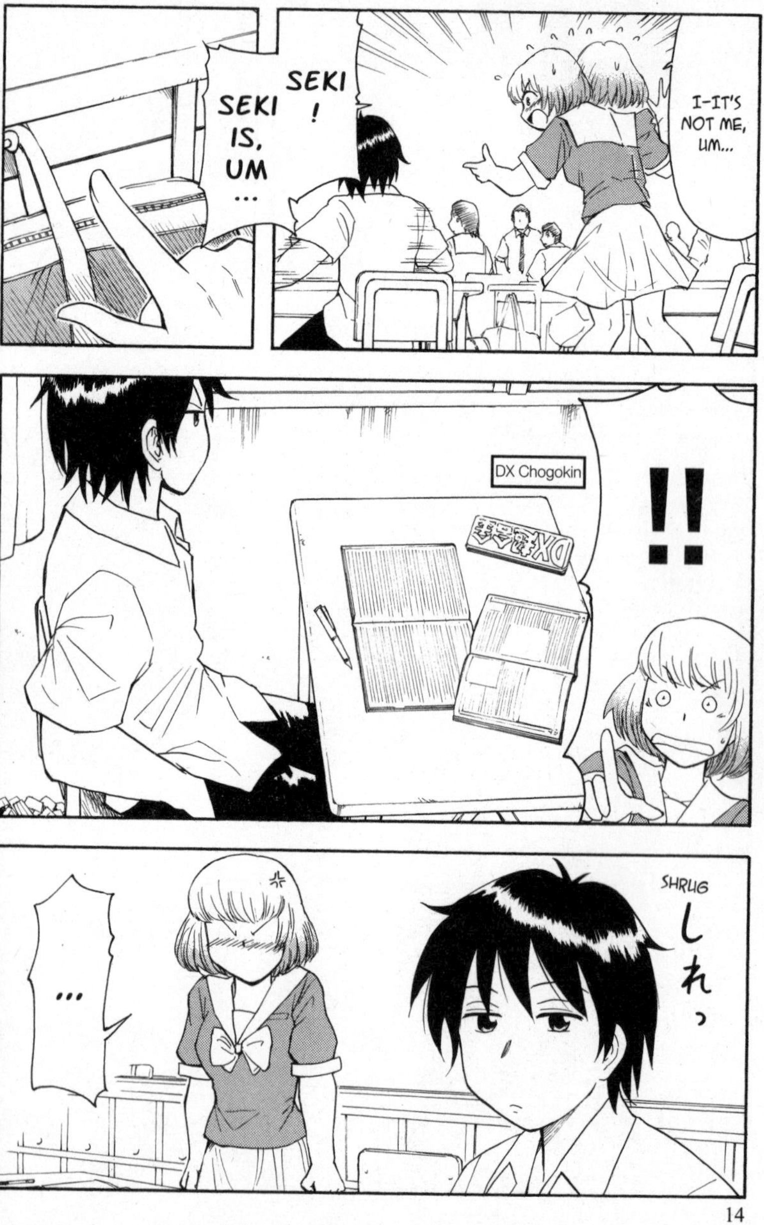
I-IT'S NOT ME, UM...
SEKI !
SEKI IS, UM ...
!!
DX Chogokin
DX超合金
SHRUG
しれっ
...

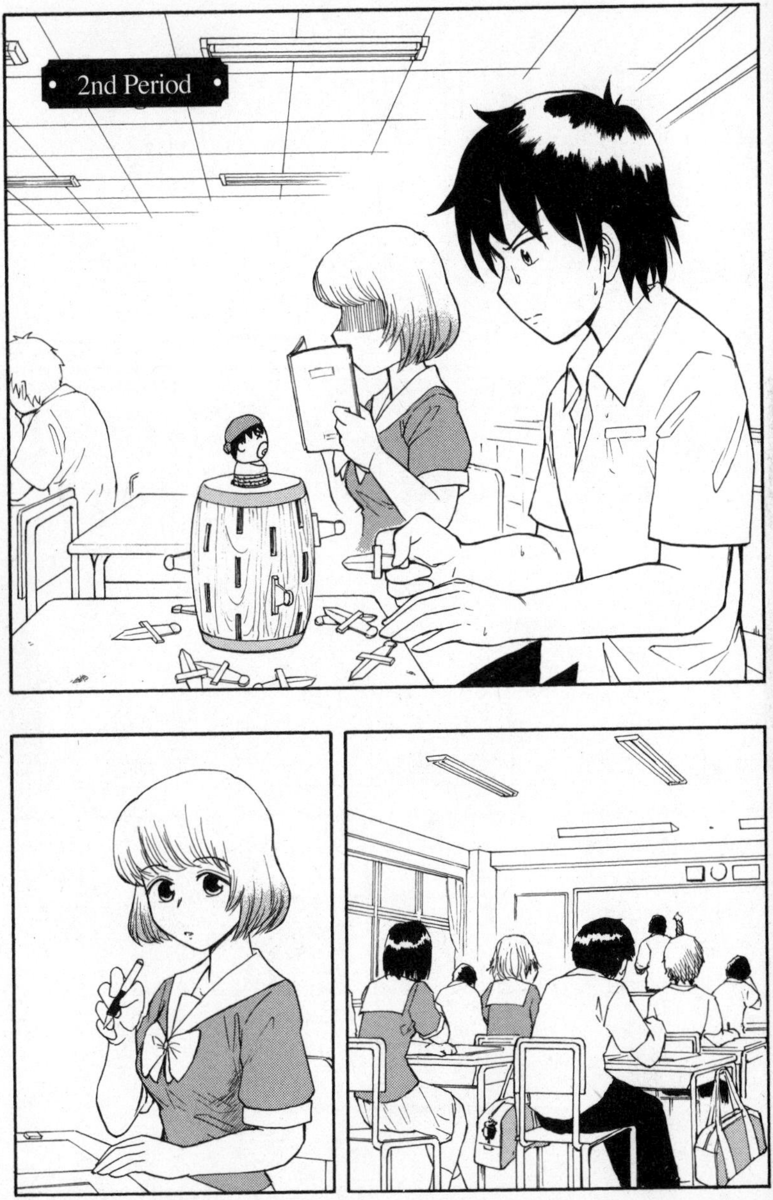
2nd Period

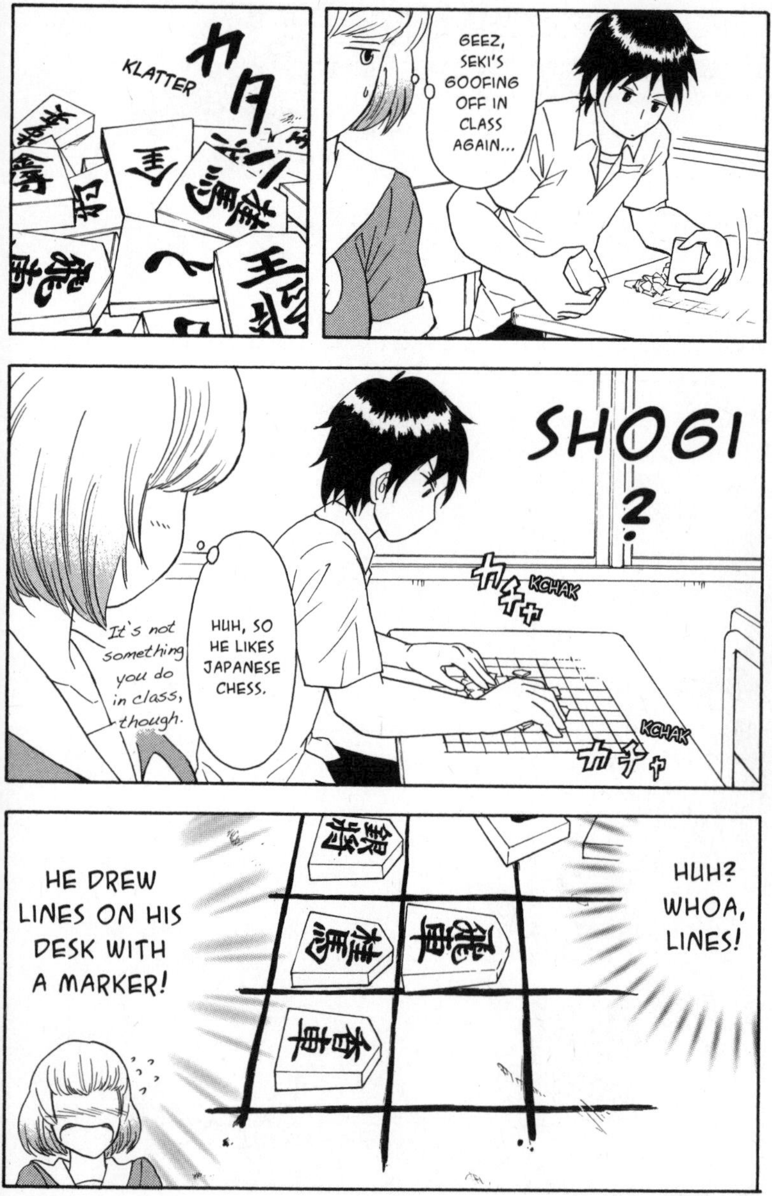
GEEZ, SEKI'S GOOFING OFF IN CLASS AGAIN...
KLATTER
SHOGI?
KCHAK
HUH, SO HE LIKES JAPANESE CHESS.
It's not something you do in class, though.
KCHAK
HUH? WHOA, LINES!
HE DREW LINES ON HIS DESK WITH A MARKER!

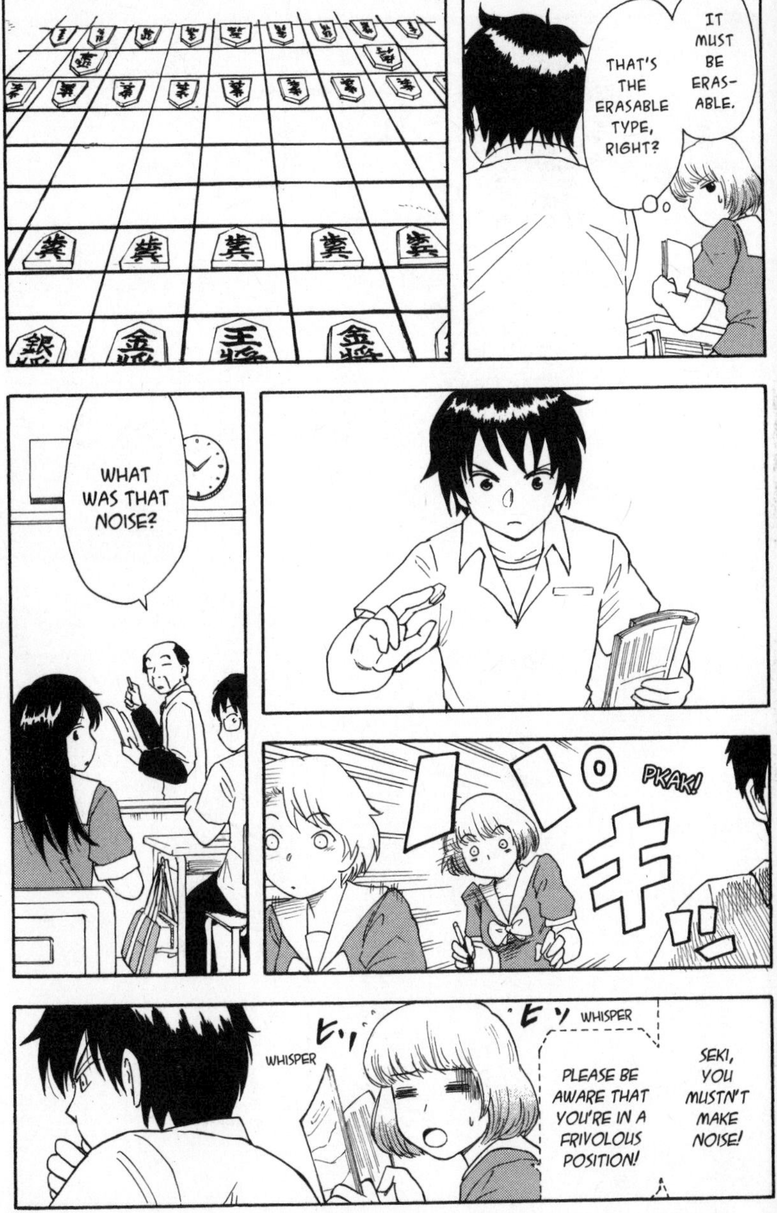
IT MUST BE ERASABLE.
THAT'S THE ERASABLE TYPE, RIGHT?
PKAK!
WHAT WAS THAT NOISE?
WHISPER
SEKI, YOU MUSTN'T MAKE NOISE!
PLEASE BE AWARE THAT YOU'RE IN A FRIVOLOUS POSITION!
WHISPER

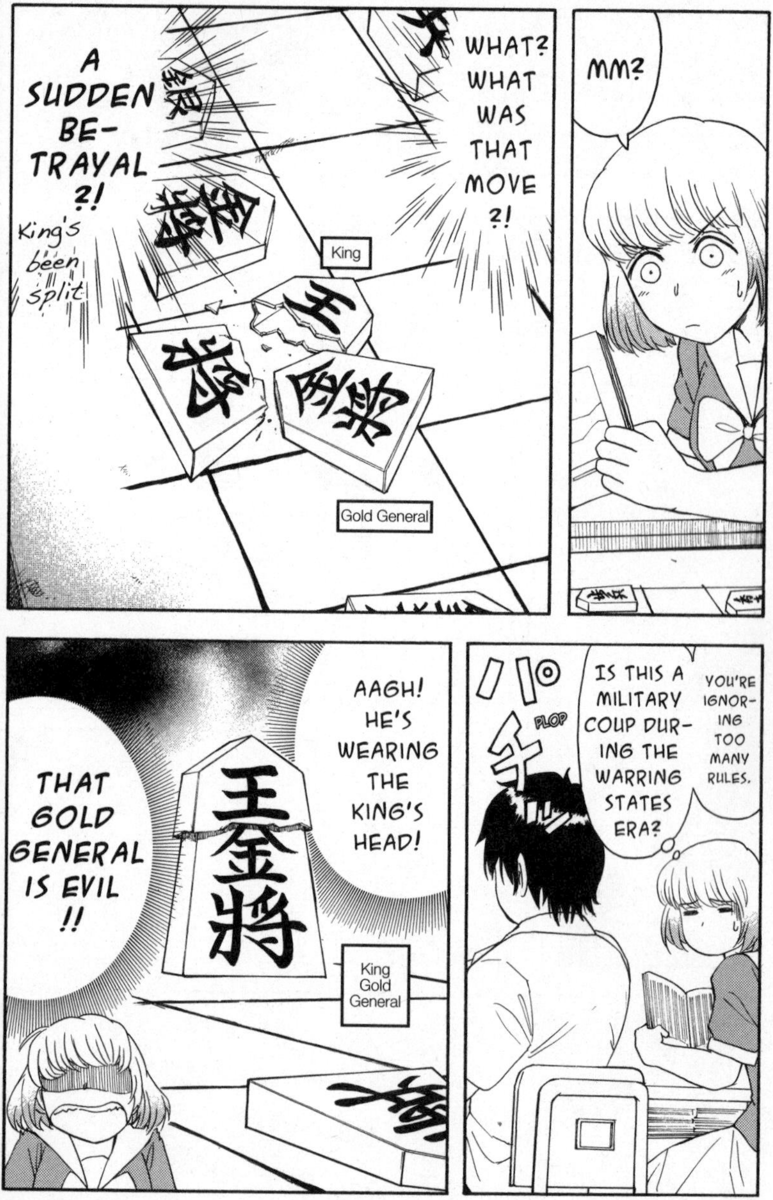
MM?
WHAT? WHAT WAS THAT MOVE?!
A SUDDEN BE-TRAYAL?!
King's been split
King
Gold General
IS THIS A MILITARY COUP DUR-ING THE WARRING STATES ERA?
YOU'RE IGNOR-ING TOO MANY RULES.
PLOP
AAGH! HE'S WEARING THE KING'S HEAD!
THAT GOLD GENERAL IS EVIL!!
King Gold General

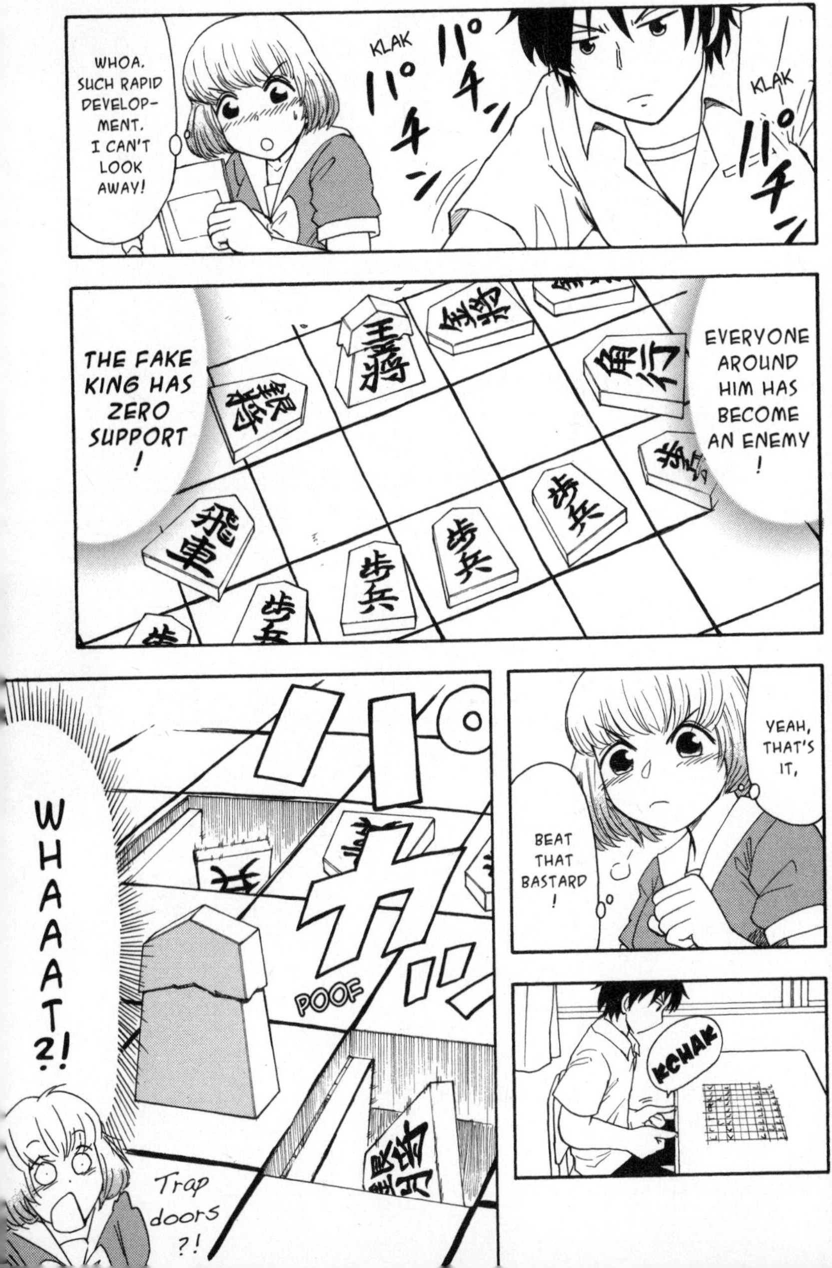
KLAK
パチン
KLAK
パチン
パチン
WHOA. SUCH RAPID DEVELOPMENT. I CAN'T LOOK AWAY!
EVERYONE AROUND HIM HAS BECOME AN ENEMY!
THE FAKE KING HAS ZERO SUPPORT!
YEAH, THAT'S IT,
BEAT THAT BASTARD!
KCHAK
POOF
WHAAAAT?!
Trap doors?!

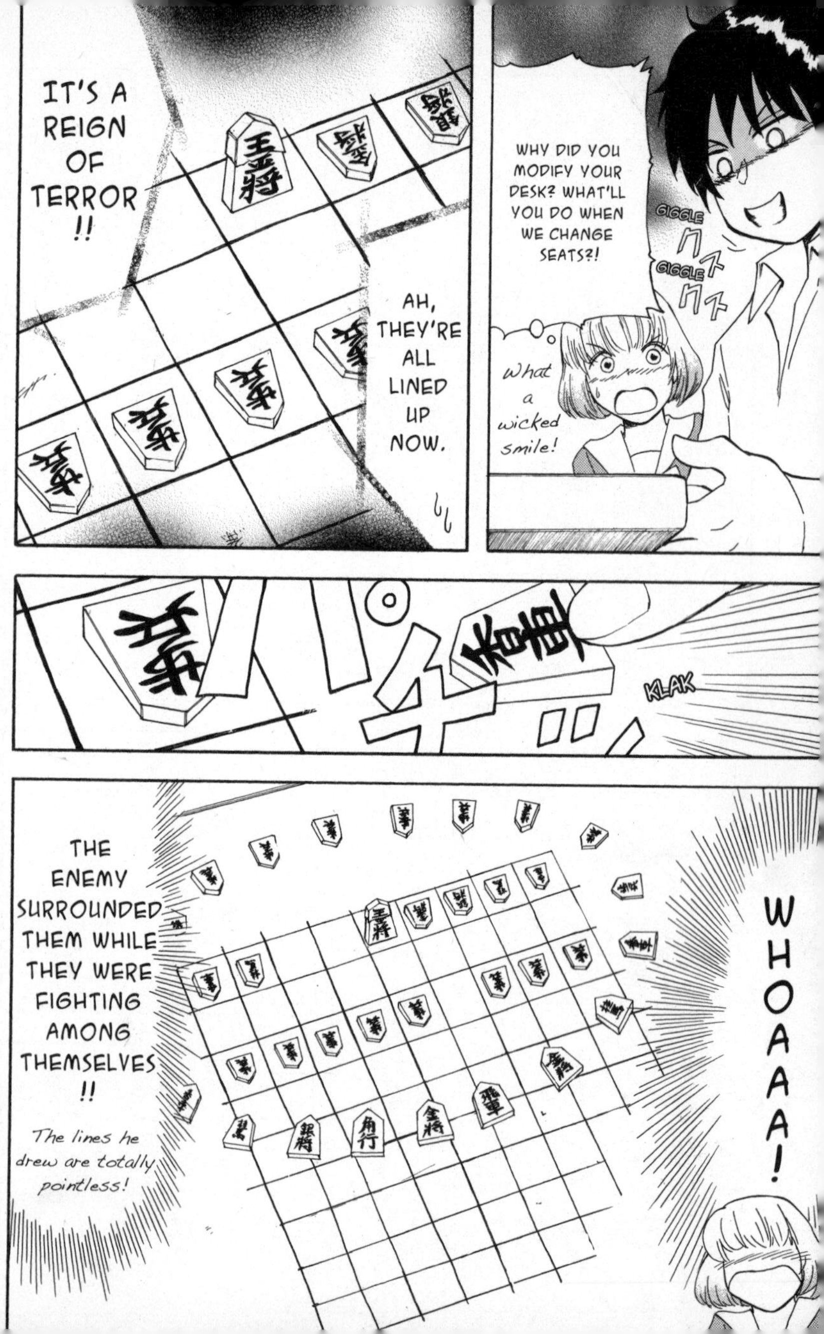
WHY DID YOU MODIFY YOUR DESK? WHAT'LL YOU DO WHEN WE CHANGE SEATS?!
GIGGLE
GIGGLE
What a wicked smile!
AH, THEY'RE ALL LINED UP NOW.
IT'S A REIGN OF TERROR !!
KLAK
WHOAAAA!
THE ENEMY SURROUNDED THEM WHILE THEY WERE FIGHTING AMONG THEMSELVES !!
The lines he drew are totally pointless!

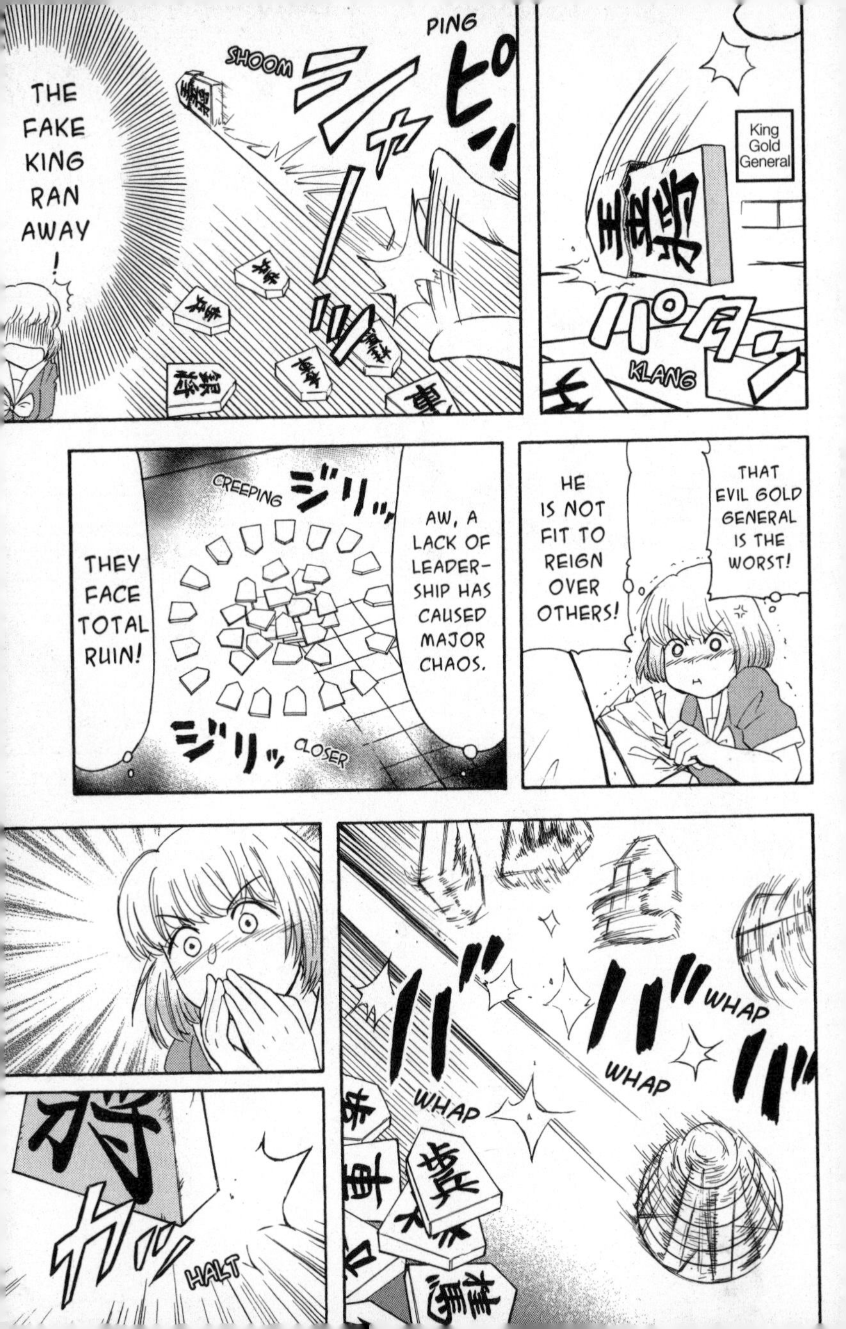
King
Gold
General
KLANG
PING
SHOOM
THE FAKE KING RAN AWAY!
THAT EVIL GOLD GENERAL IS THE WORST!
HE IS NOT FIT TO REIGN OVER OTHERS!
AW, A LACK OF LEADER-SHIP HAS CAUSED MAJOR CHAOS.
CREEPING
THEY FACE TOTAL RUIN!
CLOSER
WHAP
WHAP
WHAP
HALT

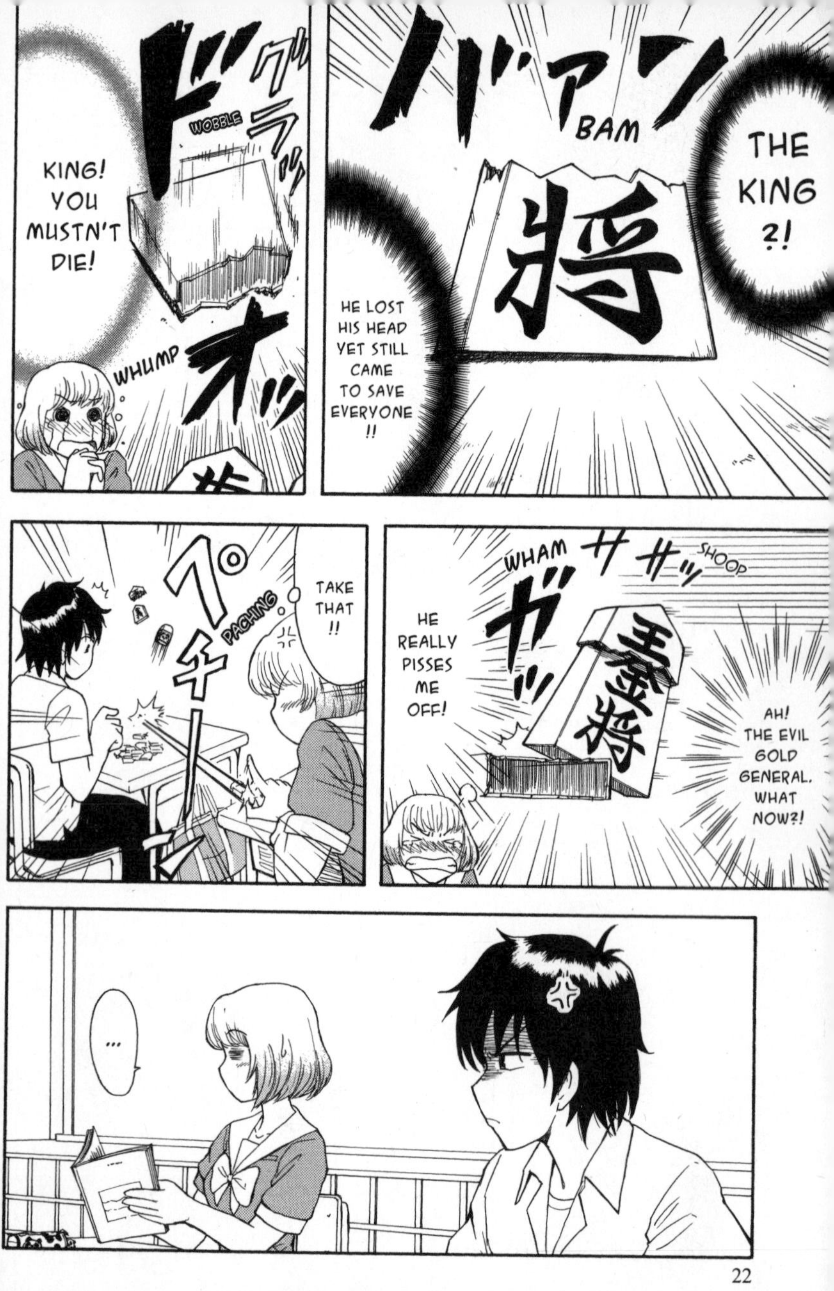
BAM
THE KING ?!
HE LOST HIS HEAD YET STILL CAME TO SAVE EVERYONE !!
WOBBLE
KING! YOU MUSTN'T DIE!
WHUMP
SHOOP
WHAM
AH! THE EVIL GOLD GENERAL. WHAT NOW?!
HE REALLY PISSES ME OFF!
TAKE THAT !!
PACHING
...

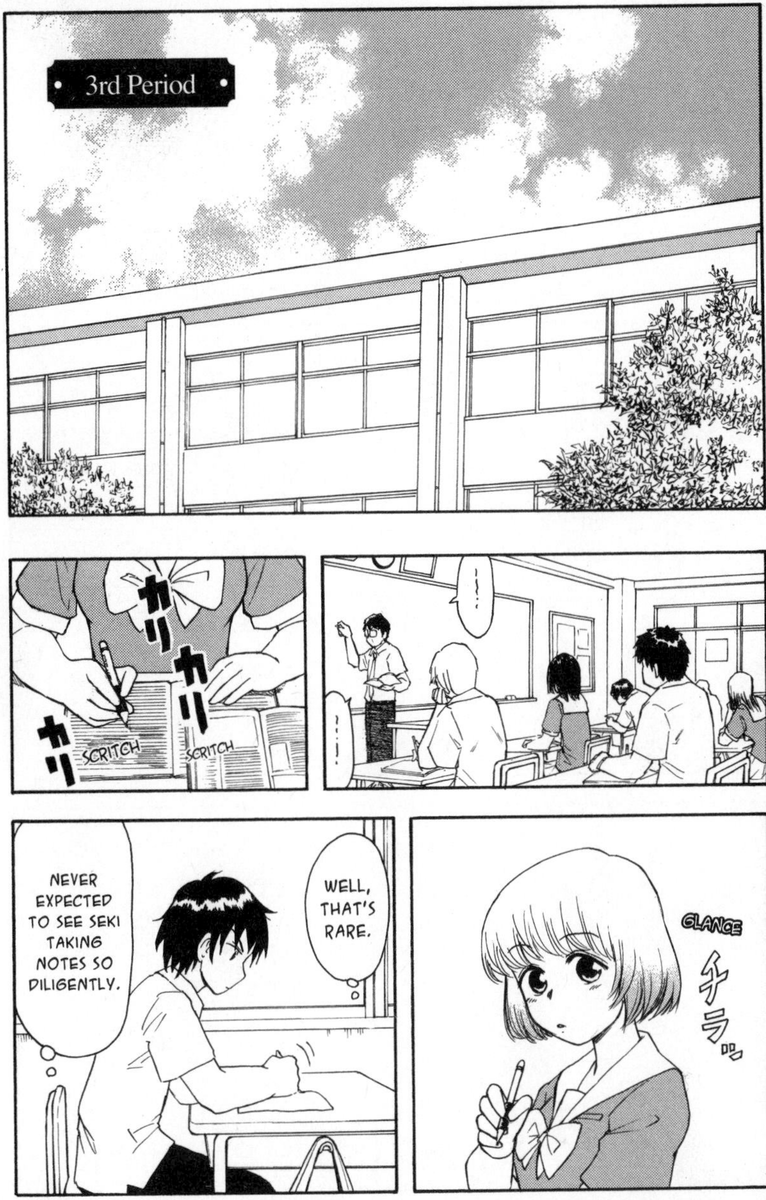
3rd Period
カリ
カリ
カリ
SCRITCH
SCRITCH
GLANCE
チラッ
WELL, THAT'S RARE.
NEVER EXPECTED TO SEE SEKI TAKING NOTES SO DILIGENTLY.

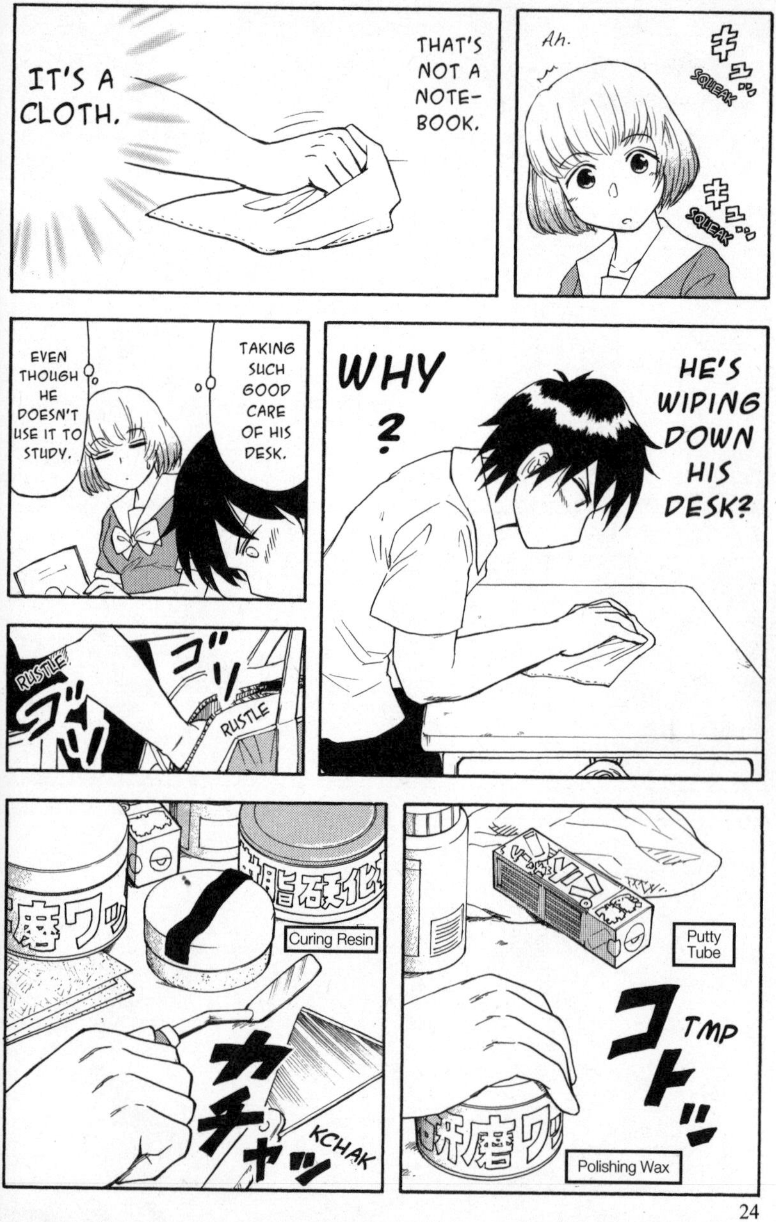
Ah.
キュ
SQUEAK
キュ
SQUEAK
THAT'S NOT A NOTE-BOOK.
IT'S A CLOTH.
HE'S WIPING DOWN HIS DESK?
WHY?
TAKING SUCH GOOD CARE OF HIS DESK.
EVEN THOUGH HE DOESN'T USE IT TO STUDY.
ゴソ
RUSTLE
ゴソ
RUSTLE
Putty Tube
コトッ
TMP
Polishing Wax
Curing Resin
カチャッ
KCHAK

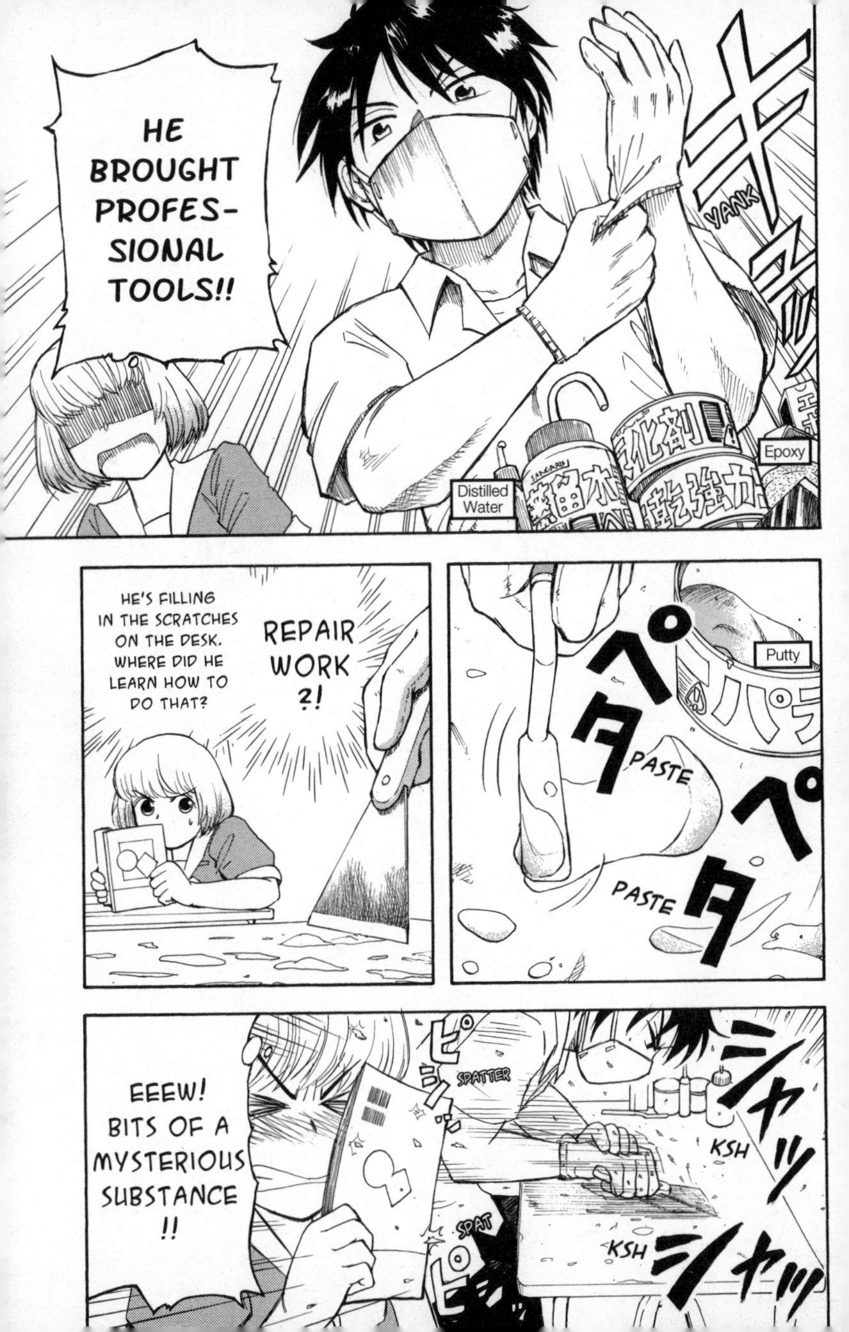
YANK
HE BROUGHT PROFES-SIONAL TOOLS!!
Epoxy
Distilled Water
Putty
PASTE
PASTE
REPAIR WORK ?!
HE'S FILLING IN THE SCRATCHES ON THE DESK. WHERE DID HE LEARN HOW TO DO THAT?
KSH
SPATTER
EEEW! BITS OF A MYSTERIOUS SUBSTANCE !!
KSH
SPAT

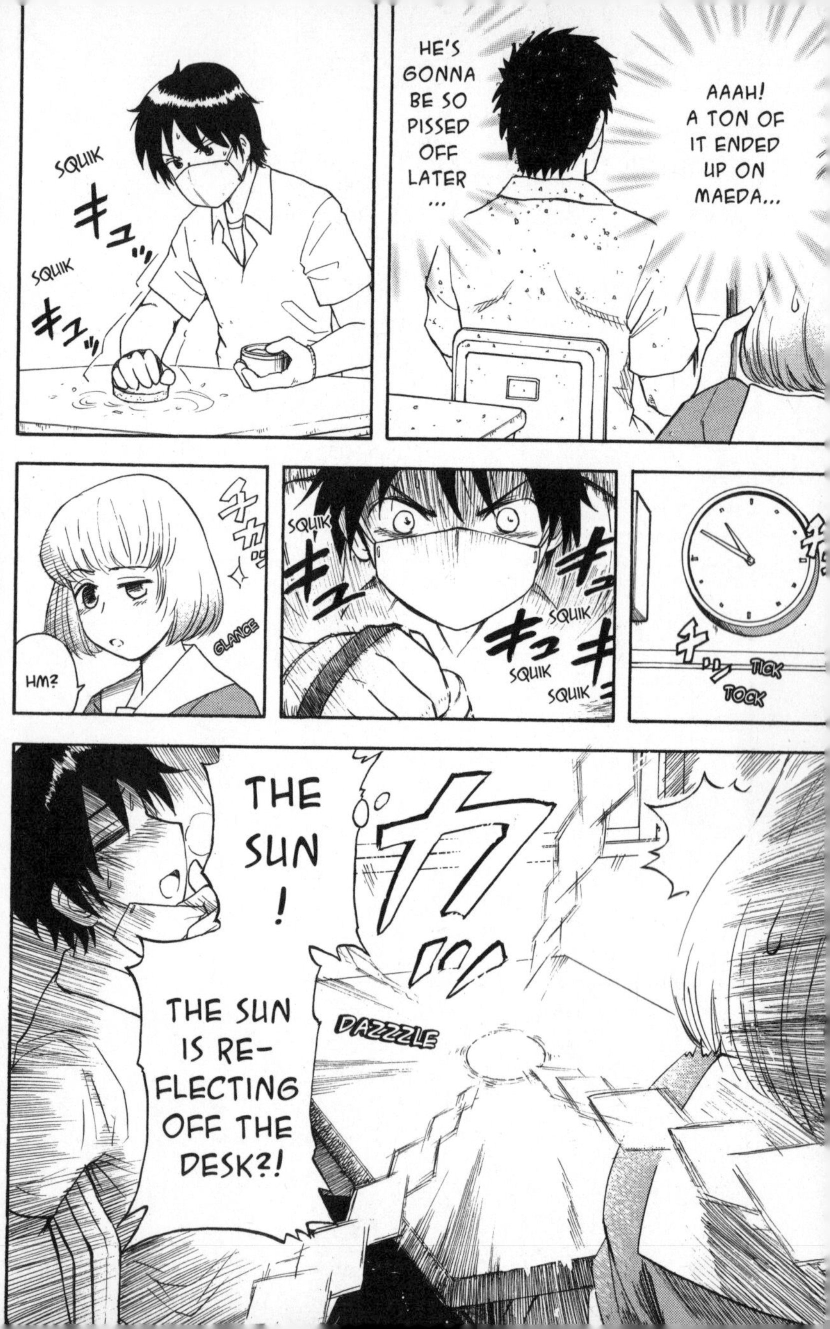
AAAH! A TON OF IT ENDED UP ON MAEDA...
HE'S GONNA BE SO PISSED OFF LATER...
SQUIK
キュッ
SQUIK
キュッ
チッ
TICK
TOCK
SQUIK
キュ
キュ
SQUIK
キュ
SQUIK
SQUIK
チカッ
GLANCE
HM?
THE SUN!
THE SUN IS RE-FLECTING OFF THE DESK?!
DAZZZLE

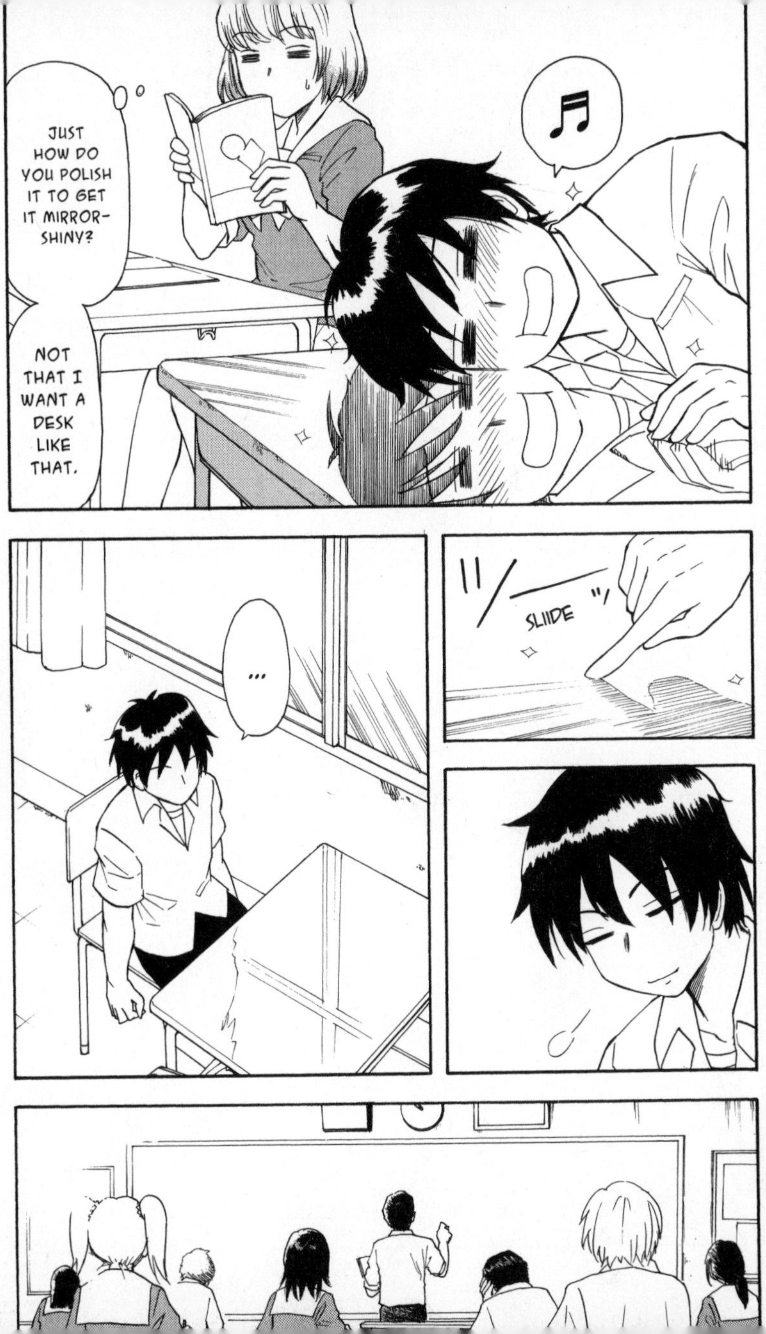
♬
JUST HOW DO YOU POLISH IT TO GET IT MIRROR-SHINY?
NOT THAT I WANT A DESK LIKE THAT.
SLIIDE
...

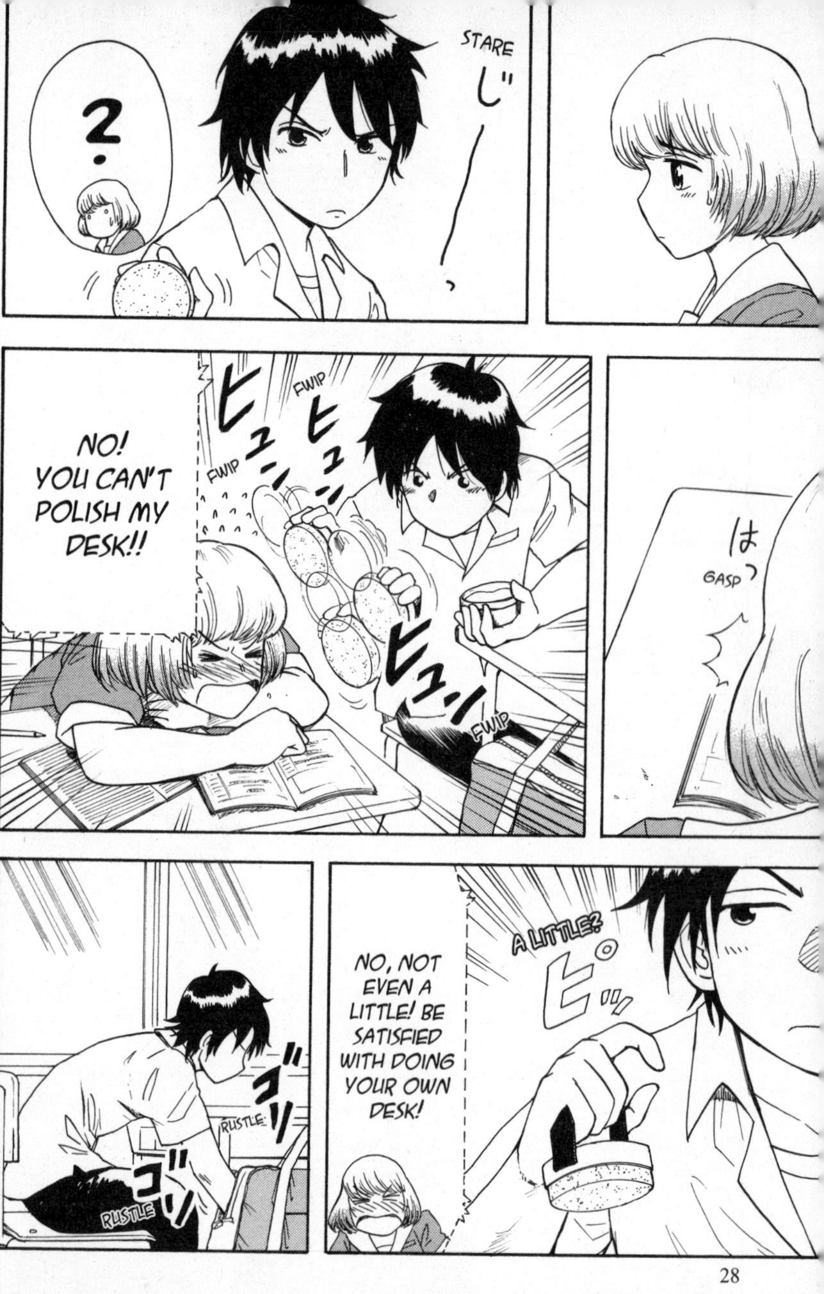
STARE
じ
?
は
GASP
FWIP
ヒュン
FWIP
ヒュン
NO! YOU CAN'T POLISH MY DESK!!
ヒュン
FWIP
A LITTLE?
ピッ
NO, NOT EVEN A LITTLE! BE SATISFIED WITH DOING YOUR OWN DESK!
ゴソ
RUSTLE
ゴソ
RUSTLE

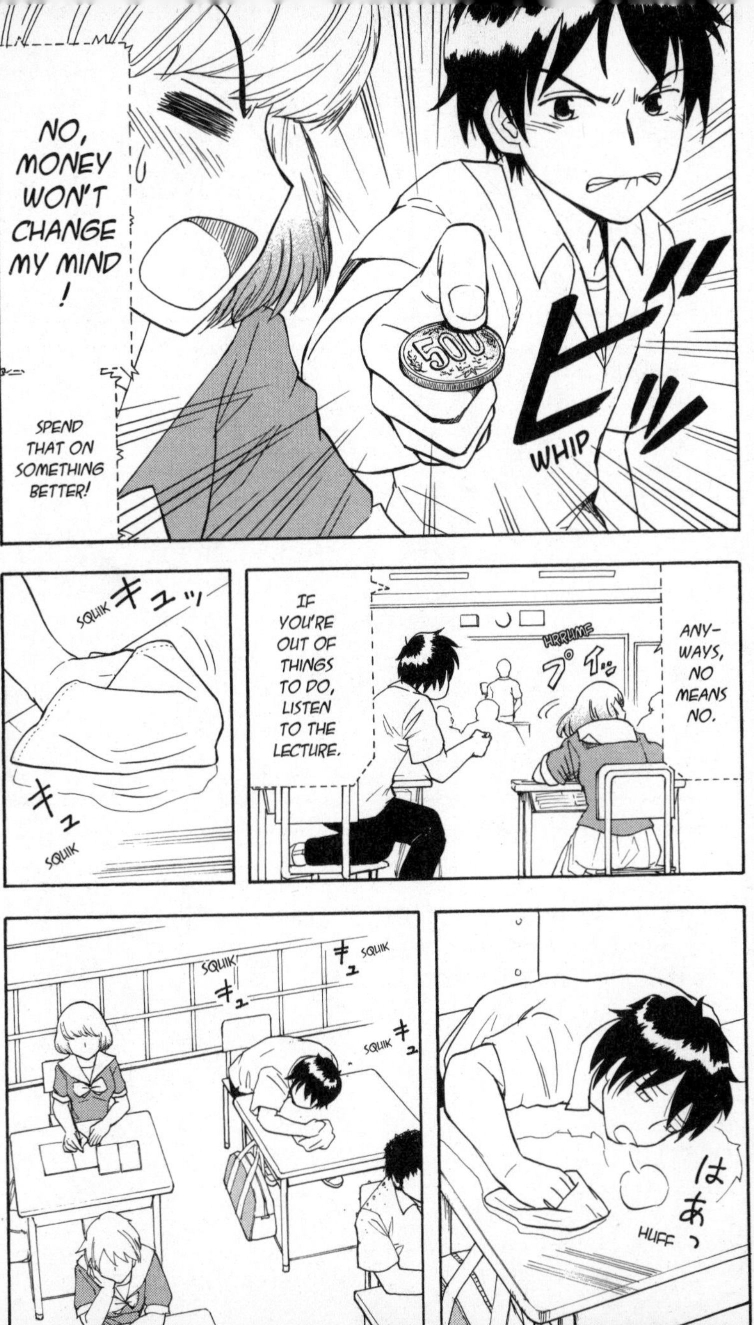
ビッ
WHIP
NO, MONEY WON'T CHANGE MY MIND!
SPEND THAT ON SOMETHING BETTER!
ANY-WAYS, NO MEANS NO.
プイッ
HRRUMF
IF YOU'RE OUT OF THINGS TO DO, LISTEN TO THE LECTURE.
キュッ
SQUIK
キュ
SQUIK
はあっ
HUFF
キュ
SQUIK
キュ
SQUIK
キュ
SQUIK

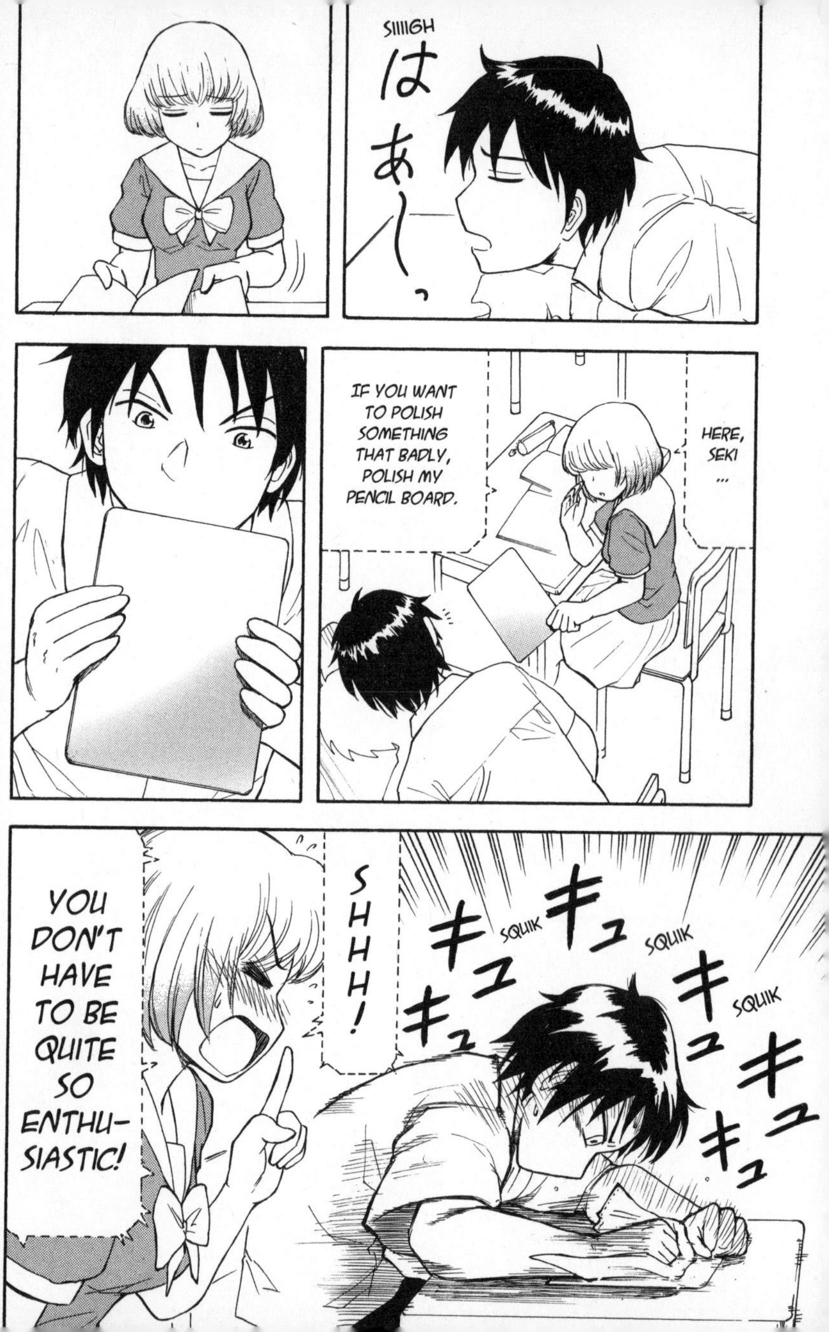
SIIIGH
はあ〜っ
HERE, SEKI ...
IF YOU WANT TO POLISH SOMETHING THAT BADLY, POLISH MY PENCIL BOARD.
キュ キュ キュ キュ キュ キュ
SQUIK
SQUIK
SQUIK
SHHHH!
YOU DON'T HAVE TO BE QUITE SO ENTHU-SIASTIC!

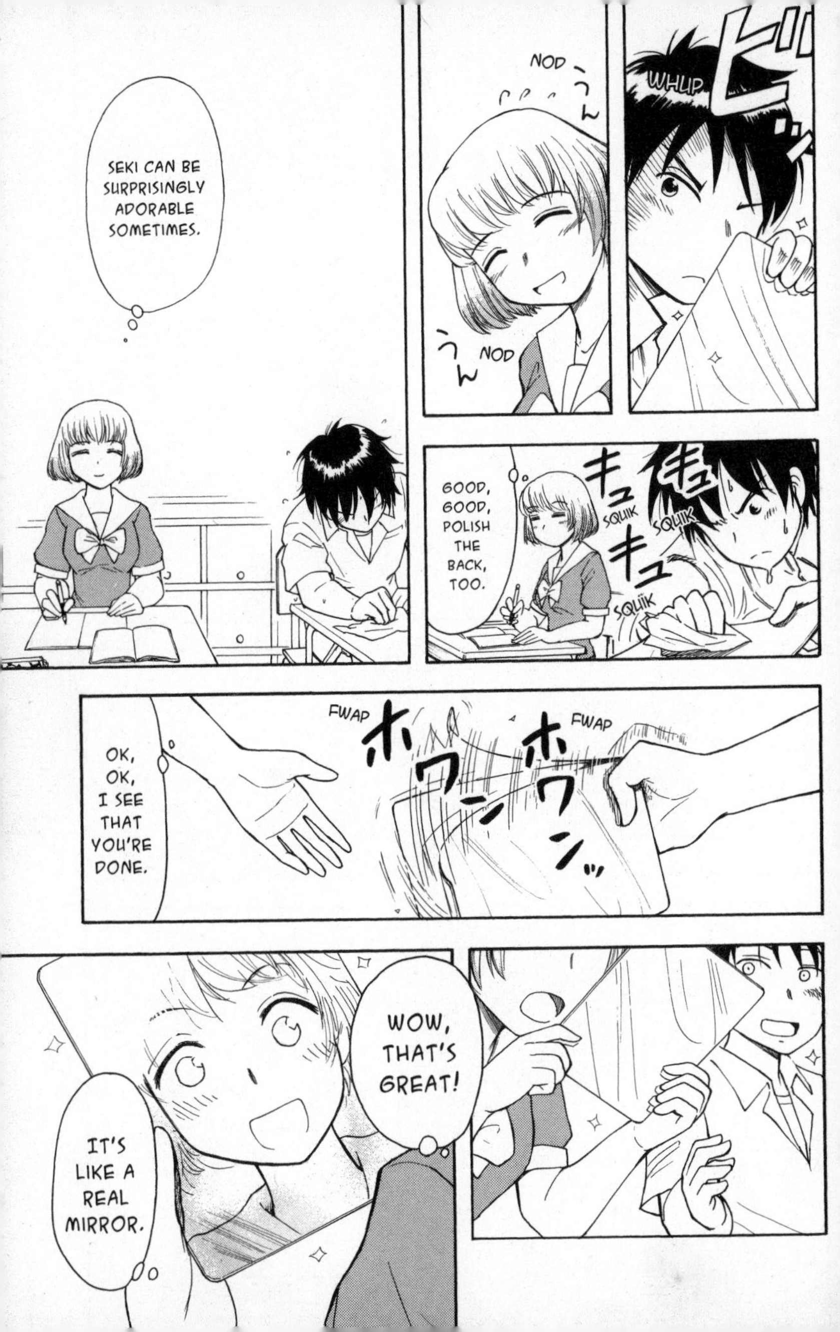

WHLIP
ビッ
NOD
うん
うん
NOD
キュ
SQUIK
SQUIK
キュ
SQUIK
GOOD, GOOD, POLISH THE BACK, TOO.
SEKI CAN BE SURPRISINGLY ADORABLE SOMETIMES.
FWAP
ホワン
FWAP
ホワンッ
OK, OK, I SEE THAT YOU'RE DONE.
WOW, THAT'S GREAT!
IT'S LIKE A REAL MIRROR.

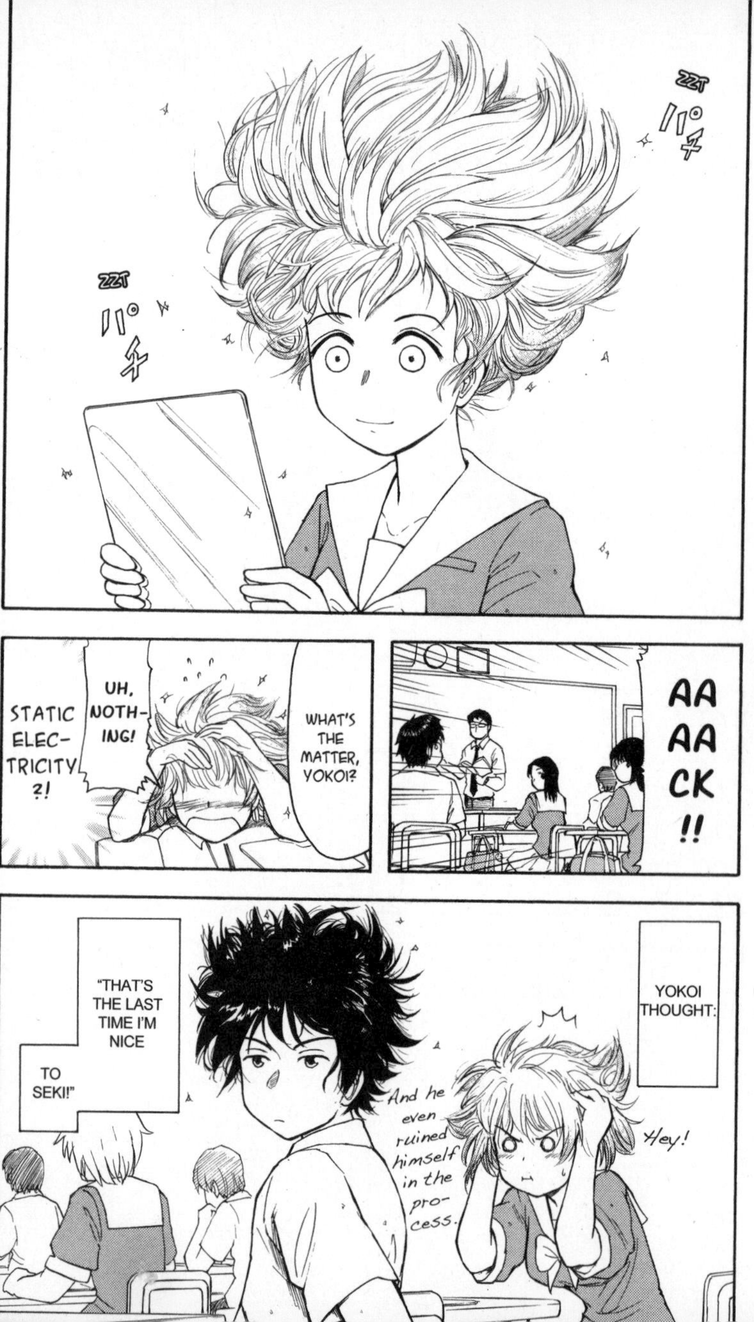
ZZT
パチ
ZZT
パチ
AAAACK!!
WHAT'S THE MATTER, YOKOI!?
UH, NOTHING!
STATIC ELECTRICITY?!
YOKOI THOUGHT:
"THAT'S THE LAST TIME I'M NICE TO SEKI!"
Hey!
And he even ruined himself in the process.

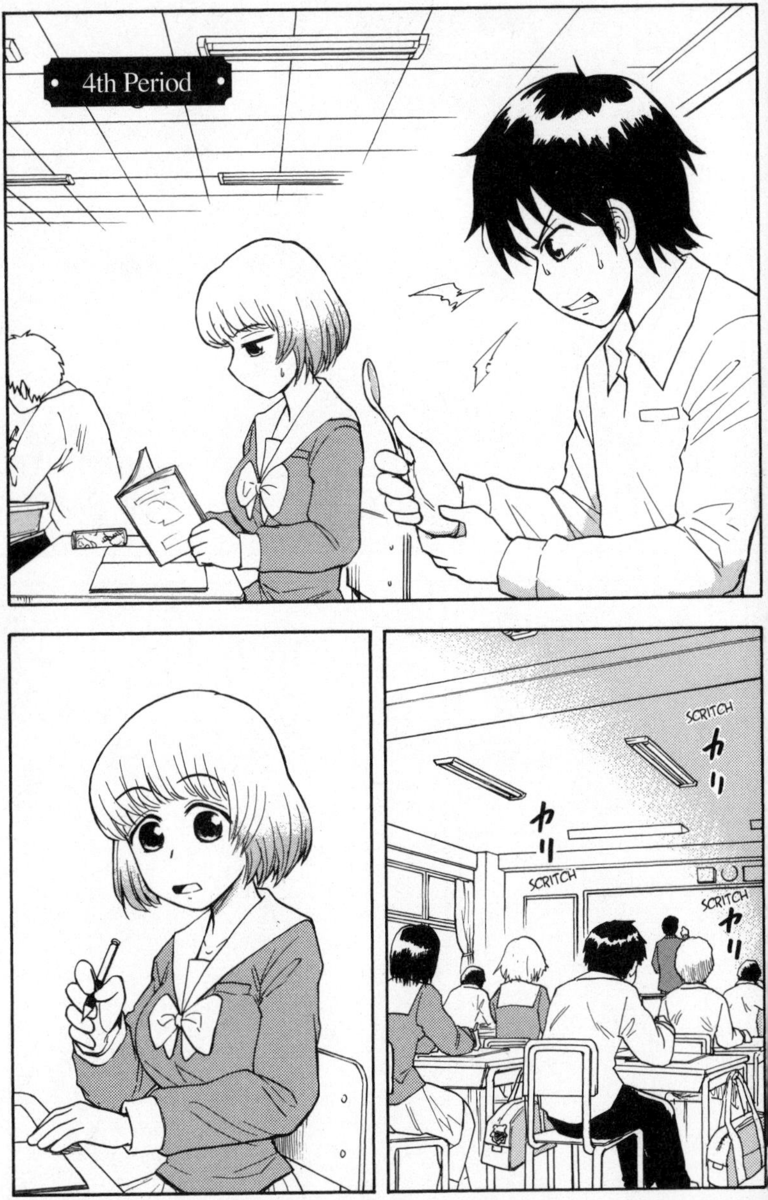
4th Period
SCRITCH
カリ
カリ
SCRITCH
SCRITCH
カリ

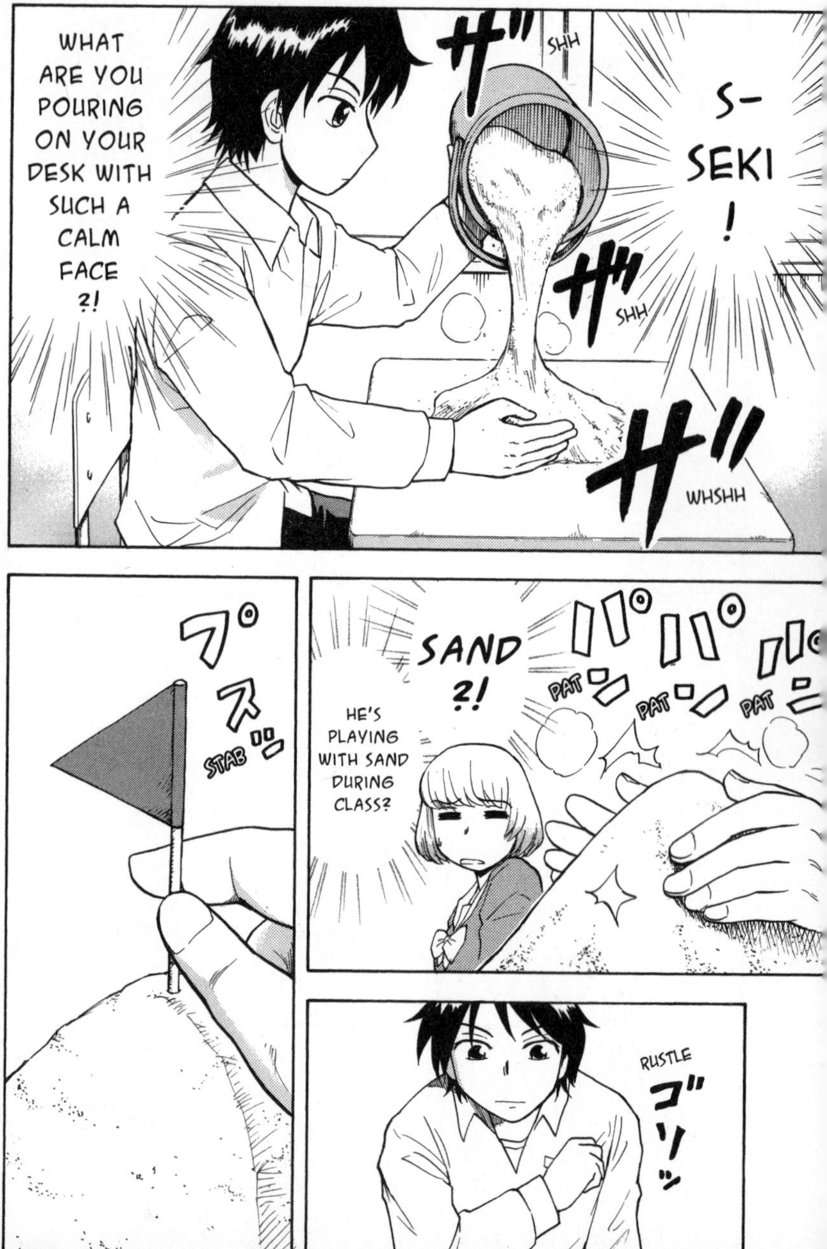
S-SEKI!
ザ SHH
ザ SHH
ザ WHSHH
WHAT ARE YOU POURING ON YOUR DESK WITH SUCH A CALM FACE?!
パ PAT パ PAT パ PAT
SAND?!
HE'S PLAYING WITH SAND DURING CLASS?
ゴソッ RUSTLE
プス STAB

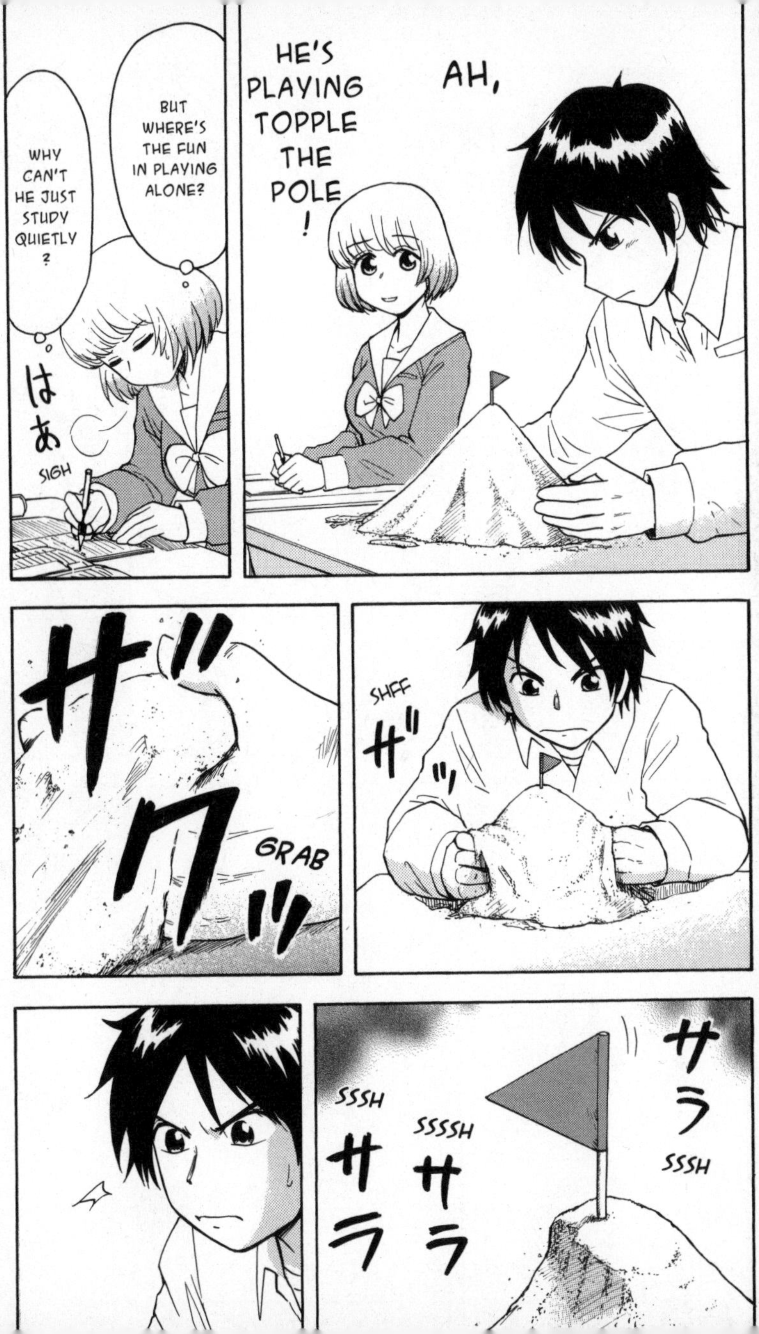
AH,
HE'S PLAYING TOPPLE THE POLE!
BUT WHERE'S THE FUN IN PLAYING ALONE?
WHY CAN'T HE JUST STUDY QUIETLY?
はぁ
SIGH
ザッ
SHFF
ザクッ
GRAB
サラ
SSSH
サラ
SSSSH
サラ
SSSH

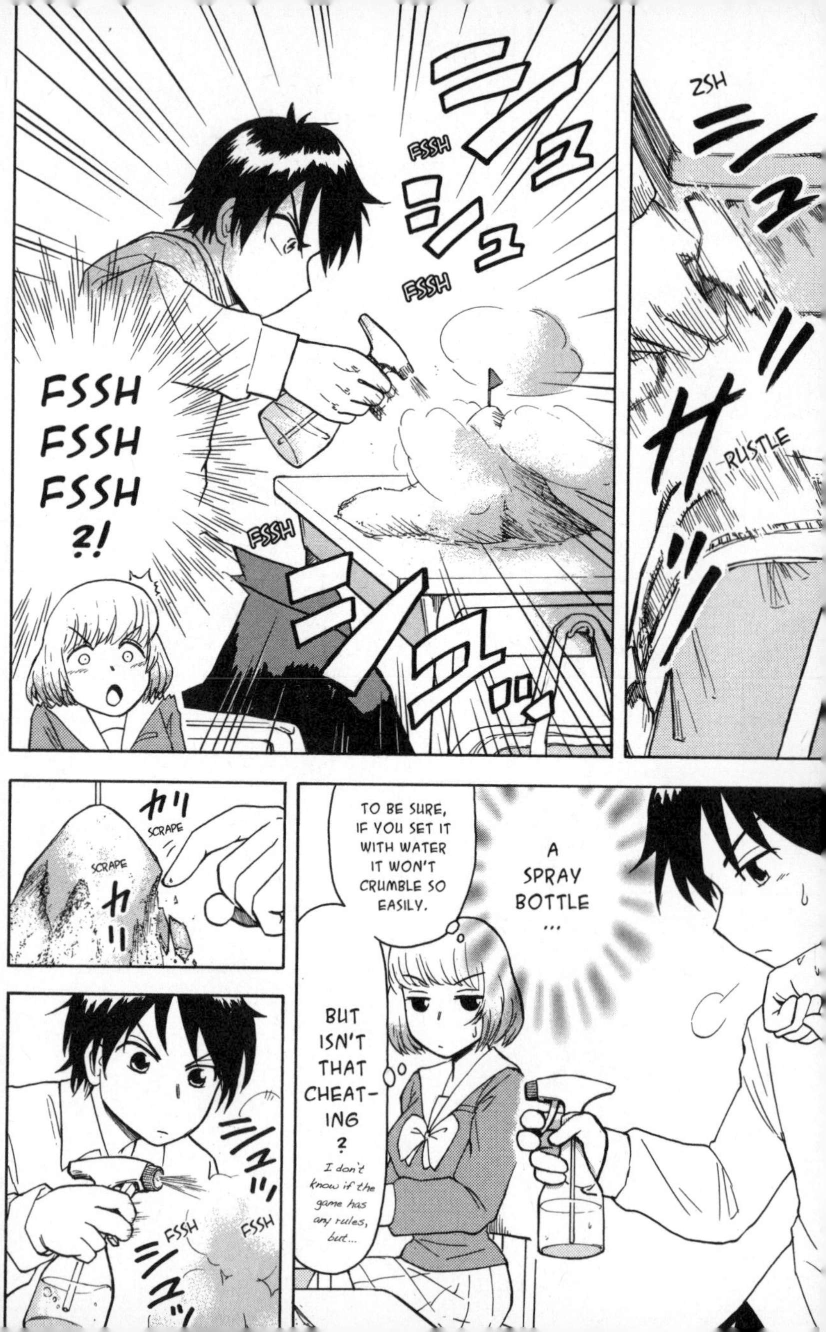
ZSH
RUSTLE
FSSH
FSSH
FSSH
FSSH
FSSH
?!
FSSH
A SPRAY BOTTLE ...
TO BE SURE, IF YOU SET IT WITH WATER IT WON'T CRUMBLE SO EASILY.
BUT ISN'T THAT CHEATING?
I don't know if the game has any rules, but...
SCRAPE
SCRAPE
FSSH
FSSH

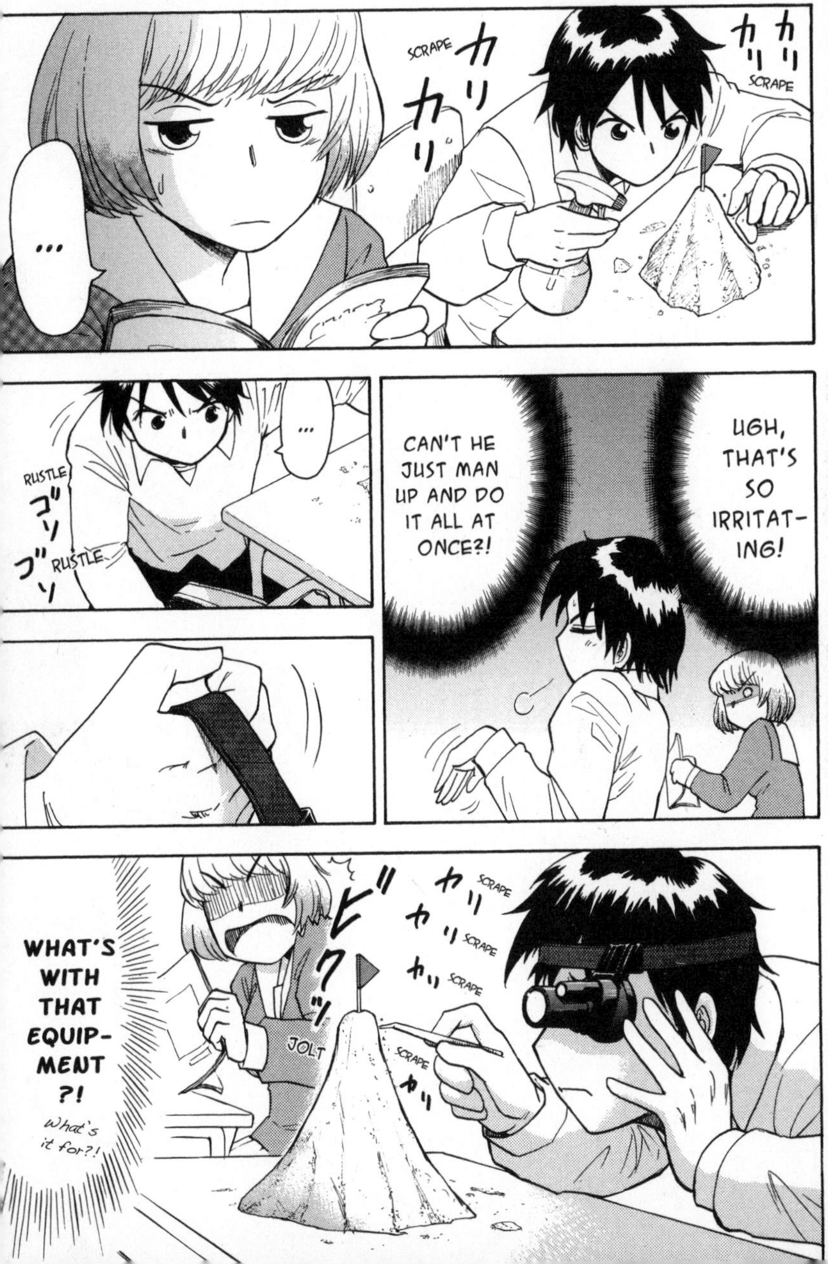

カリカリ
SCRAPE
SCRAPE
カリカリ
...
UGH, THAT'S SO IRRITATING!
CAN'T HE JUST MAN UP AND DO IT ALL AT ONCE?!
...
RUSTLE
ゴソゴソ
RUSTLE
SCRAPE
ヤリヤリヤリ
SCRAPE
SCRAPE
SCRAPE
ヤリ
ビクッ
JOLT
WHAT'S WITH THAT EQUIPMENT?!
What's it for?!

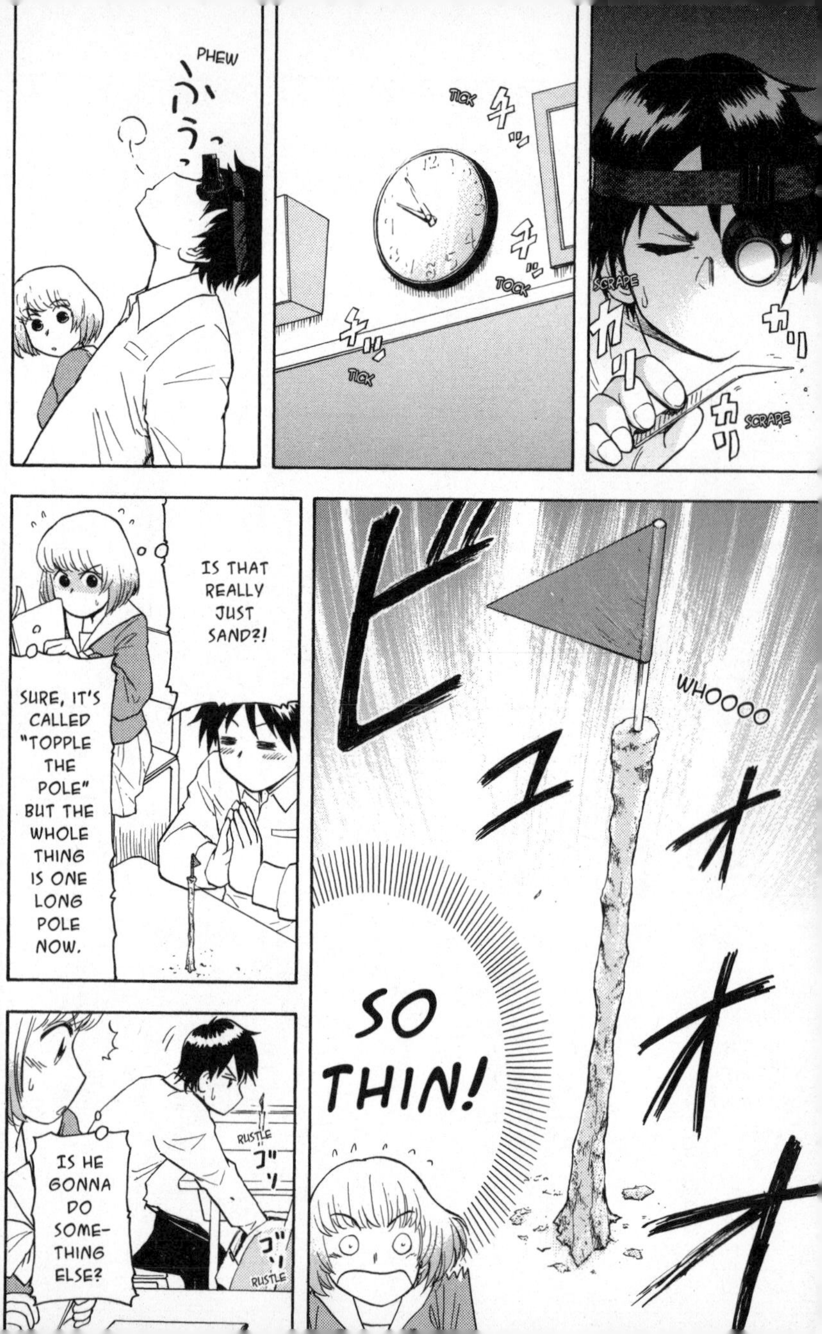
SCRAPE
カリ
カリ
SCRAPE
TICK
チッ
TOCK
チッ
TICK
チッ
PHEW
ふうっ
ビュオオオ
WHOOOO
SO THIN!
IS THAT REALLY JUST SAND?!
SURE, IT'S CALLED "TOPPLE THE POLE" BUT THE WHOLE THING IS ONE LONG POLE NOW.
IS HE GONNA DO SOME-THING ELSE?
RUSTLE
ゴソ
ゴソ
RUSTLE

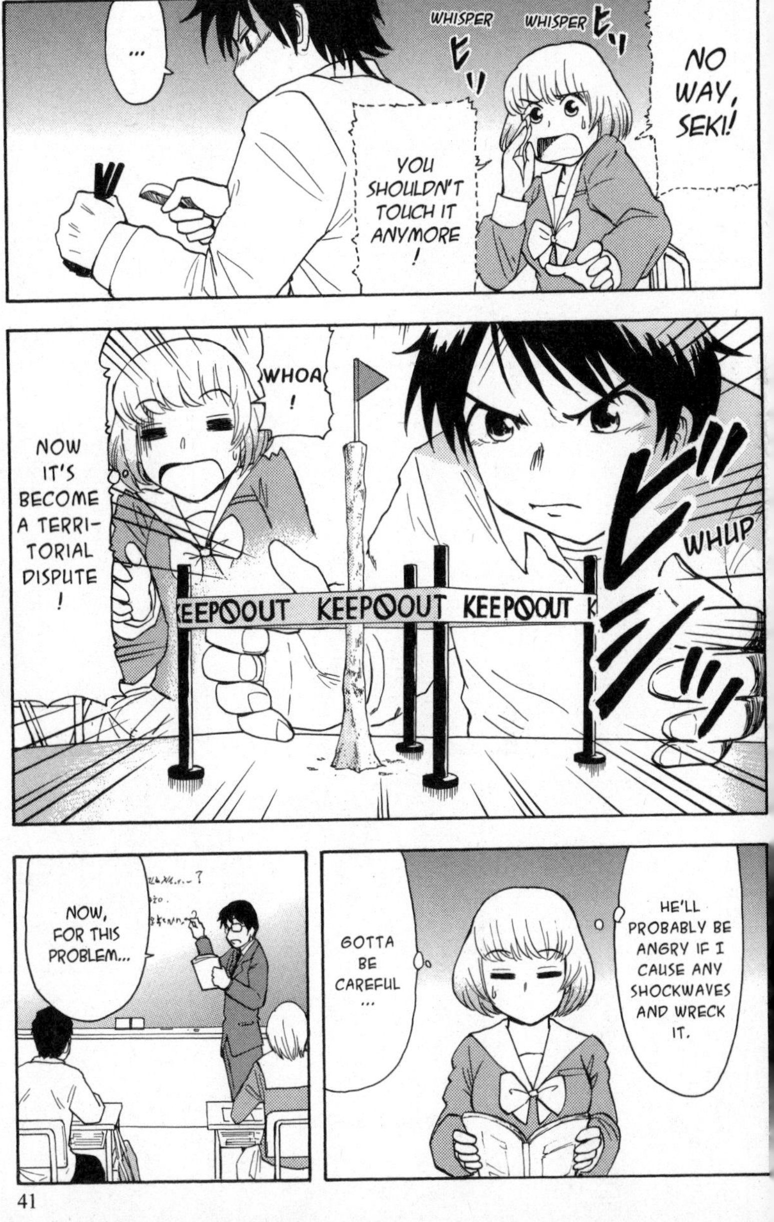
NO WAY, SEKI!
WHISPER ヒッ
WHISPER ヒッ
YOU SHOULDN'T TOUCH IT ANYMORE!
...
WHUP
KEEP OUT KEEP OUT KEEP OUT
WHOA!
NOW IT'S BECOME A TERRI-TORIAL DISPUTE!
HE'LL PROBABLY BE ANGRY IF I CAUSE ANY SHOCKWAVES AND WRECK IT.
GOTTA BE CAREFUL...
NOW, FOR THIS PROBLEM...

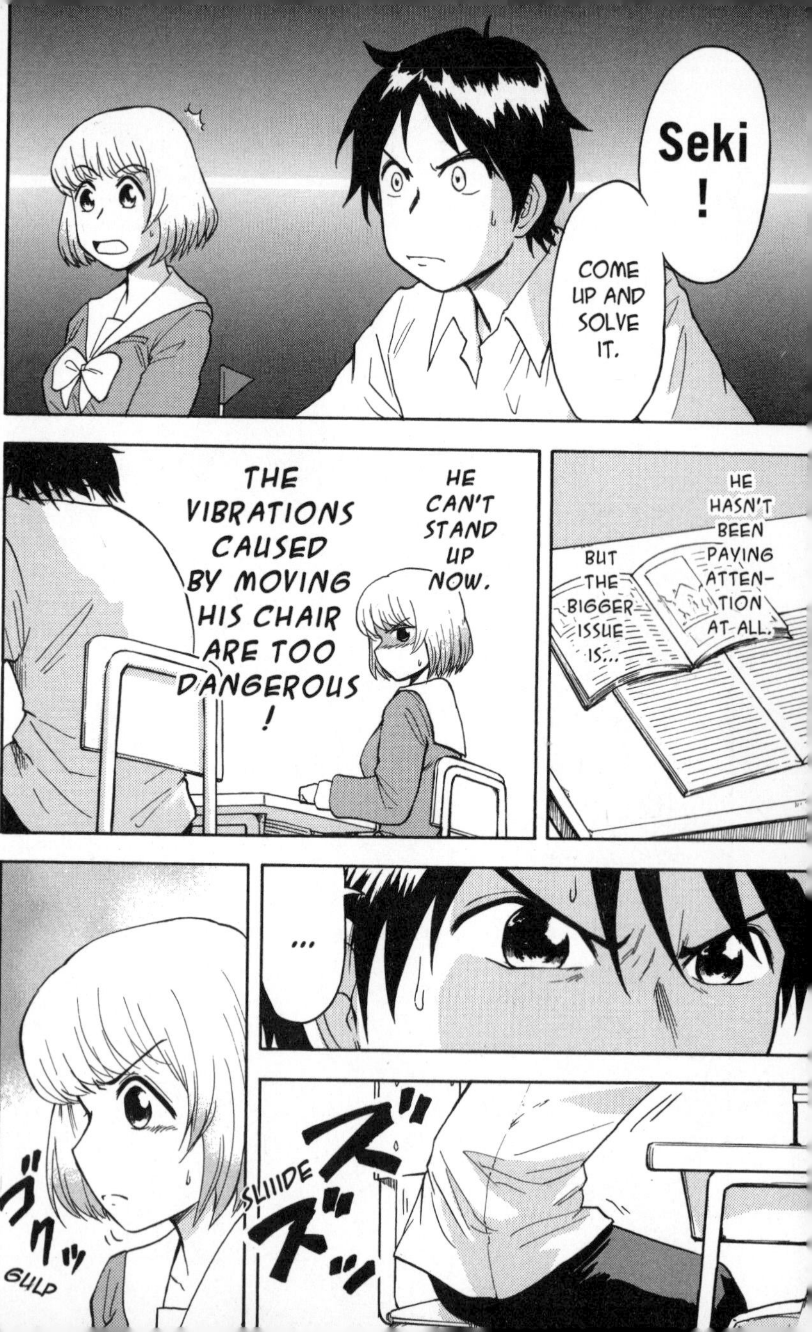
Seki!
COME UP AND SOLVE IT.
HE HASN'T BEEN PAYING ATTENTION AT ALL.
BUT THE BIGGER ISSUE IS...
HE CAN'T STAND UP NOW.
THE VIBRATIONS CAUSED BY MOVING HIS CHAIR ARE TOO DANGEROUS!
...
ズズッ
SLIIIDE
ゴクッ
GULP

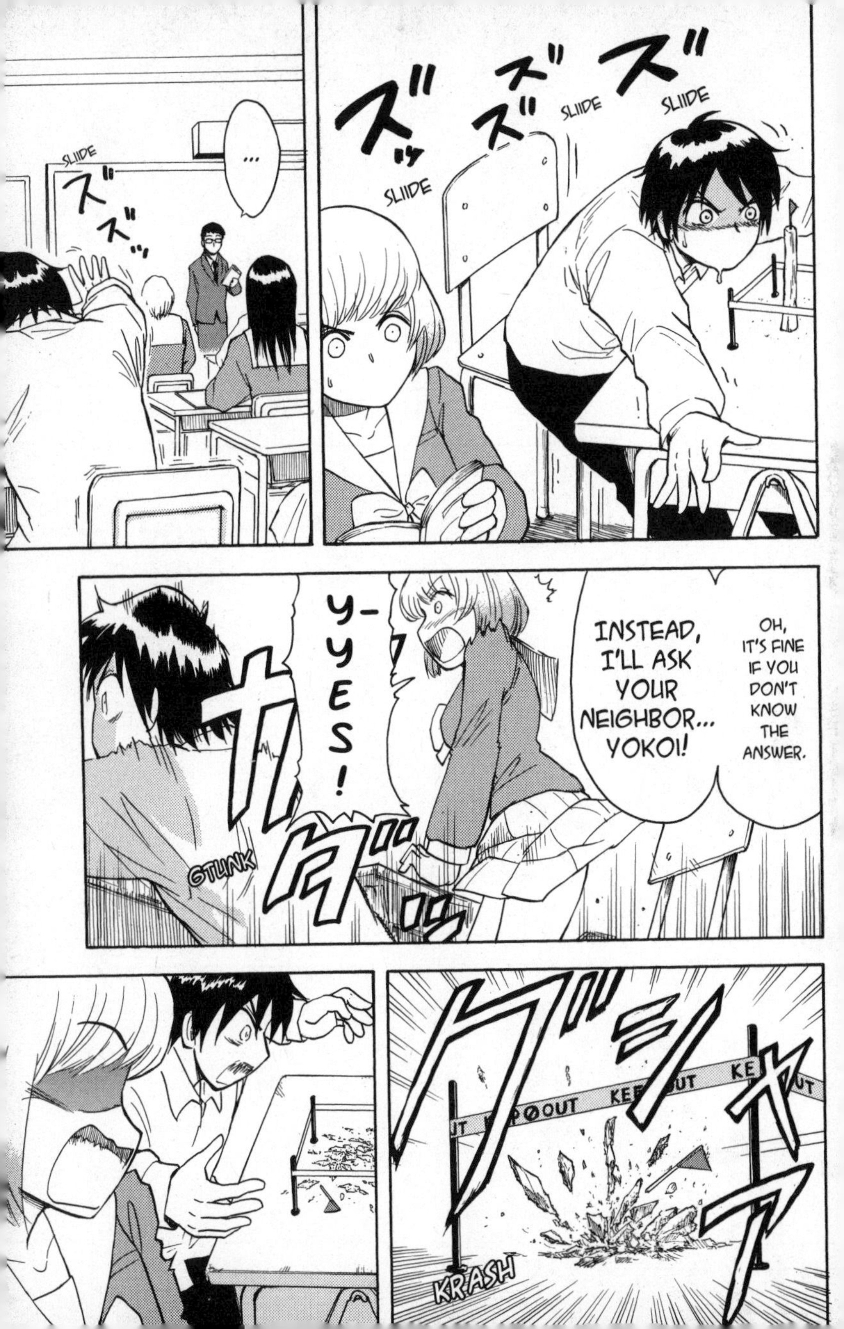
ズッズズ
SLIIDE
SLIIDE
SLIIDE
...
SLIIDE
ズズッ
OH, IT'S FINE IF YOU DON'T KNOW THE ANSWER.
INSTEAD, I'LL ASK YOUR NEIGHBOR... YOKOI!
Y-YYES!
GTUNK
KEEP OUT
KRASH

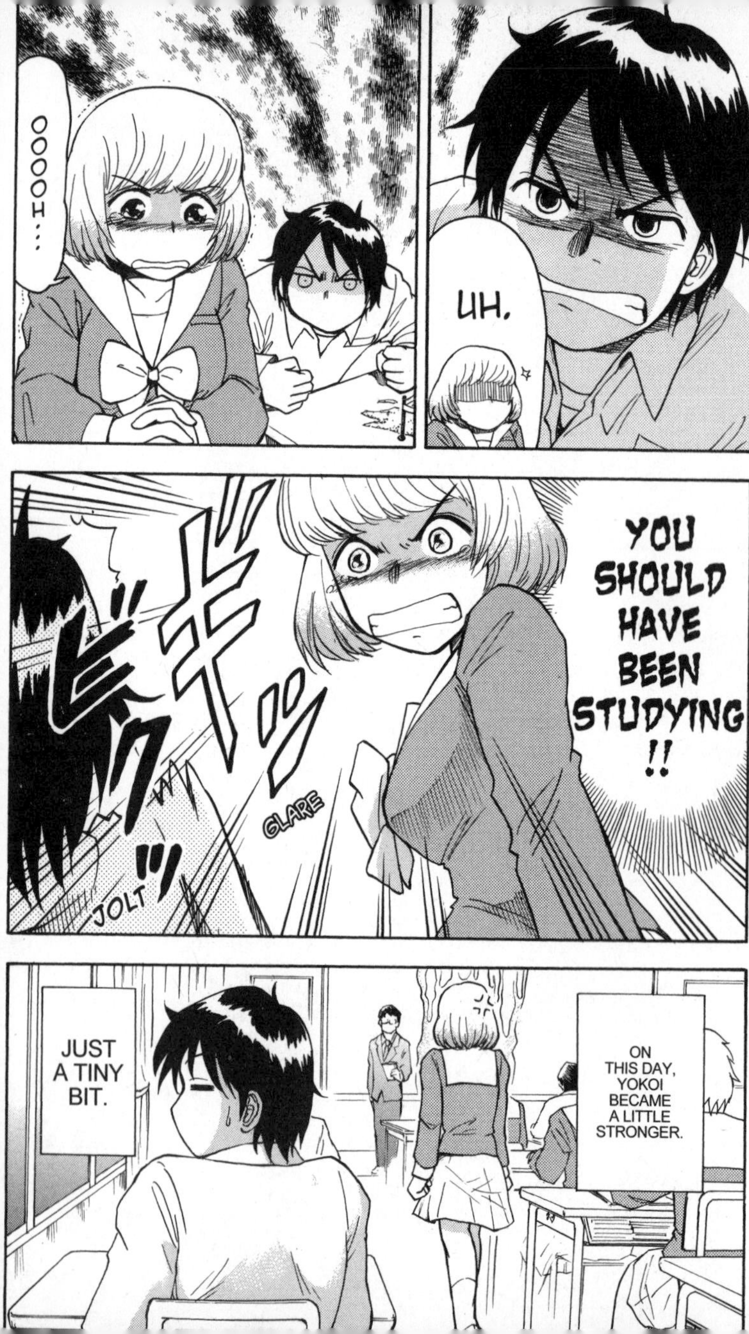
UH.
OOOOH...
YOU SHOULD HAVE BEEN STUDYING!!
GLARE
JOLT
ON THIS DAY, YOKOI BECAME A LITTLE STRONGER.
JUST A TINY BIT.

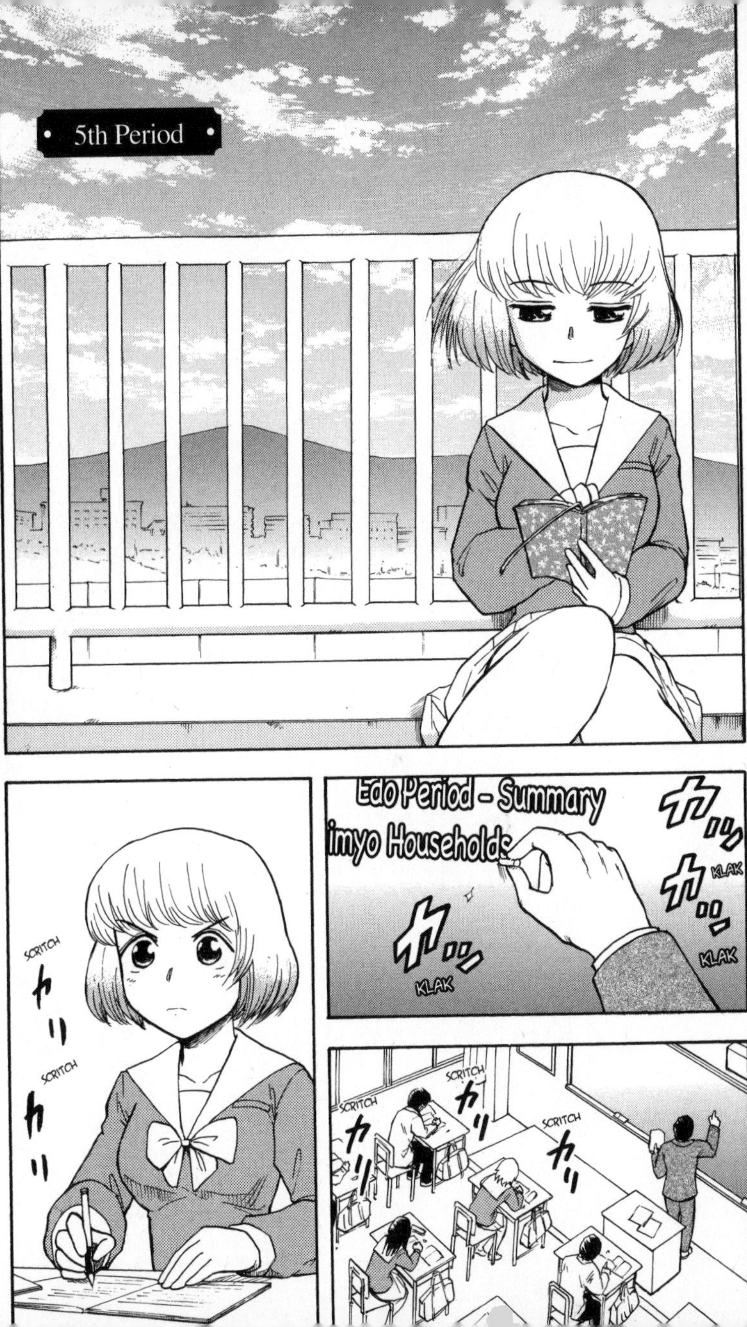
5th Period
Edo Period – Summary
imyo Households
カッ
KLAK
カッ
KLAK
カッ
KLAK
SCRITCH
カリ
SCRITCH
カリ
SCRITCH
カリ
SCRITCH
カリ
SCRITCH
カリ

IT'S AMAZING THAT HE CAN PLAY AROUND SO BOLDLY IN THIS SERIOUS ENVIRONMENT.

KACHAK

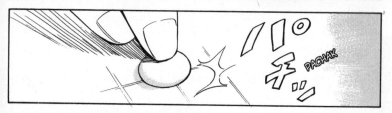

PACHAK

YET ANOTHER NOISY THING.

A GAME OF GO.

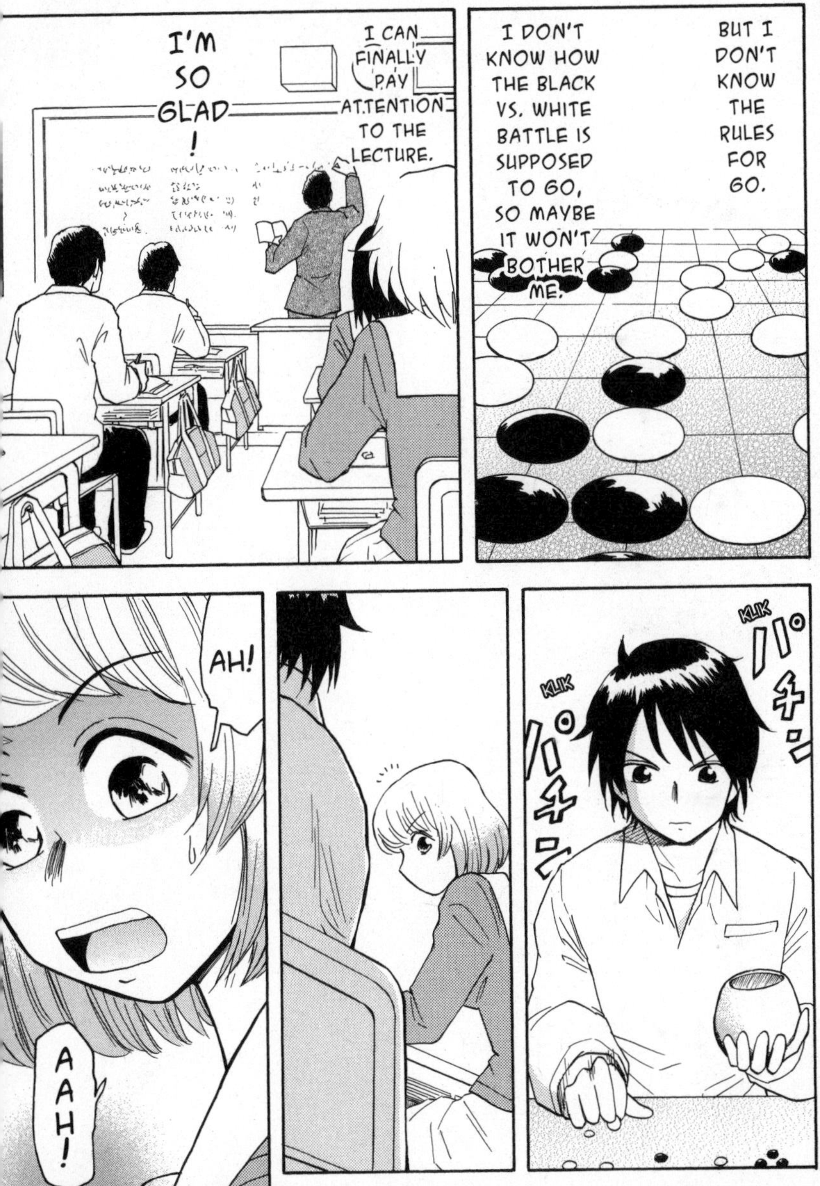
BUT I DON'T KNOW THE RULES FOR GO.
I DON'T KNOW HOW THE BLACK VS. WHITE BATTLE IS SUPPOSED TO GO, SO MAYBE IT WON'T BOTHER ME.
I CAN FINALLY PAY ATTENTION TO THE LECTURE.
I'M SO GLAD!
KLIK
パチ
KLIK
パチ
AH!
AAH!

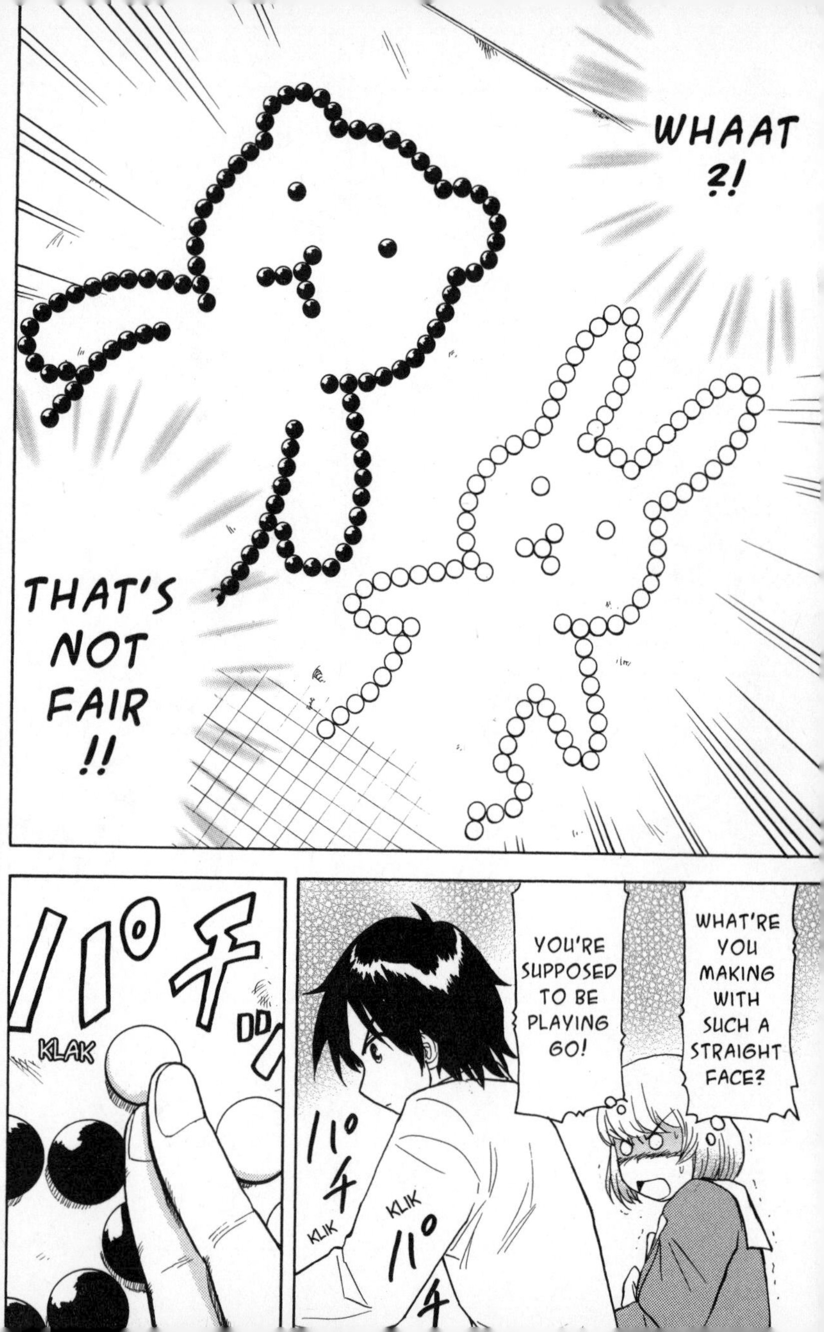
WHAAT ?!
THAT'S NOT FAIR !!
WHAT'RE YOU MAKING WITH SUCH A STRAIGHT FACE?
YOU'RE SUPPOSED TO BE PLAYING GO!
パチ
KLIK
パチ
KLIK
パチ
KLAK

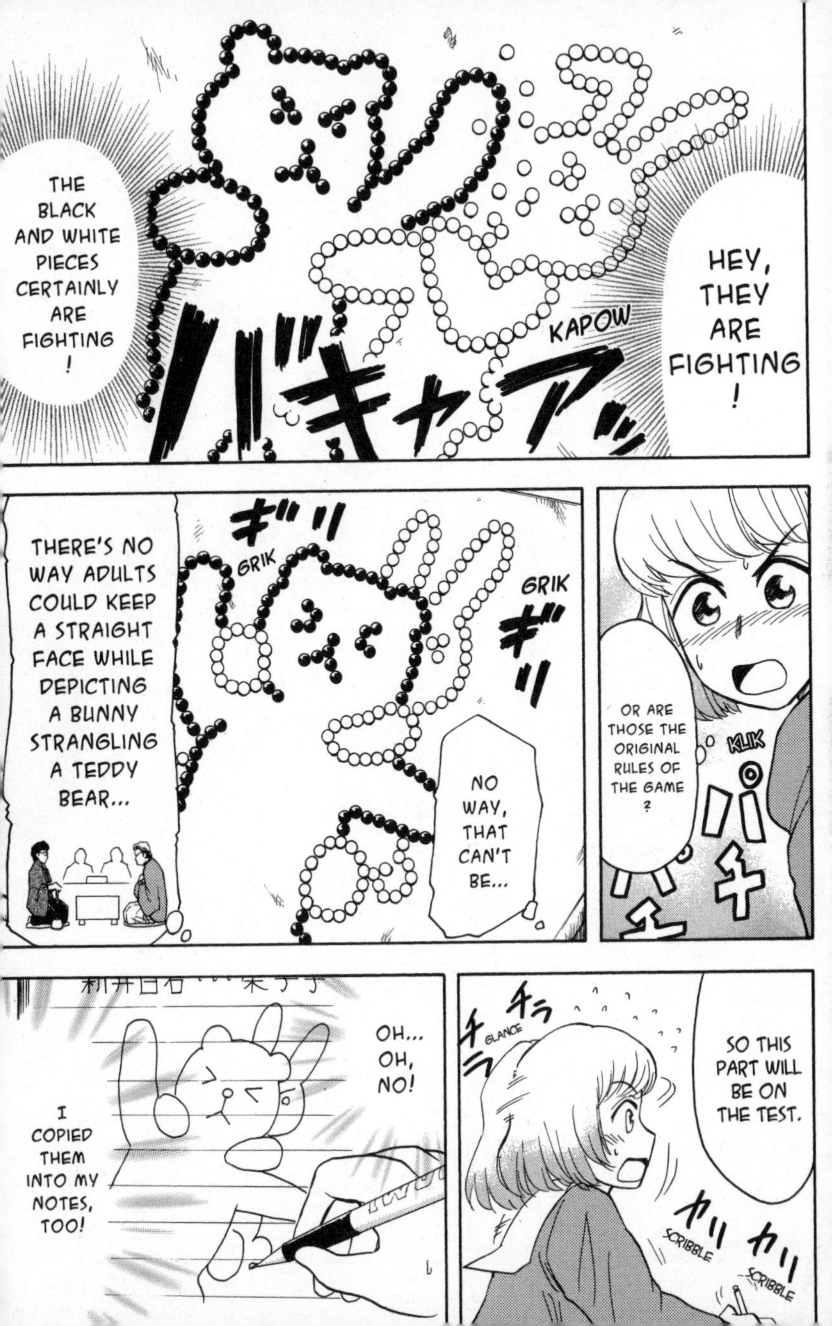
HEY, THEY ARE FIGHTING!
KAPOW
THE BLACK AND WHITE PIECES CERTAINLY ARE FIGHTING!
OR ARE THOSE THE ORIGINAL RULES OF THE GAME?
KLIK
GRIK
GRIK
NO WAY, THAT CAN'T BE...
THERE'S NO WAY ADULTS COULD KEEP A STRAIGHT FACE WHILE DEPICTING A BUNNY STRANGLING A TEDDY BEAR...
SO THIS PART WILL BE ON THE TEST.
GLANCE
SCRIBBLE
SCRIBBLE
OH... OH, NO!
I COPIED THEM INTO MY NOTES, TOO!

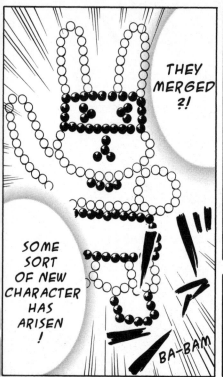

ARGH, RATS.
IT'S ALL A MESS, I CAN'T TELL WHAT'S GOING ON!
KLIK
KLIK
THEY MERGED ?!
SOME SORT OF NEW CHARACTER HAS ARISEN !
BA-BAM
HAS THEIR BATTLE ENDED FOR NOW?
SCRITCH
ANYWAYS, GOTTA GET BACK TO TAKING NOTES.
SCRITCH
KLIK
KLIK

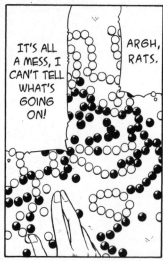

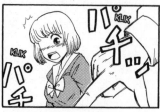

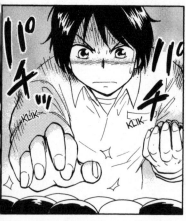

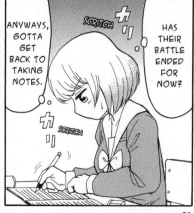

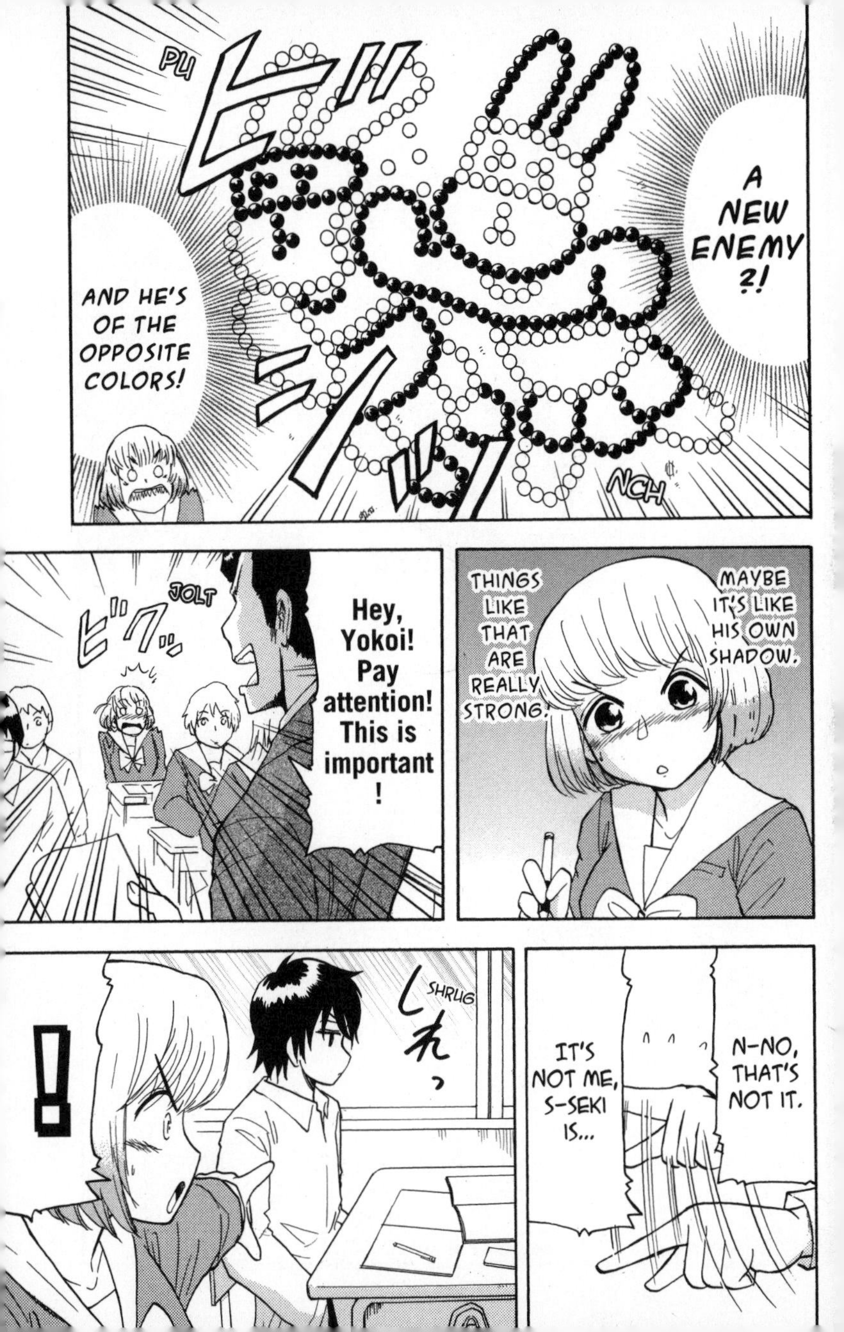
A NEW ENEMY ?!
PU
AND HE'S OF THE OPPOSITE COLORS!
NCH
MAYBE IT'S LIKE HIS OWN SHADOW.
THINGS LIKE THAT ARE REALLY STRONG.
Hey, Yokoi! Pay attention! This is important!
JOLT
N-NO, THAT'S NOT IT.
IT'S NOT ME, S-SEKI IS...
SHRUG
!

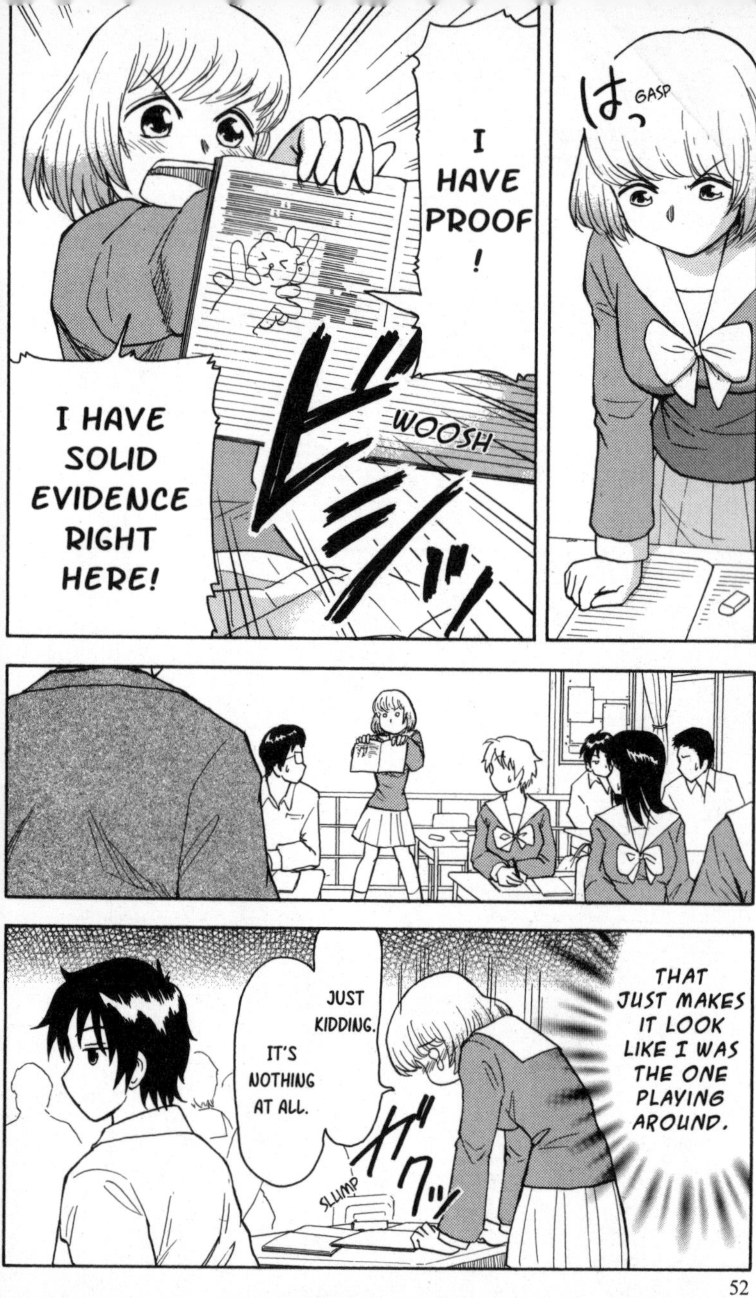
はっ
GASP
I HAVE PROOF!
I HAVE SOLID EVIDENCE RIGHT HERE!
WOOSH
ビシッ
THAT JUST MAKES IT LOOK LIKE I WAS THE ONE PLAYING AROUND.
JUST KIDDING.
IT'S NOTHING AT ALL.
ガクッ
SLUMP

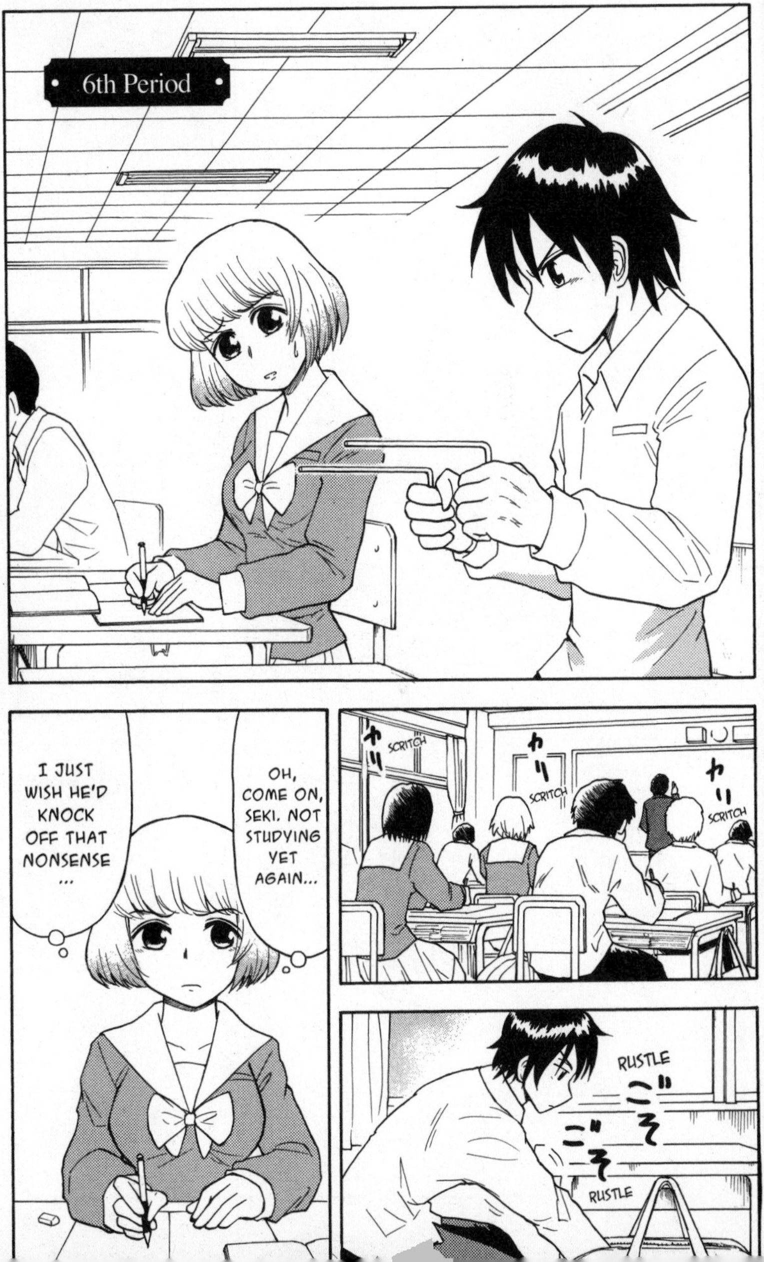
6th Period
カリ
SCRITCH
カリ
SCRITCH
カリ
SCRITCH
RUSTLE
ごそ
ごそ
RUSTLE
OH, COME ON, SEKI. NOT STUDYING YET AGAIN...
I JUST WISH HE'D KNOCK OFF THAT NONSENSE ...

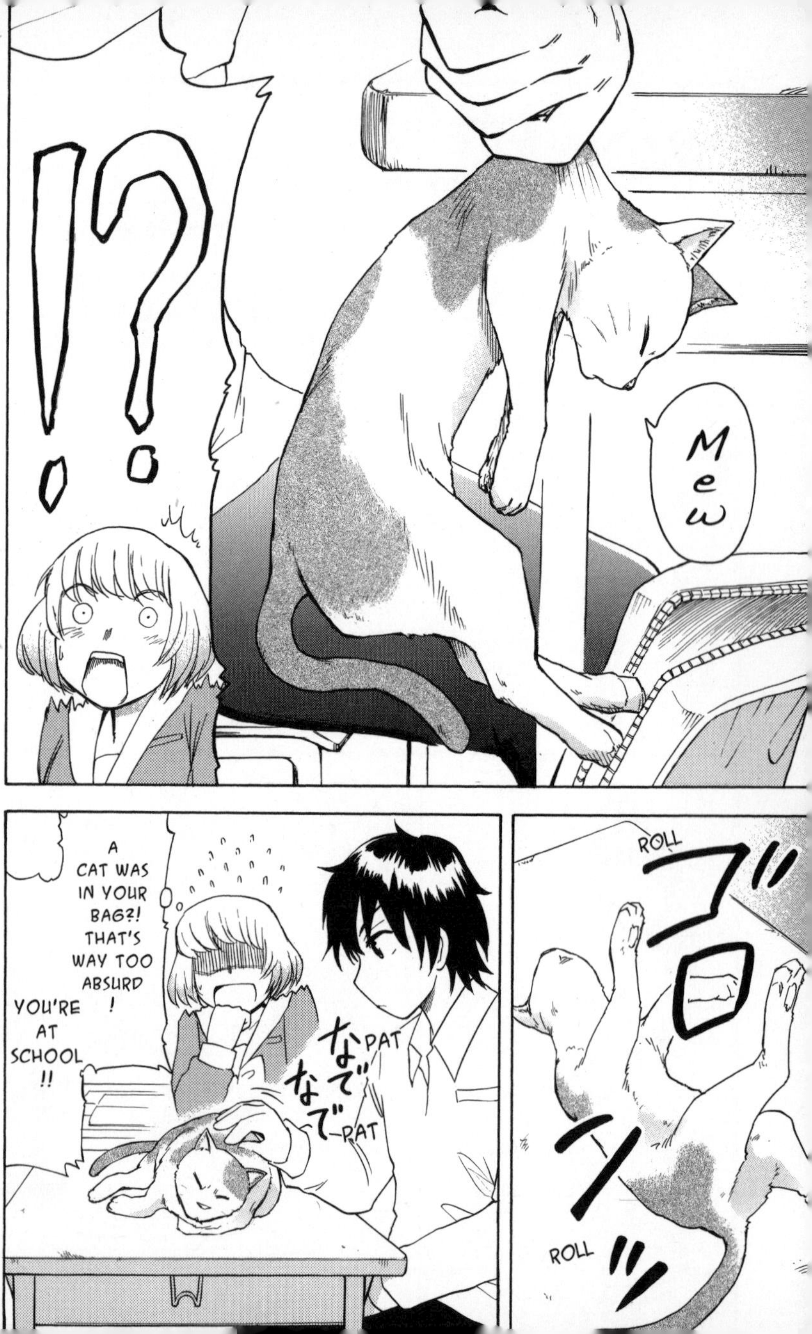
Mew
!?
ゴロンッ
ROLL
ROLL
A CAT WAS IN YOUR BAG?! THAT'S WAY TOO ABSURD!
YOU'RE AT SCHOOL!!
なでなで
PAT
PAT

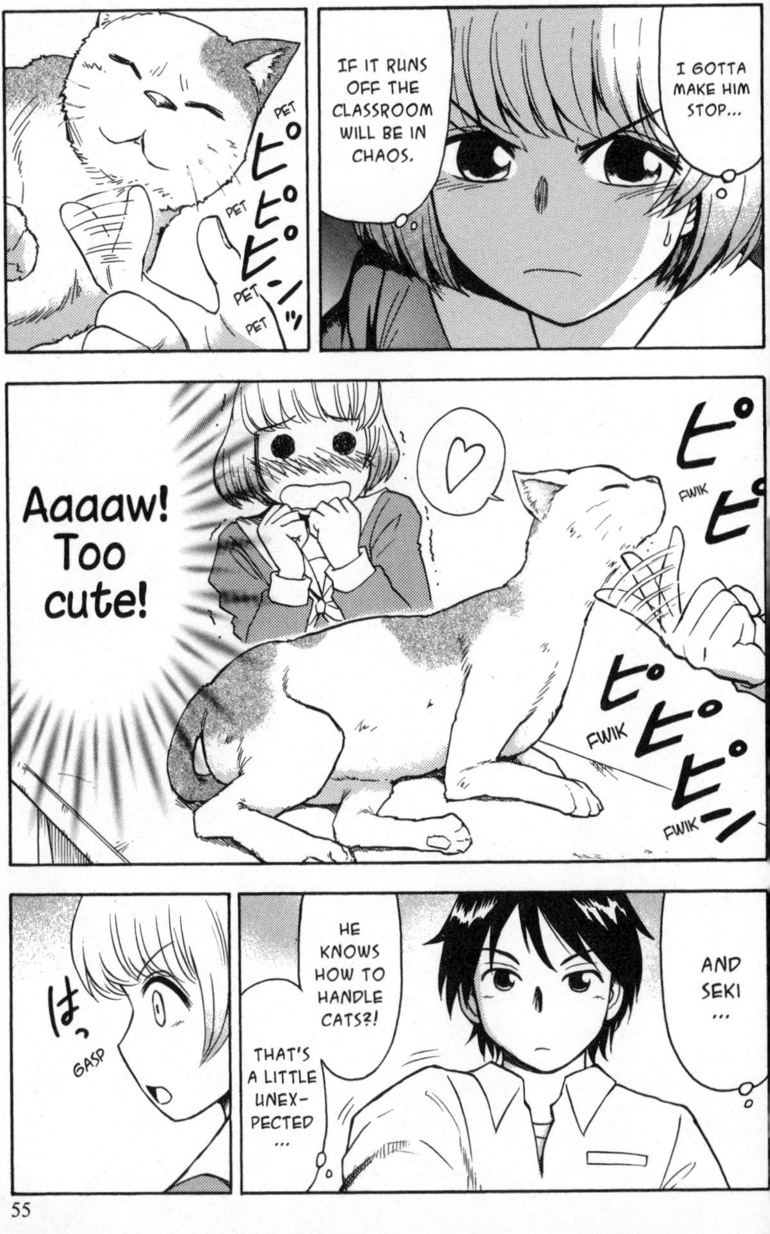
I GOTTA MAKE HIM STOP...
IF IT RUNS OFF THE CLASSROOM WILL BE IN CHAOS.
PET
PET
PET
PET
FWIK
FWIK
FWIK
Aaaaw! Too cute!
AND SEKI...
HE KNOWS HOW TO HANDLE CATS?!
THAT'S A LITTLE UNEX-PECTED...
GASP

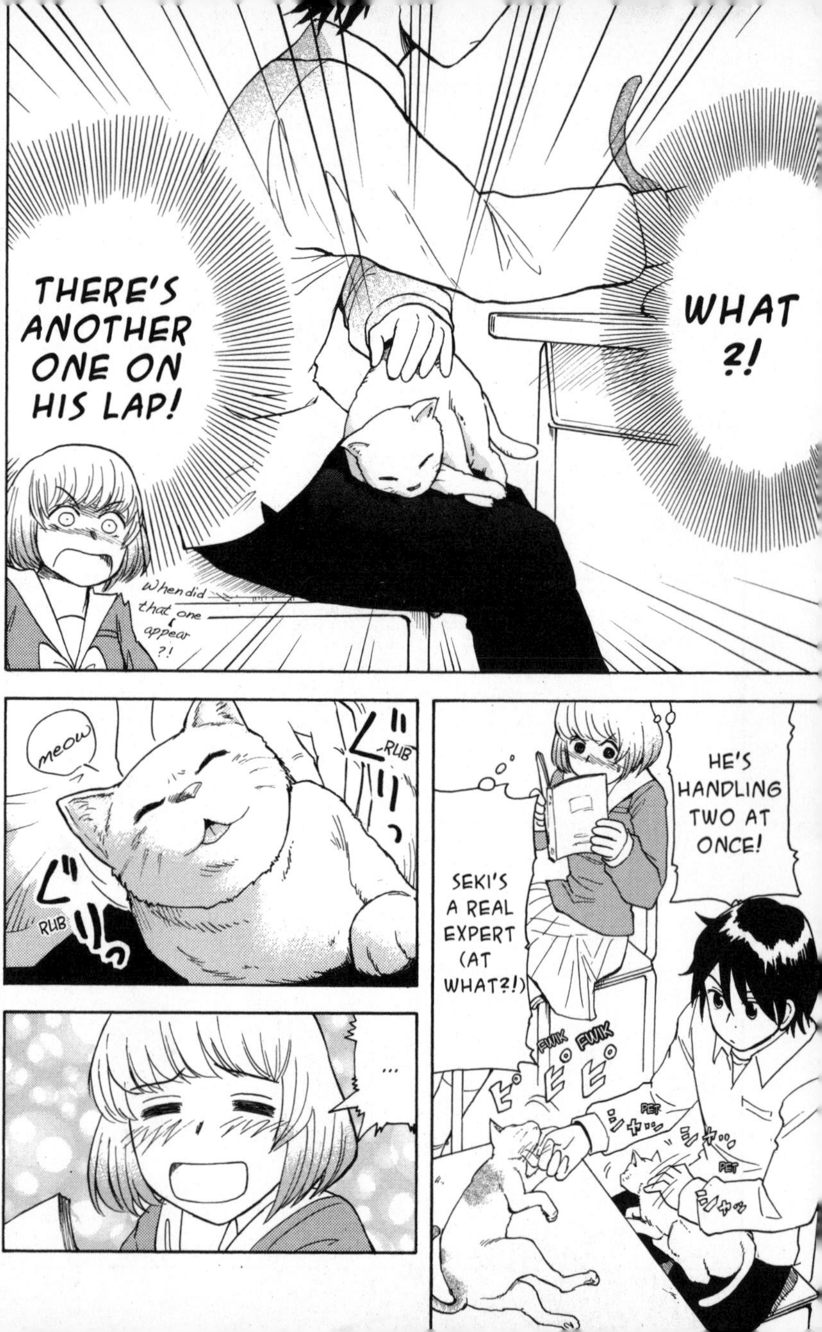
WHAT ?!
THERE'S ANOTHER ONE ON HIS LAP!
When did that one appear ?!
HE'S HANDLING TWO AT ONCE!
SEKI'S A REAL EXPERT (AT WHAT?!)
FWIK FWIK
PET
PET
RUB
meow
RUB
...

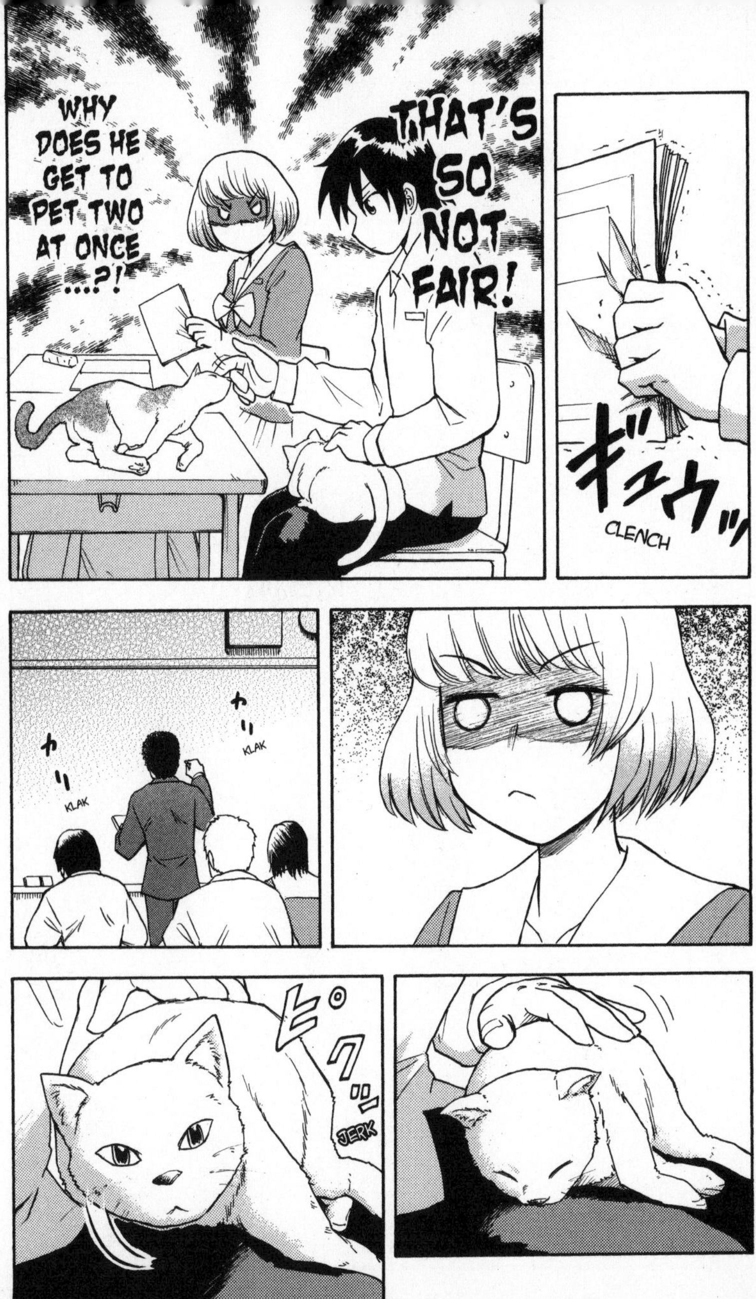
ギュウッ
CLENCH
THAT'S SO NOT FAIR!
WHY DOES HE GET TO PET TWO AT ONCE ...?!
カリ
KLAK
カリ
KLAK
ピクッ
JERK

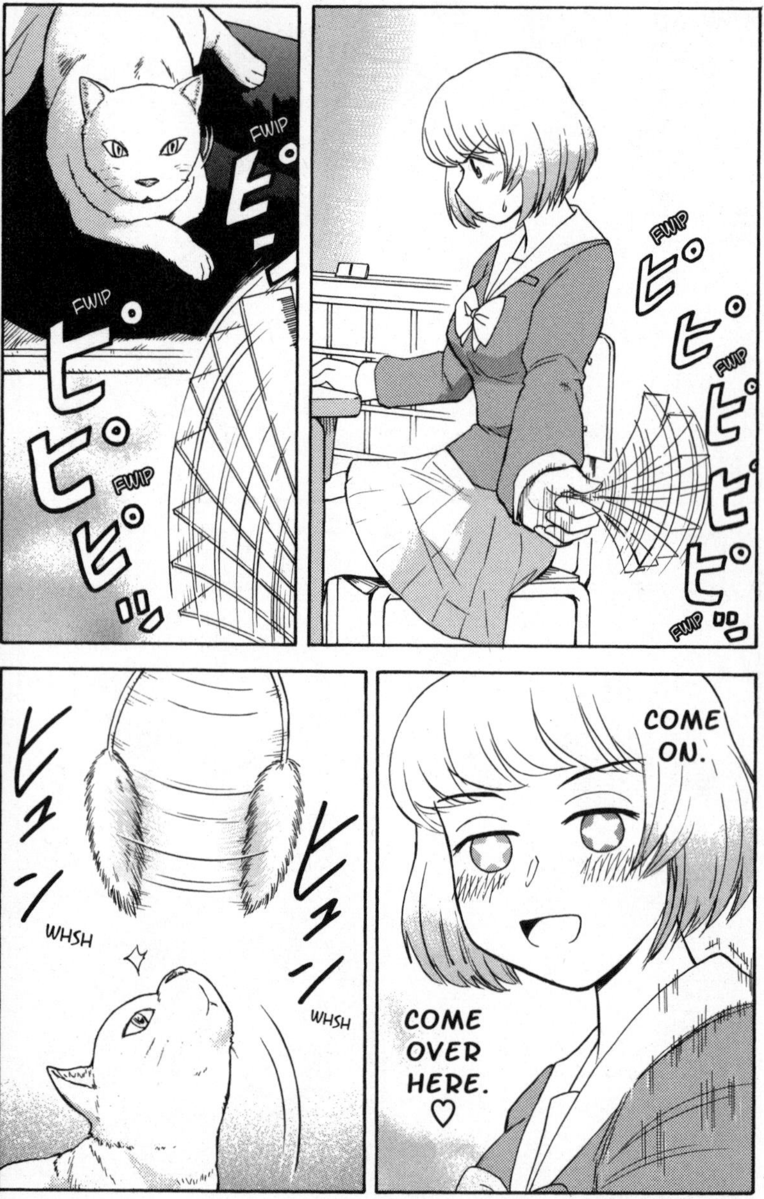
FWIP
FWIP
FWIP
FWIP
FWIP
FWIP
COME ON.
COME OVER HERE. ♡
WHSH
WHSH

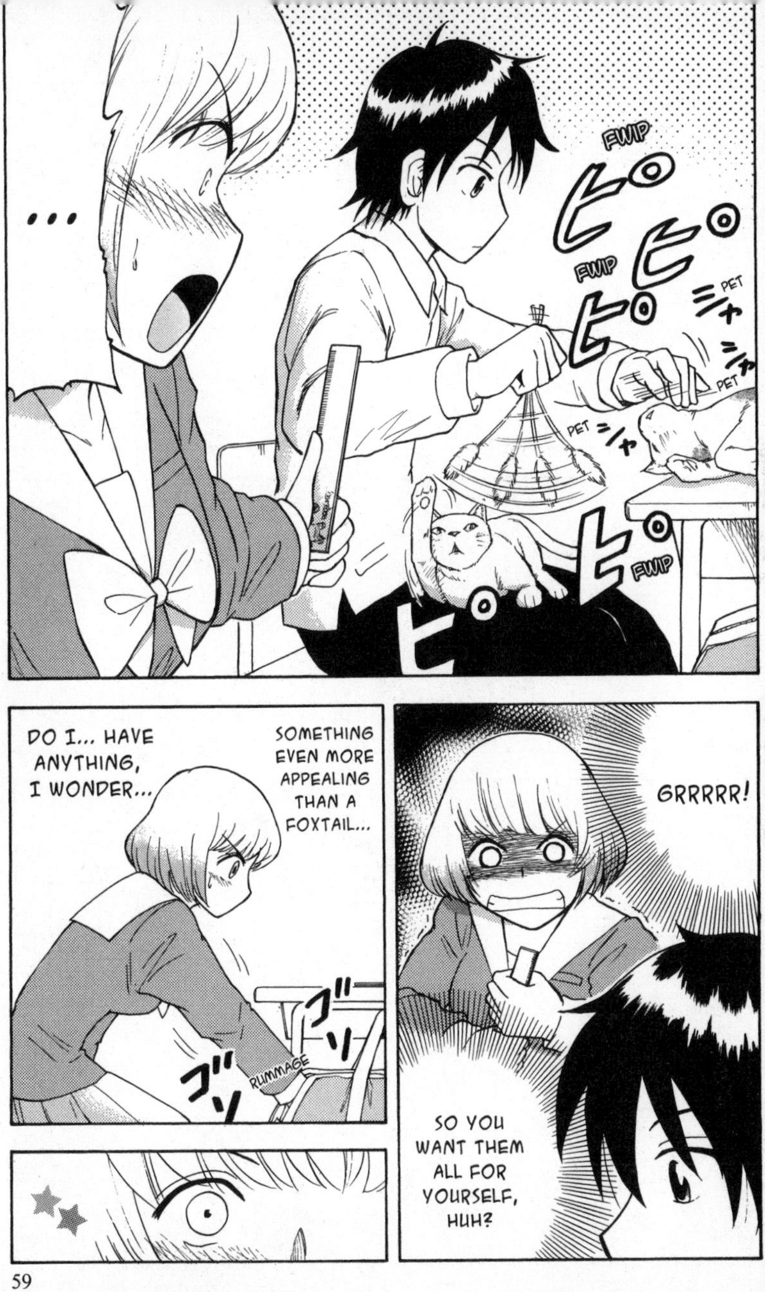
FWIP
FWIP
PET
PET
PET
FWIP
...
GRRRRR!
SO YOU WANT THEM ALL FOR YOURSELF, HUH?
SOMETHING EVEN MORE APPEALING THAN A FOXTAIL...
DO I... HAVE ANYTHING, I WONDER...
RUMMAGE

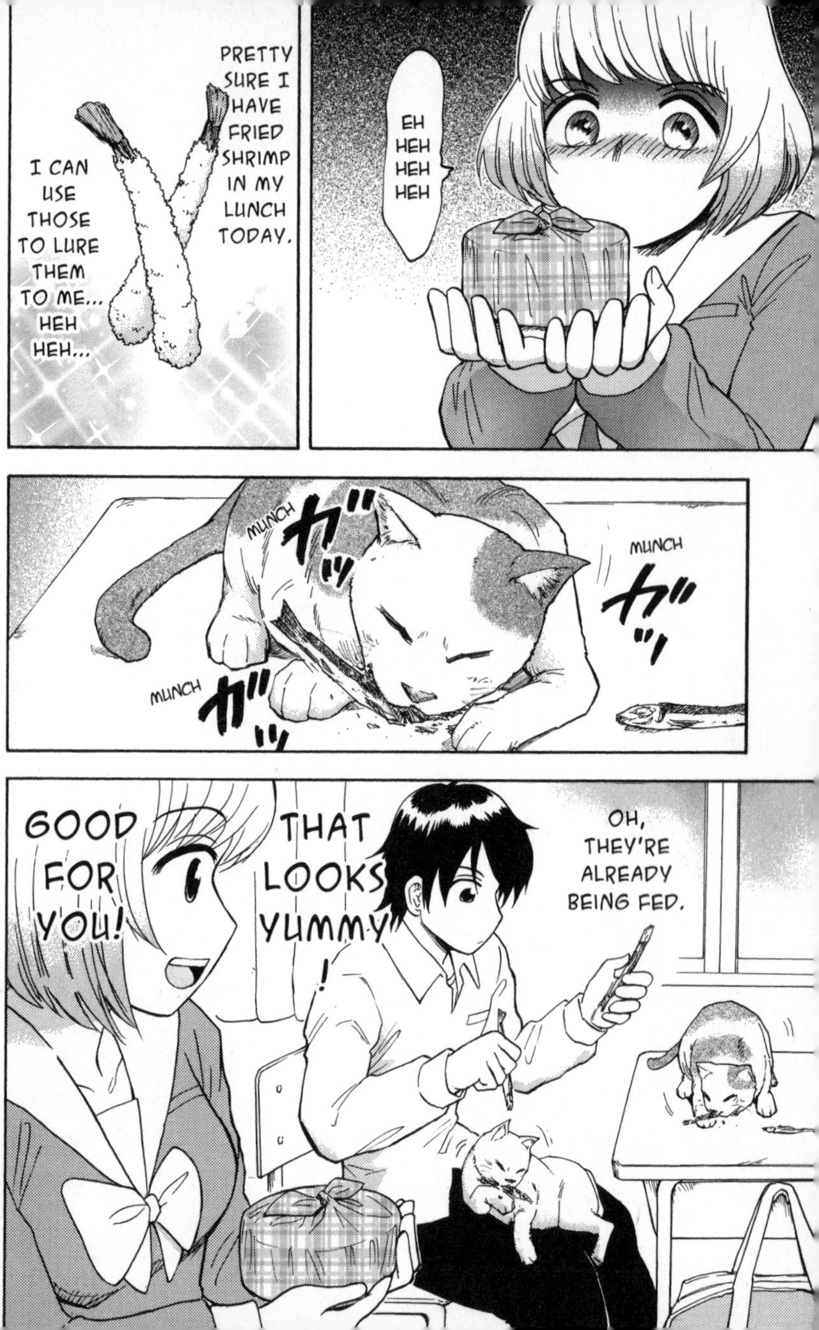
EH HEH HEH HEH
PRETTY SURE I HAVE FRIED SHRIMP IN MY LUNCH TODAY.
I CAN USE THOSE TO LURE THEM TO ME... HEH HEH...
MUNCH
ガッ
MUNCH
ガッ
MUNCH
ガッ
OH, THEY'RE ALREADY BEING FED.
THAT LOOKS YUMMY!
GOOD FOR YOU!

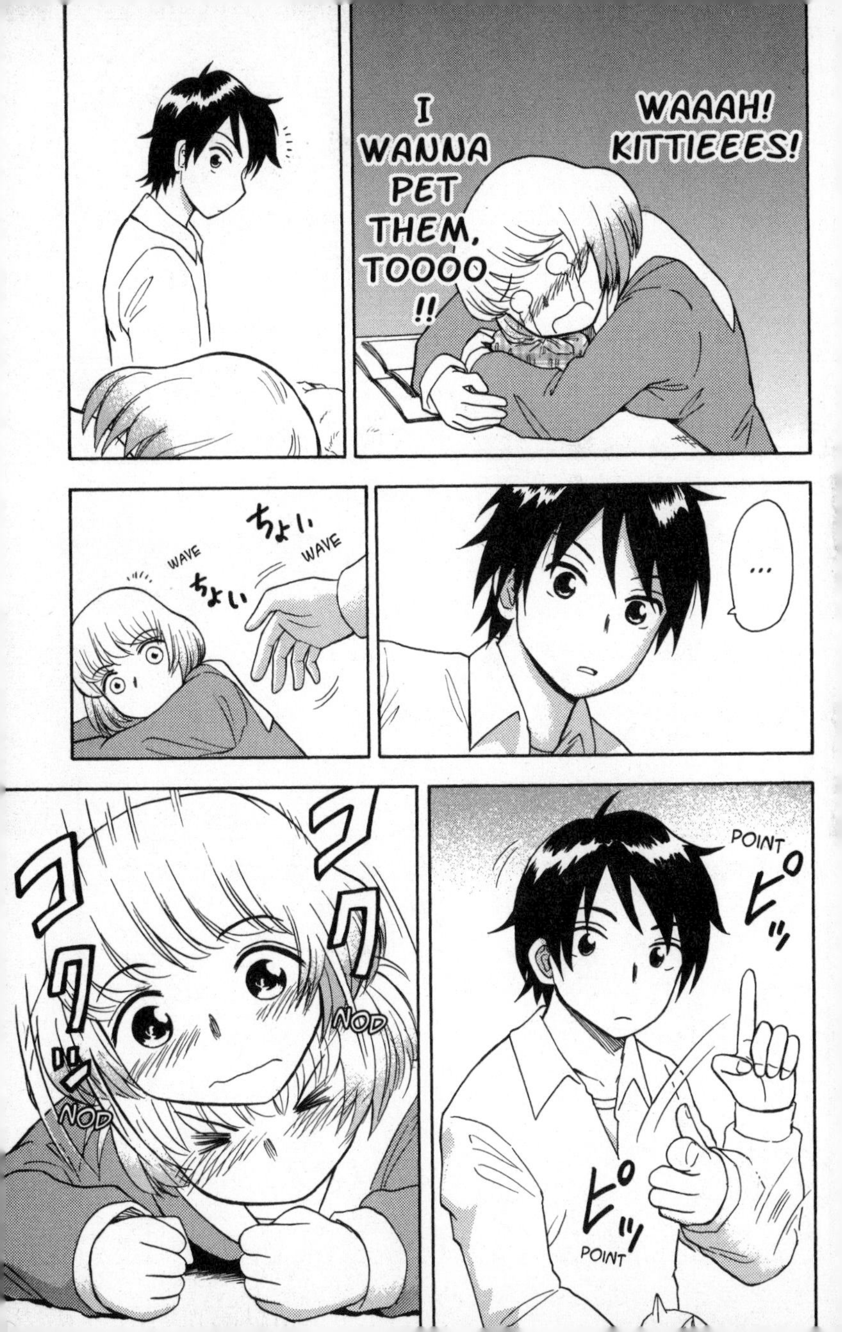
WAAAH! KITTIEEES!
I WANNA PET THEM, TOOOO!!
...
ちょい
WAVE
ちょい
WAVE
ピッ
POINT
ピッ
POINT
コク
NOD
コクッ
NOD

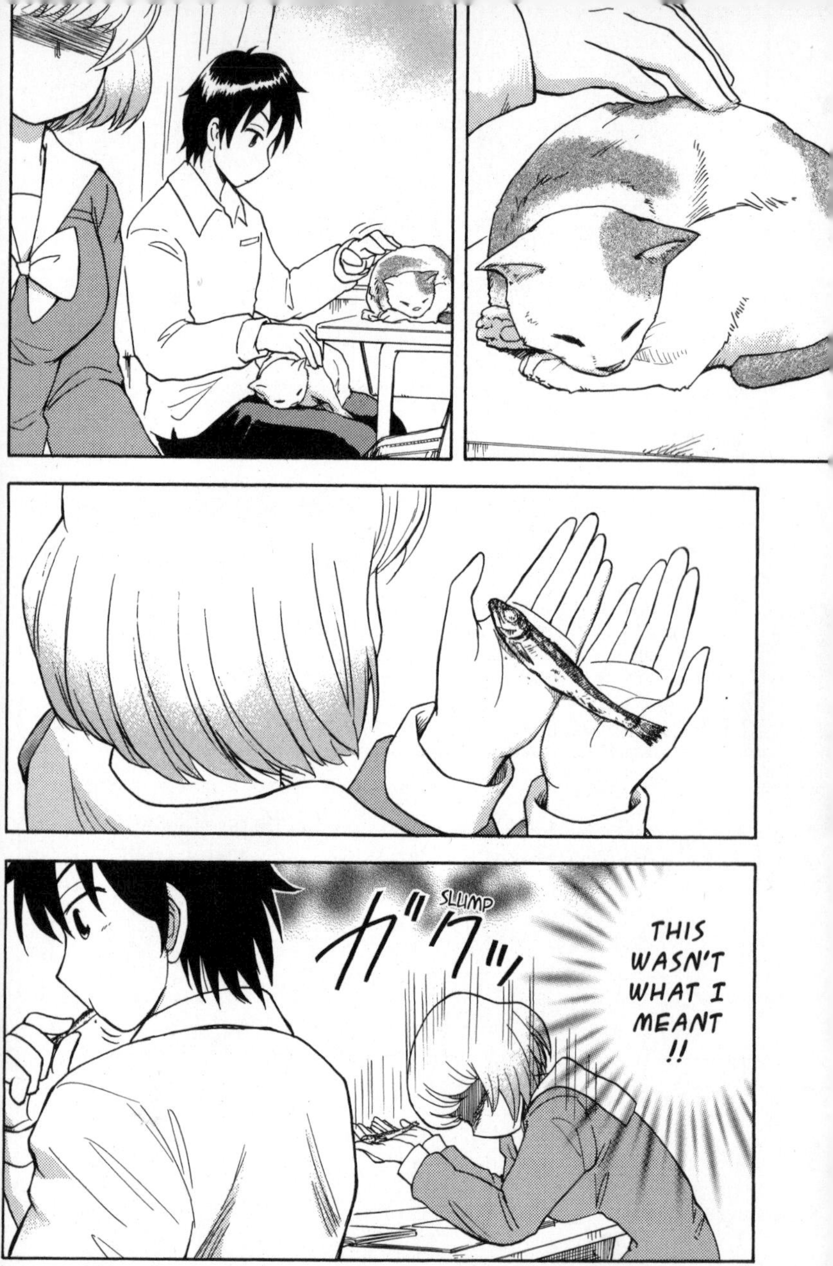
SLUMP
ガクッ
THIS WASN'T WHAT I MEANT !!

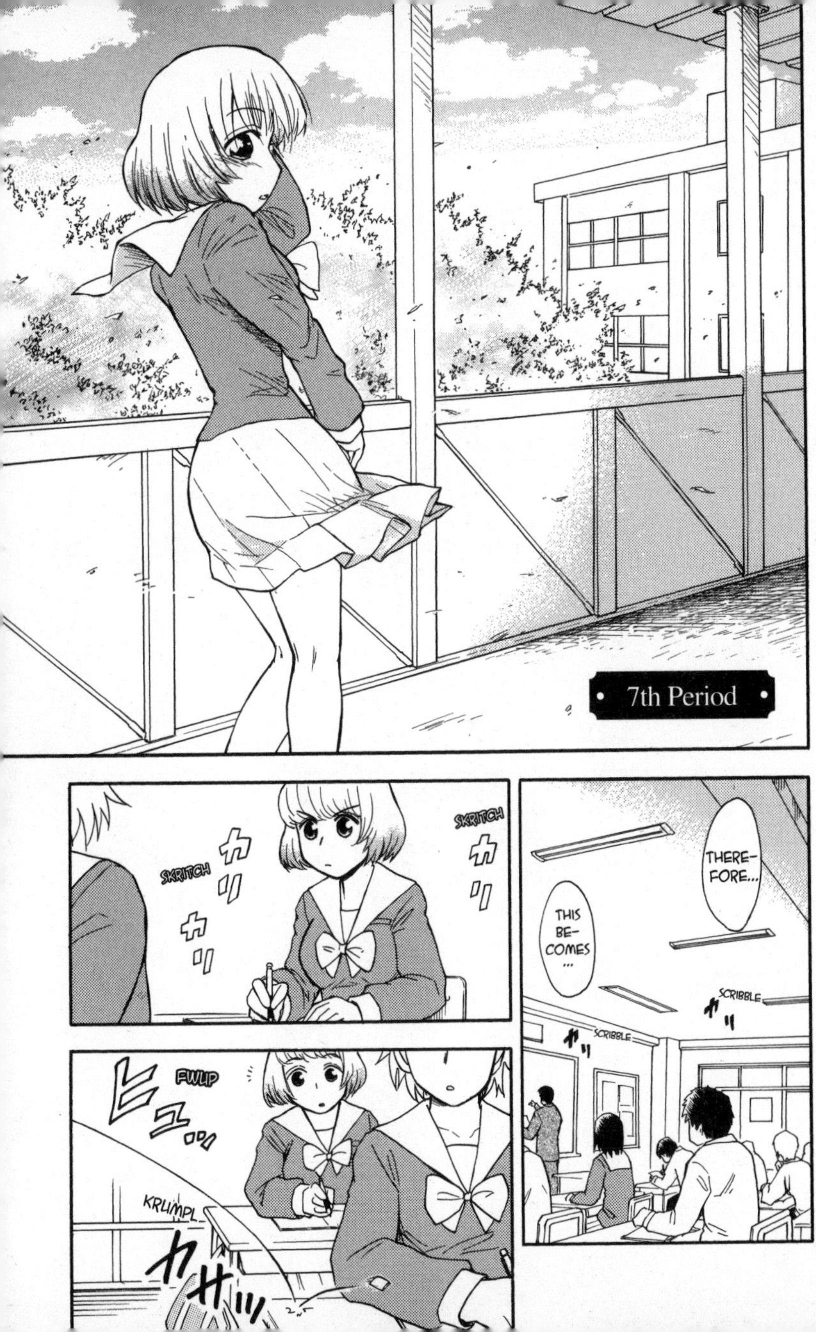
7th Period
THERE-FORE...
THIS BE-COMES ...
SCRIBBLE
SCRIBBLE
SKRITCH
カリ
SKRITCH
カリ
カリ
FWUP
KRUMPL

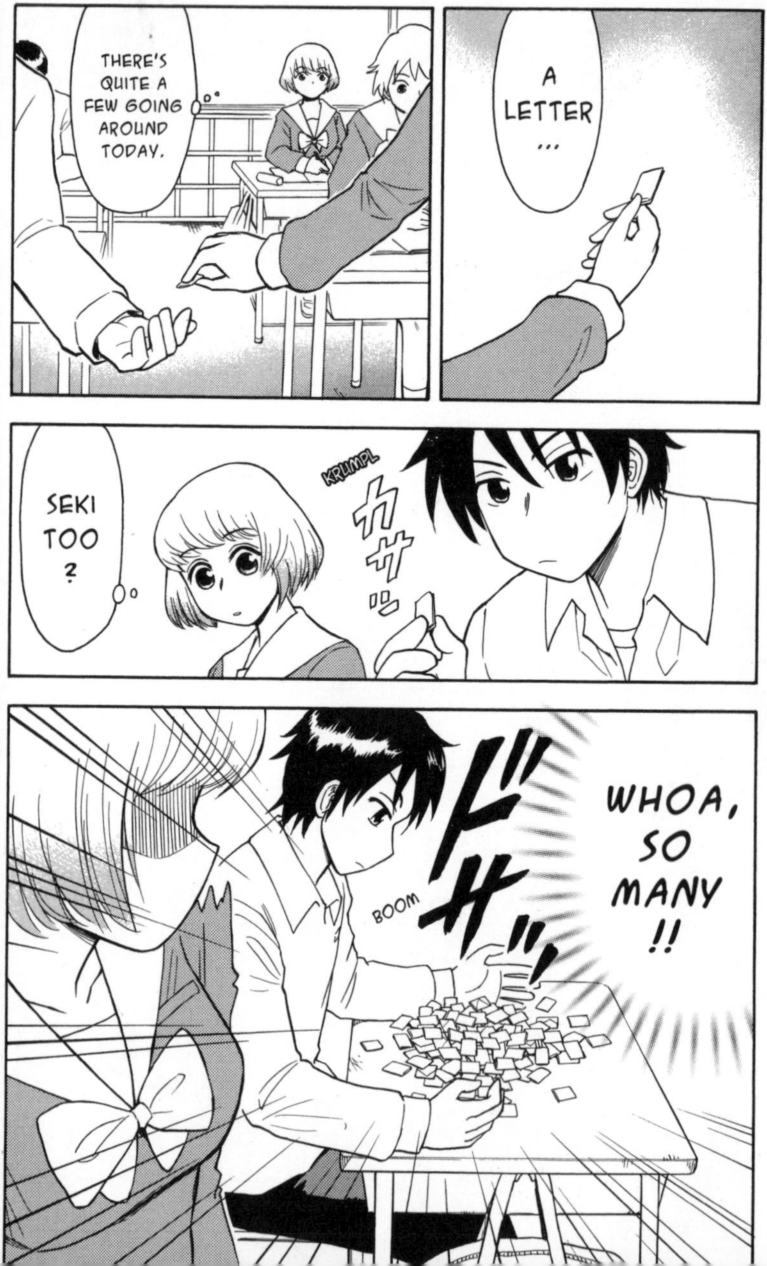
A LETTER ...
THERE'S QUITE A FEW GOING AROUND TODAY.
KRUMPL
カサッ
SEKI TOO ?
WHOA, SO MANY !!
ドサッ
BOOM

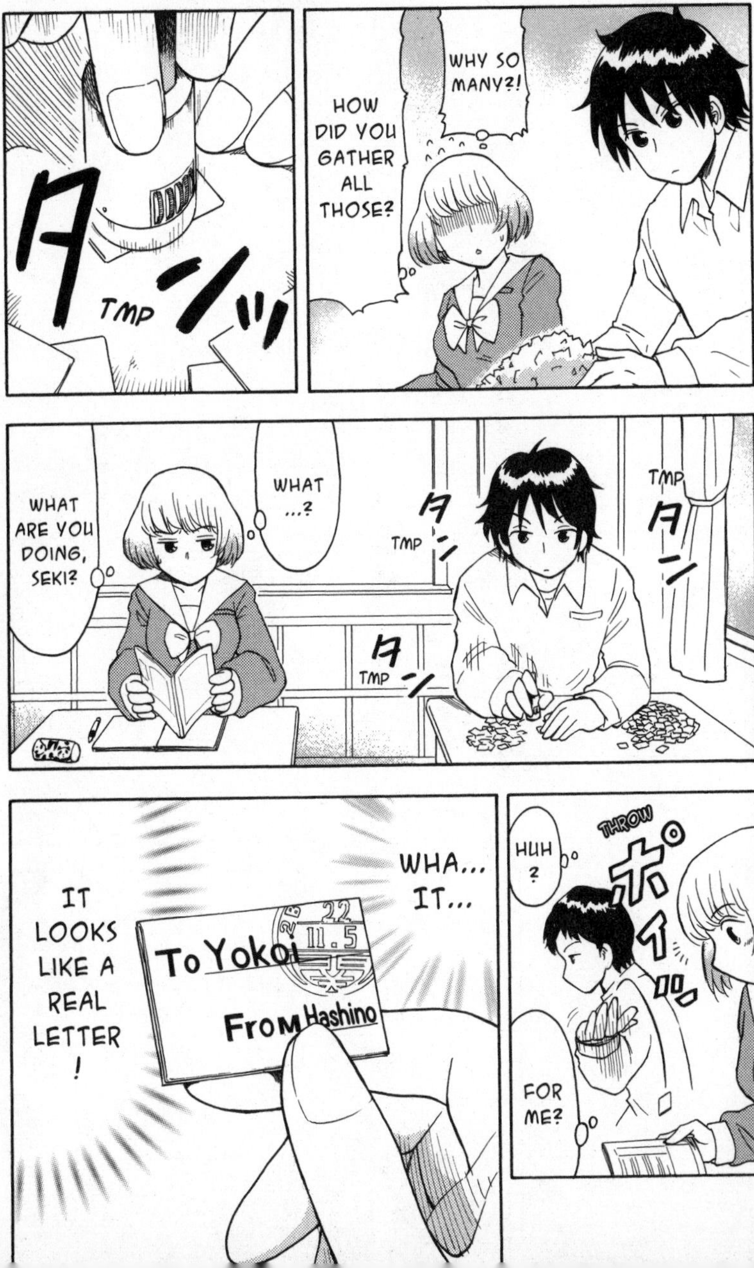
WHY SO MANY?!
HOW DID YOU GATHER ALL THOSE?
TMP
タンッ
TMP
タン
TMP
タン
WHAT ...?
WHAT ARE YOU DOING, SEKI?
TMP
タン
THROW
ポイッ
HUH?
FOR ME?
WHA... IT...
IT LOOKS LIKE A REAL LETTER!
22
11.5
To Yokoi
From Hashino

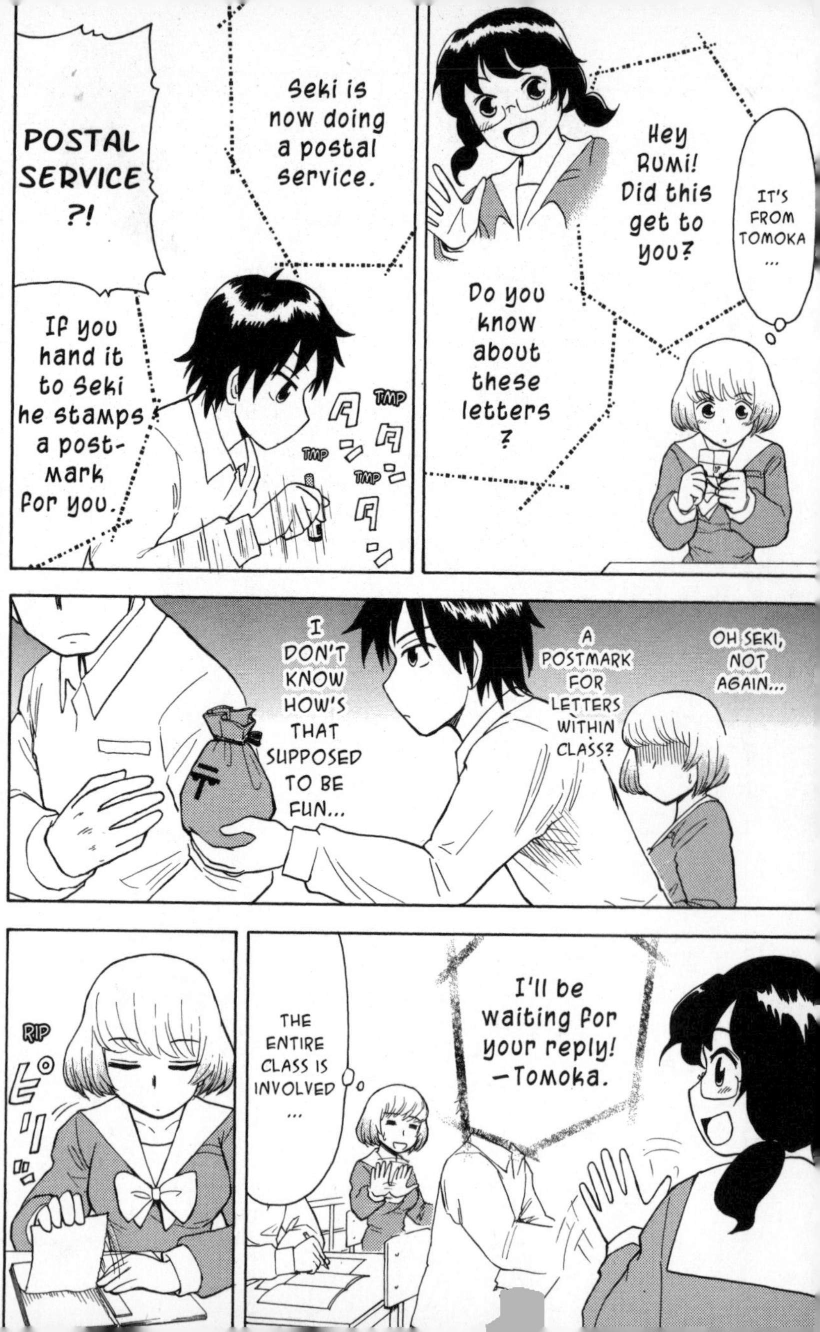
Hey Rumi! Did this get to you?
IT'S FROM TOMOKA ...
Do you know about these letters?
Seki is now doing a postal service.
POSTAL SERVICE ?!
TMP
TMP
TMP
If you hand it to Seki he stamps a post-mark for you.
OH SEKI, NOT AGAIN...
A POSTMARK FOR LETTERS WITHIN CLASS?
I DON'T KNOW HOW'S THAT SUPPOSED TO BE FUN...
I'll be waiting for your reply! —Tomoka.
THE ENTIRE CLASS IS INVOLVED ...
RIP

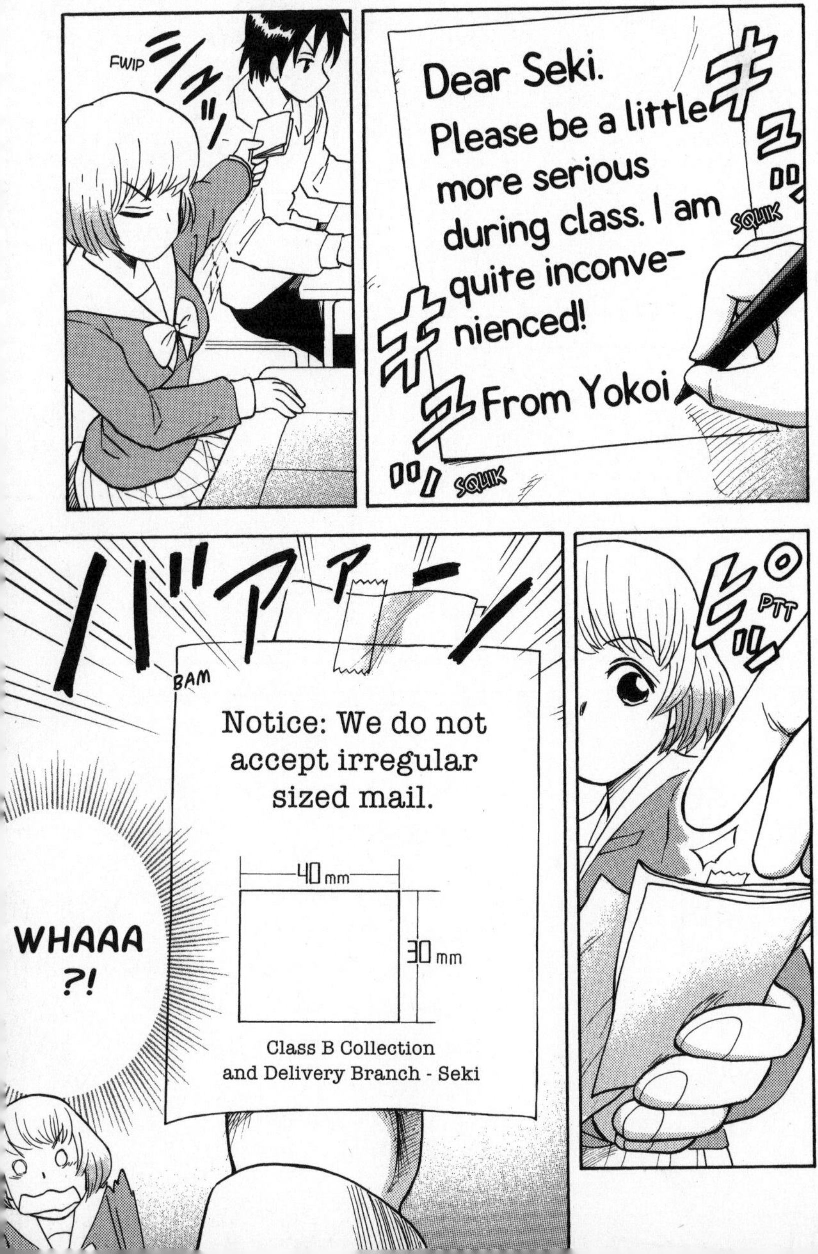
Dear Seki.
Please be a little more serious during class. I am quite inconve-nienced!
From Yokoi
SQUIK
SQUIK
FWIP
PTT
BAM
Notice: We do not accept irregular sized mail.
40mm
30mm
Class B Collection and Delivery Branch - Seki
WHAAA ?!

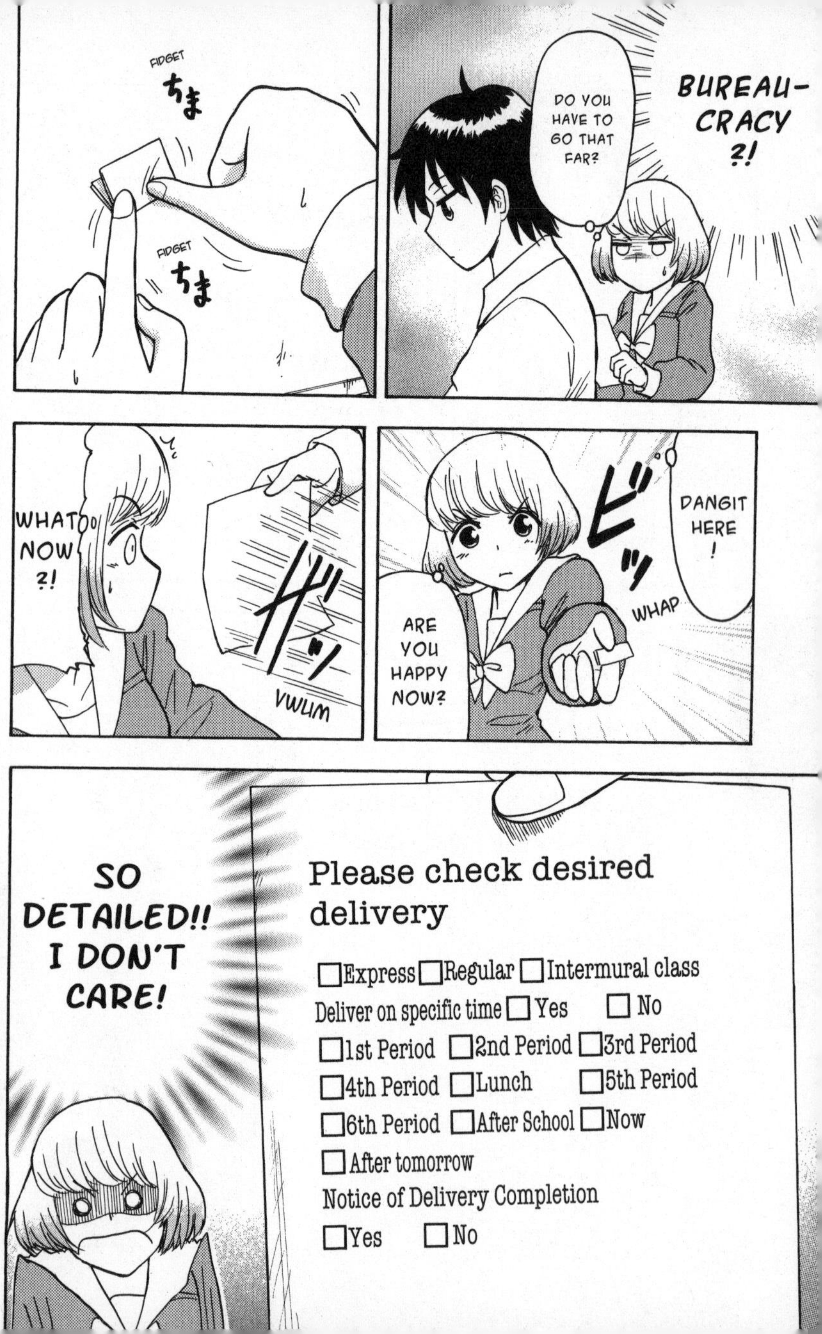
BUREAU-CRACY ?!
DO YOU HAVE TO GO THAT FAR?
FIDGET
ちま
FIDGET
ちま
DANGIT HERE!
ビッ
WHAP
ARE YOU HAPPY NOW?
WHAT NOW?!
ザッ
VWUM
SO DETAILED!! I DON'T CARE!
Please check desired delivery
Express Regular Intermural class
Deliver on specific time Yes No
1st Period 2nd Period 3rd Period
4th Period Lunch 5th Period
6th Period After School Now
After tomorrow
Notice of Delivery Completion
Yes No

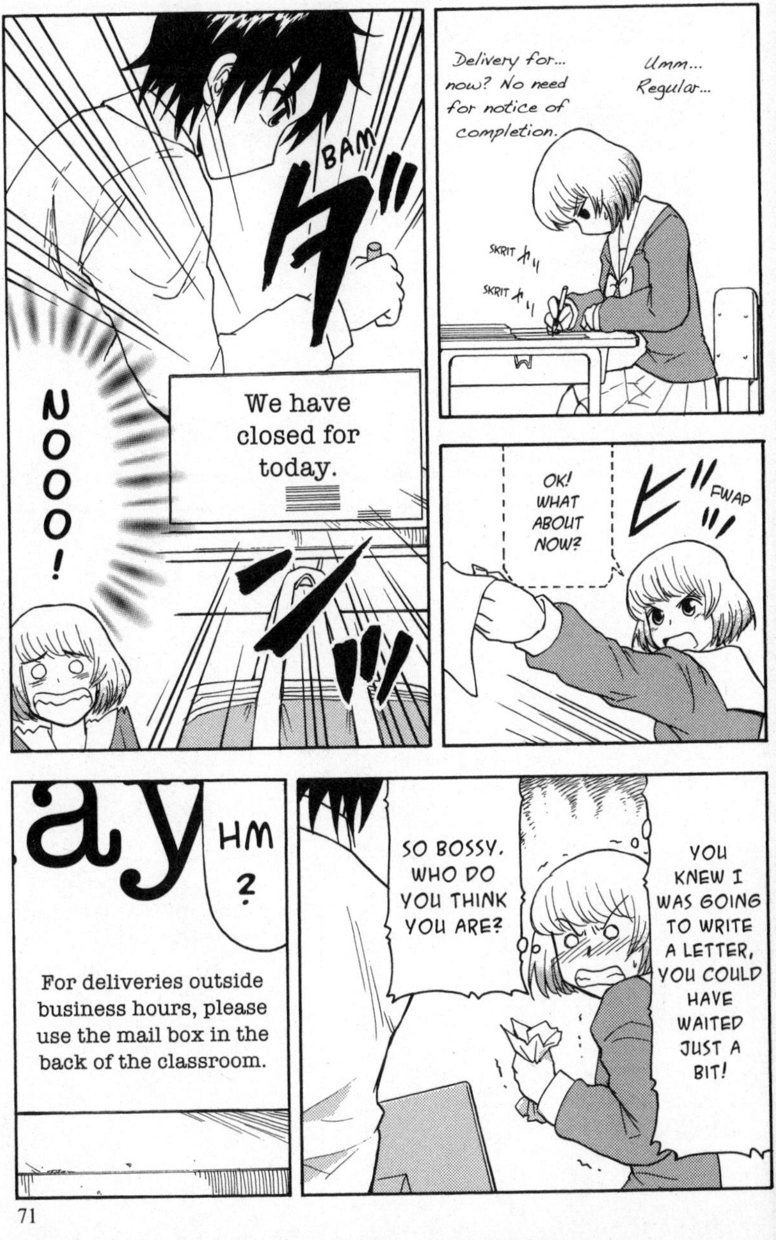
Umm... Regular...
Delivery for... now? No need for notice of completion.
SKRIT
SKRIT
FWAP
OK! WHAT ABOUT NOW?
BAM
We have closed for today.
NOOOO!
YOU KNEW I WAS GOING TO WRITE A LETTER, YOU COULD HAVE WAITED JUST A BIT!
SO BOSSY. WHO DO YOU THINK YOU ARE?
HM?
For deliveries outside business hours, please use the mail box in the back of the classroom.

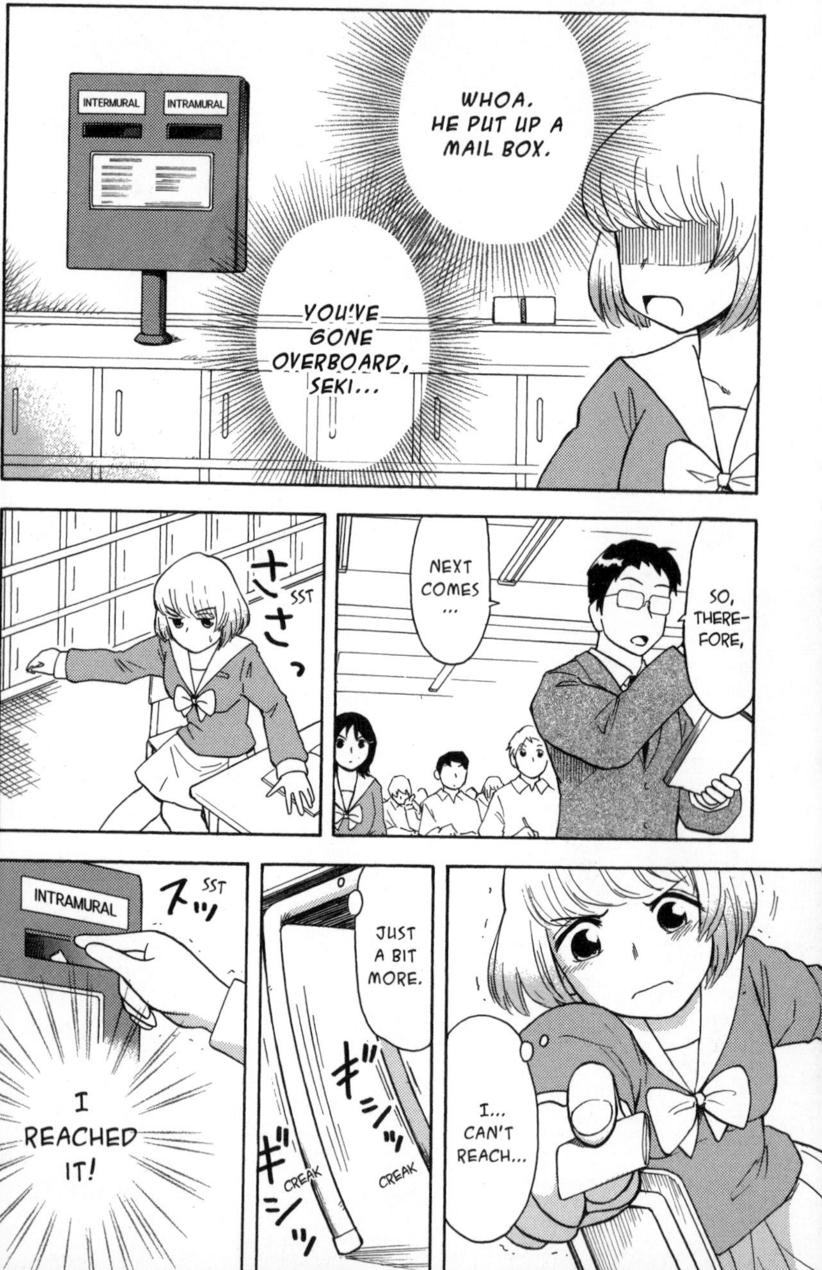
WHOA. HE PUT UP A MAIL BOX.
INTERMURAL
INTRAMURAL
YOU'VE GONE OVERBOARD, SEKI...
SO, THERE-FORE,
NEXT COMES ...
さっ
SST
I... CAN'T REACH...
JUST A BIT MORE.
ギシッ
CREAK
ギシッ
CREAK
INTRAMURAL
スッ
SST
I REACHED IT!

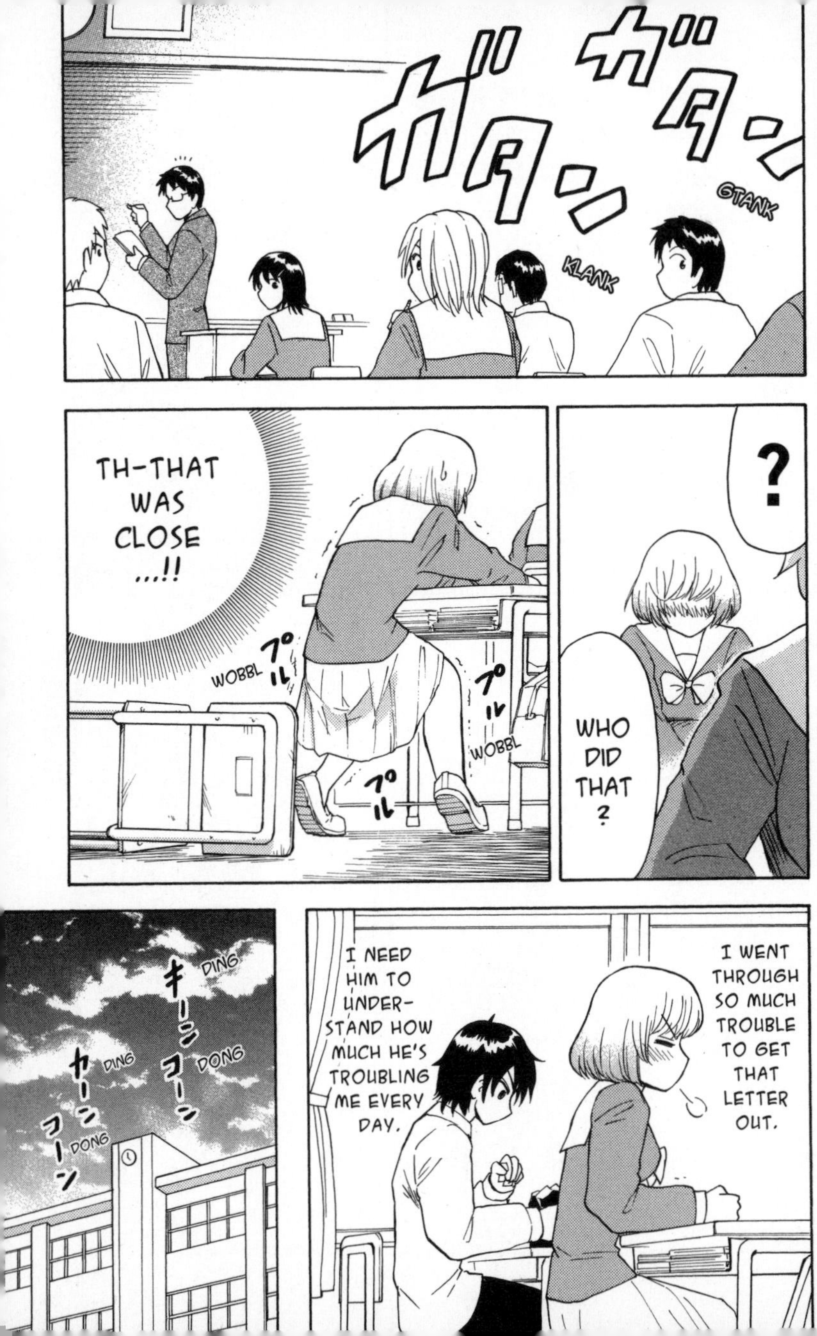
ガターン
GTANK
ガターン
KLANK
?
WHO DID THAT?
TH-THAT WAS CLOSE ...!!
プル
WOBBL
プル
WOBBL
プル
I WENT THROUGH SO MUCH TROUBLE TO GET THAT LETTER OUT.
I NEED HIM TO UNDER-STAND HOW MUCH HE'S TROUBLING ME EVERY DAY.
キーン
DING
コーン
DONG
カーン
DING
コーン
DONG

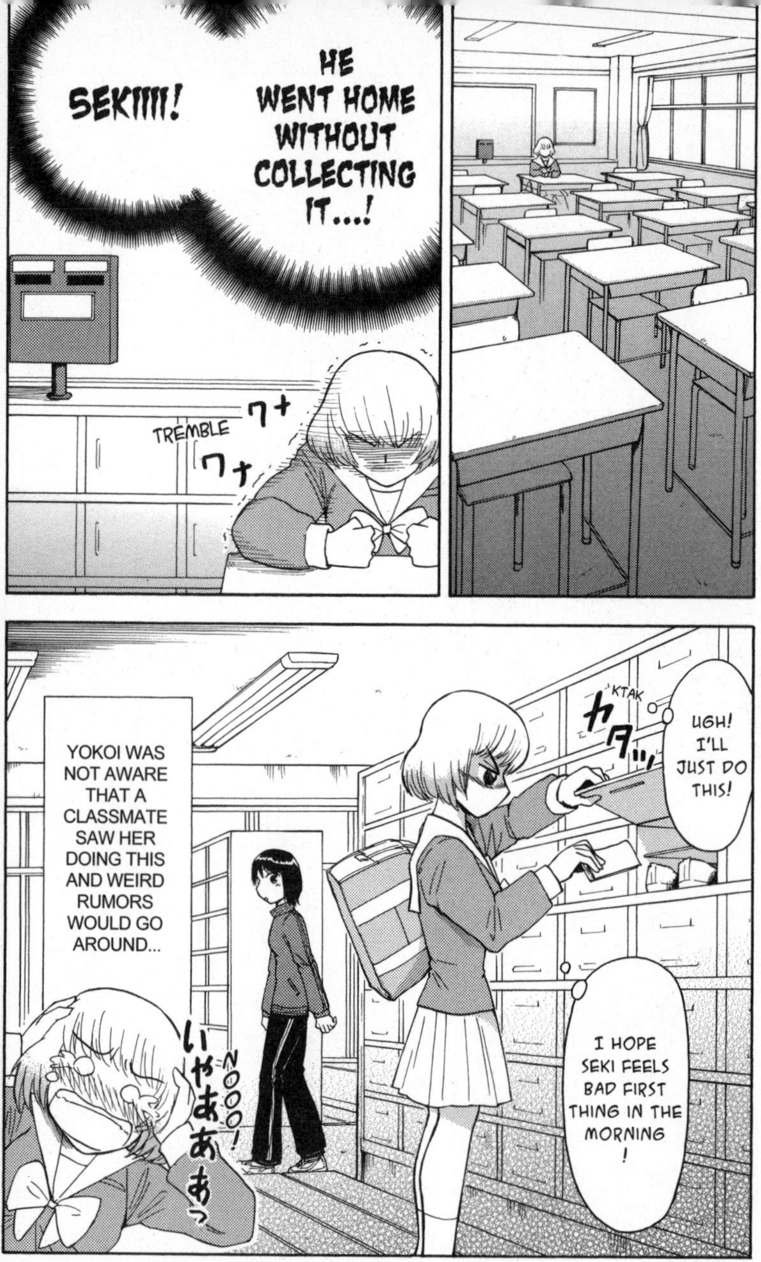
SEKIIII!
HE WENT HOME WITHOUT COLLECTING IT...!
TREMBLE
ワナワナ
KTAK
カタッ
UGH! I'LL JUST DO THIS!
I HOPE SEKI FEELS BAD FIRST THING IN THE MORNING!
YOKOI WAS NOT AWARE THAT A CLASSMATE SAW HER DOING THIS AND WEIRD RUMORS WOULD GO AROUND...
NOOOO!
いやあああっ

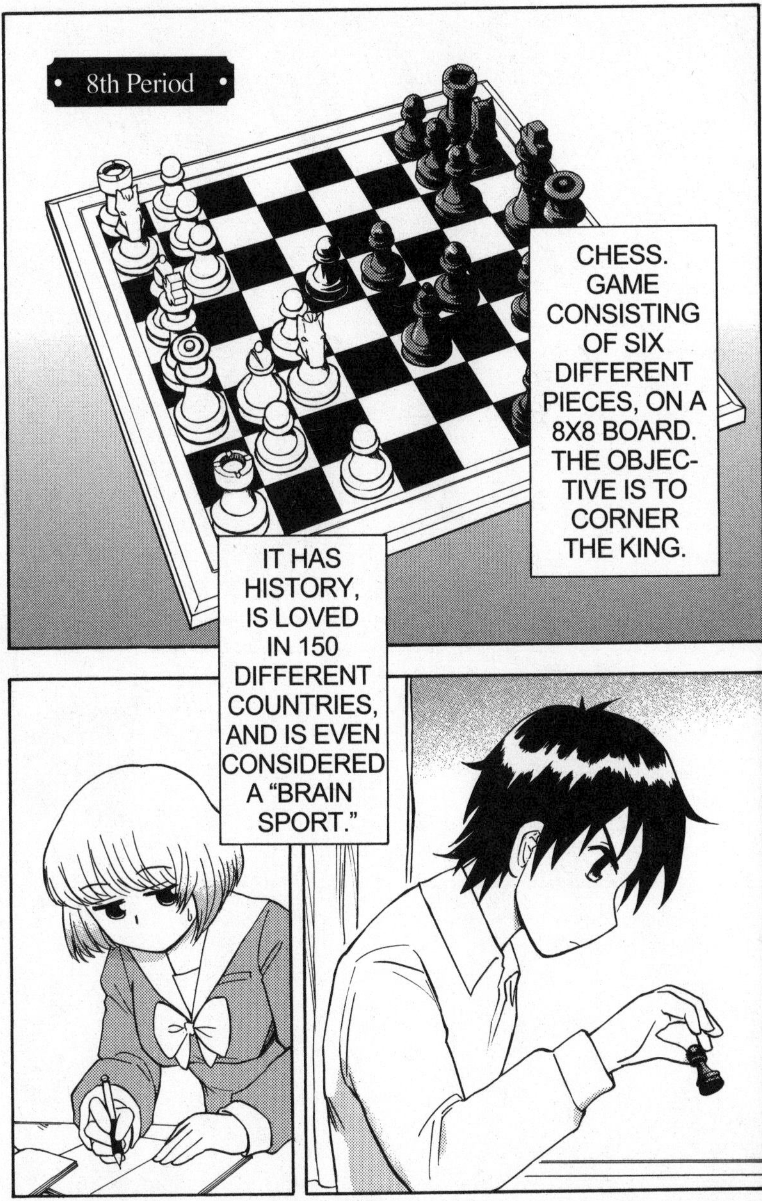
8th Period
CHESS. GAME CONSISTING OF SIX DIFFERENT PIECES, ON A 8X8 BOARD. THE OBJECTIVE IS TO CORNER THE KING.
IT HAS HISTORY, IS LOVED IN 150 DIFFERENT COUNTRIES, AND IS EVEN CONSIDERED A “BRAIN SPORT.”

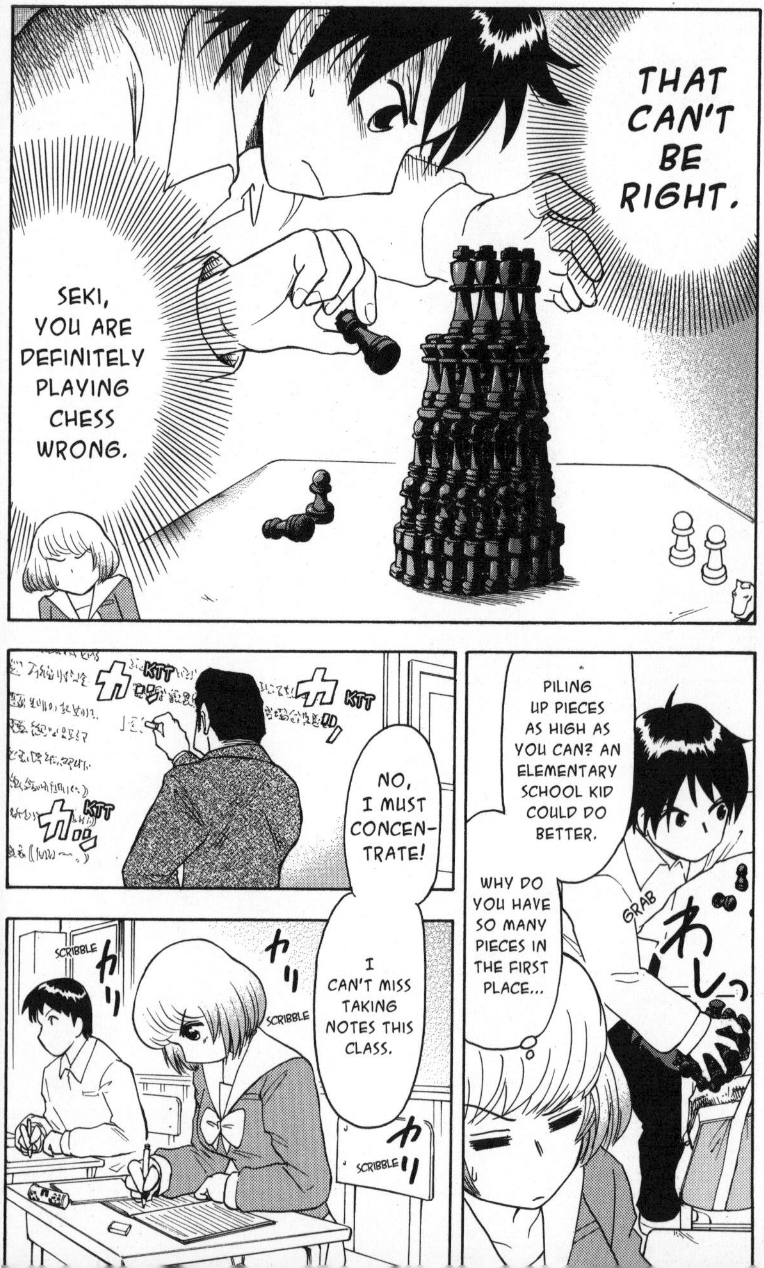
THAT CAN'T BE RIGHT.
SEKI, YOU ARE DEFINITELY PLAYING CHESS WRONG.
PILING UP PIECES AS HIGH AS YOU CAN? AN ELEMENTARY SCHOOL KID COULD DO BETTER.
GRAB
WHY DO YOU HAVE SO MANY PIECES IN THE FIRST PLACE...
KTT
KTT
KTT
NO, I MUST CONCEN-TRATE!
I CAN'T MISS TAKING NOTES THIS CLASS.
SCRIBBLE
SCRIBBLE
SCRIBBLE

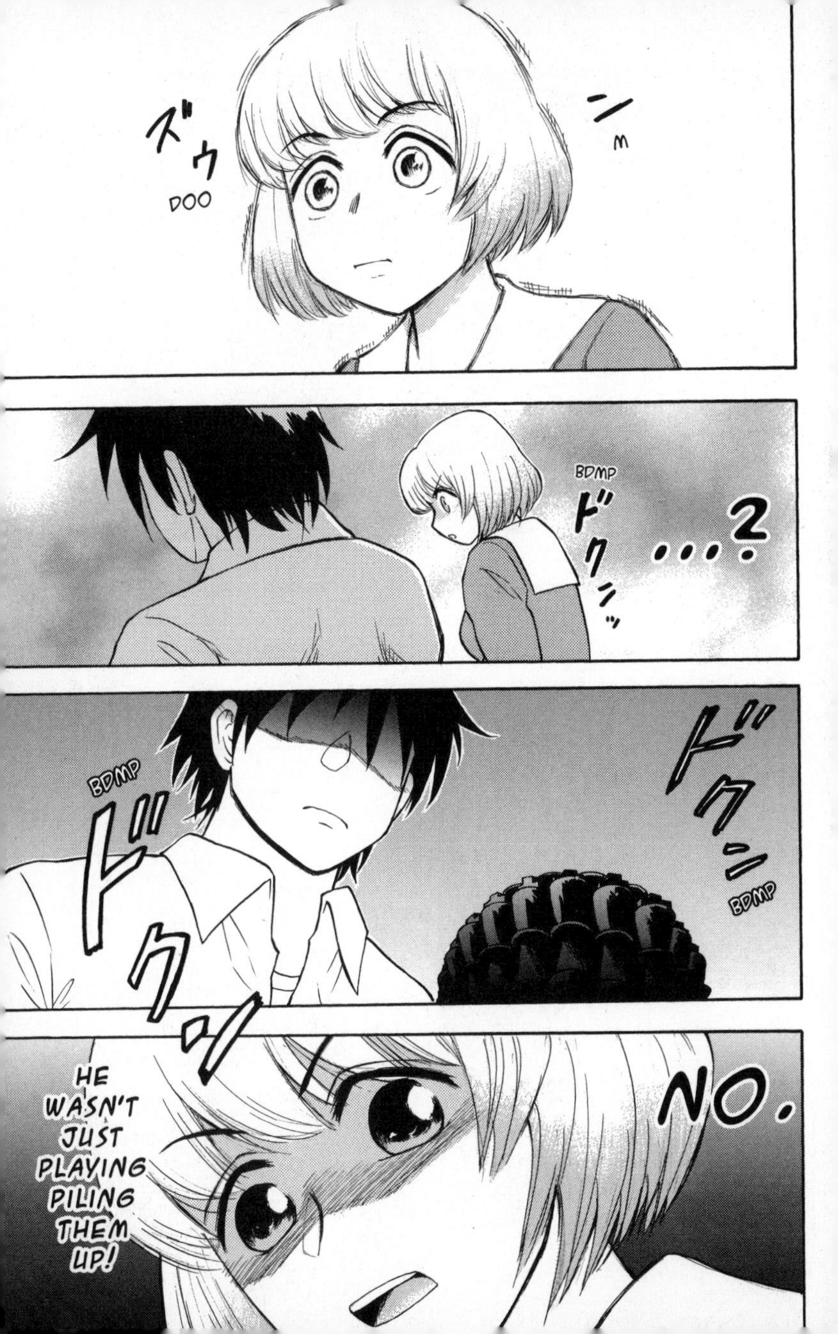
ン
m
ズウ
DOO
...?
ドクンッ
BDMP
ドクン
BDMP
ドクン
BDMP
NO.
HE WASN'T JUST PLAYING PILING THEM UP!

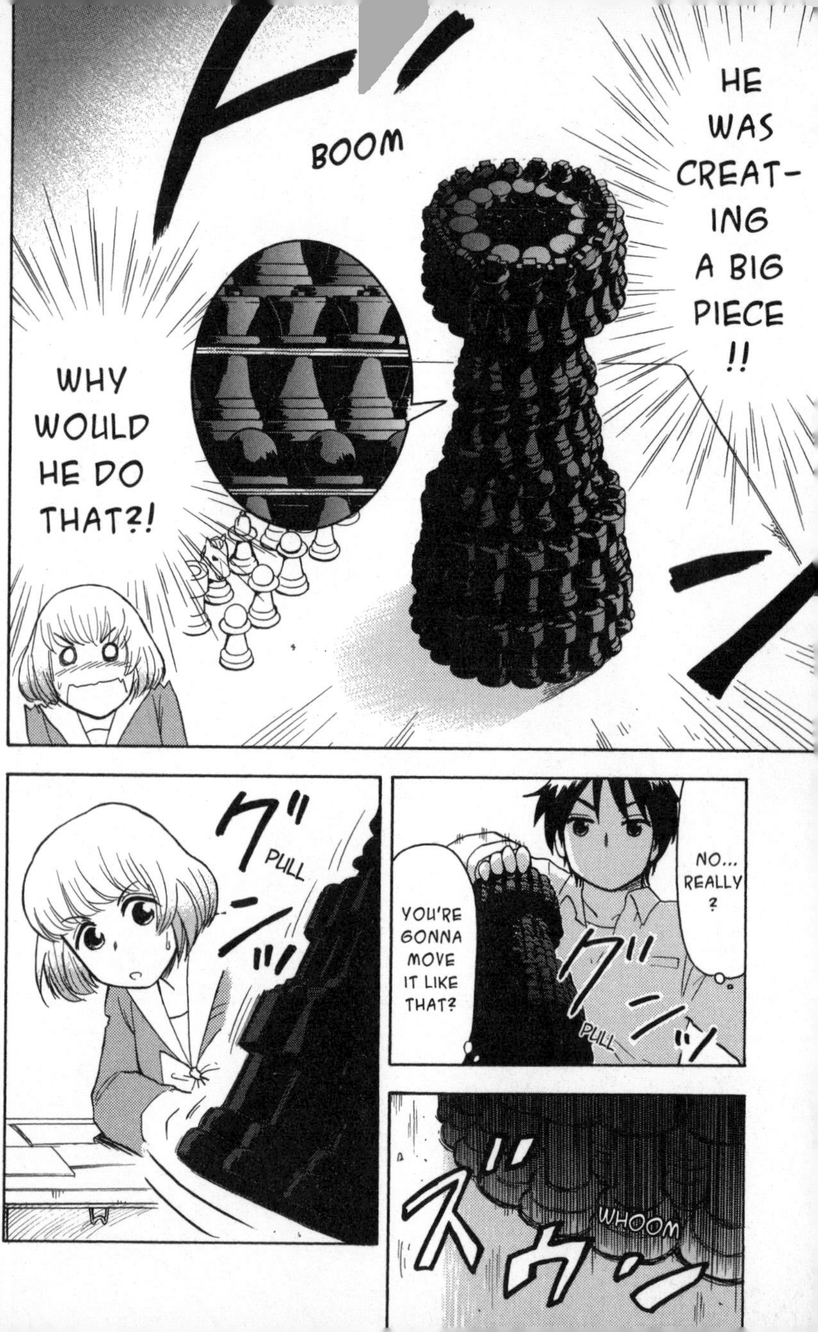
HE WAS CREATING A BIG PIECE!!
BOOM
WHY WOULD HE DO THAT?!
NO... REALLY?
YOU'RE GONNA MOVE IT LIKE THAT?
PULL
WHOOM
PULL

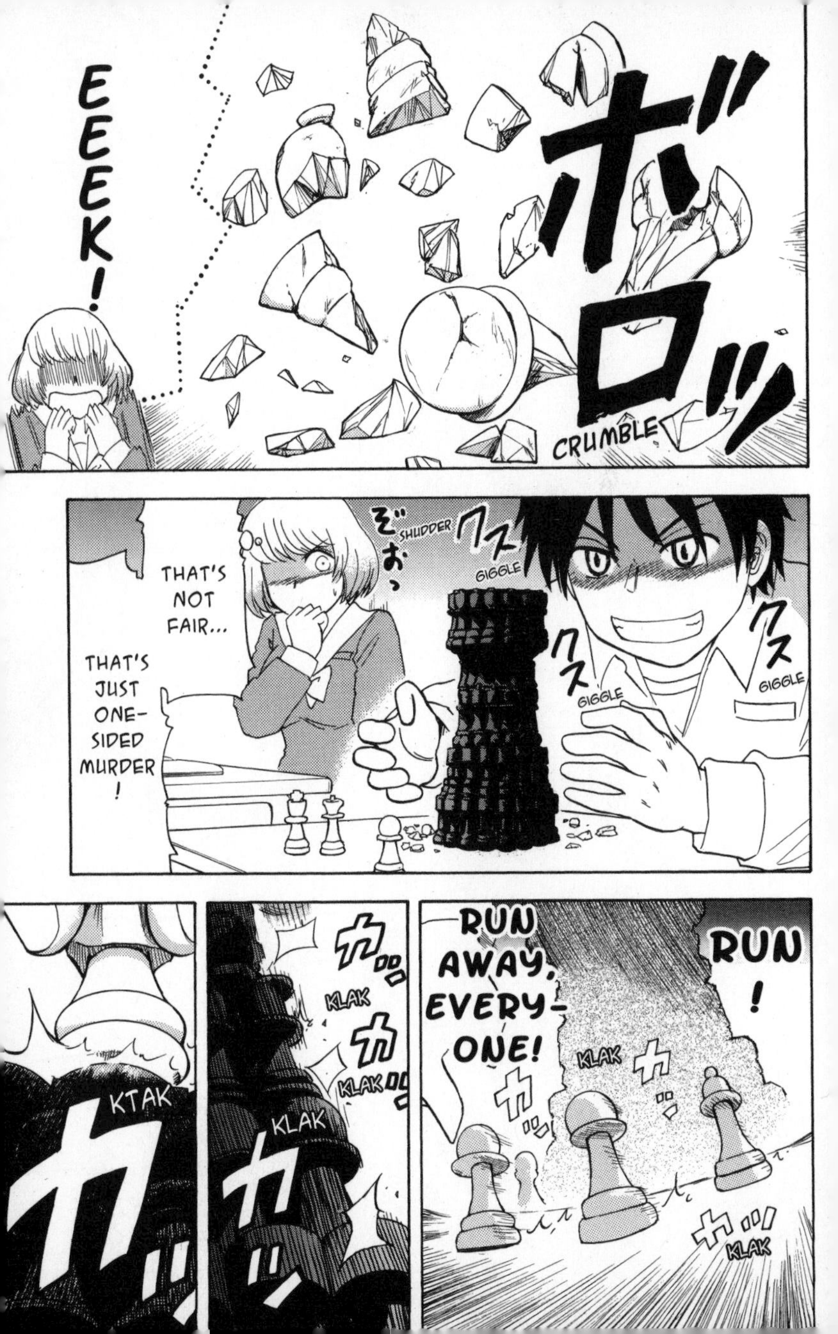

ボロッ
CRUMBLE
EEEEK!
クス
GIGGLE
クス
GIGGLE
クス
GIGGLE
ぞぉっ
SHUDDER
THAT'S NOT FAIR...
THAT'S JUST ONE-SIDED MURDER!
RUN!
RUN AWAY, EVERYONE!
カッ
KLAK
カッ
KLAK
カッ
KLAK
カッ
KLAK
カッ
KLAK
カッ
KLAK
カッ
KTAK

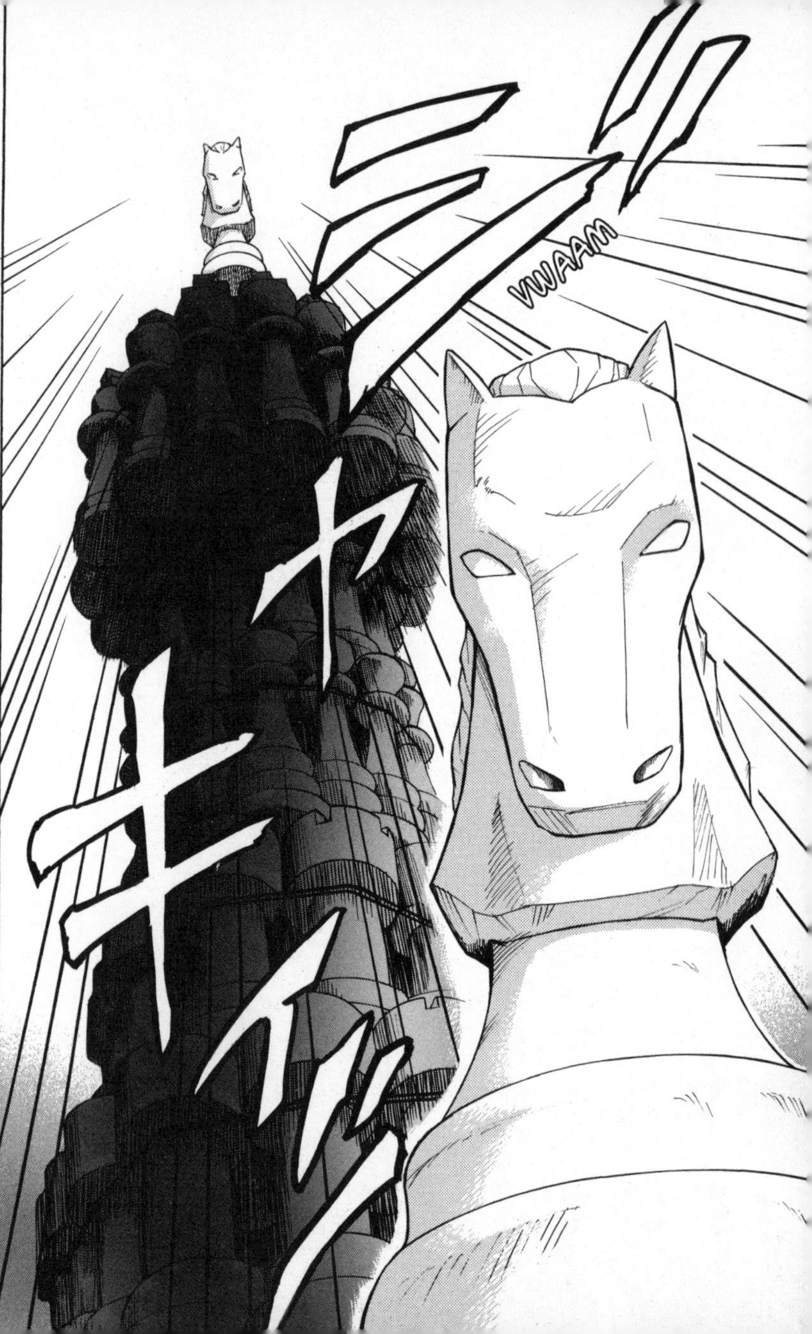
VWAAM

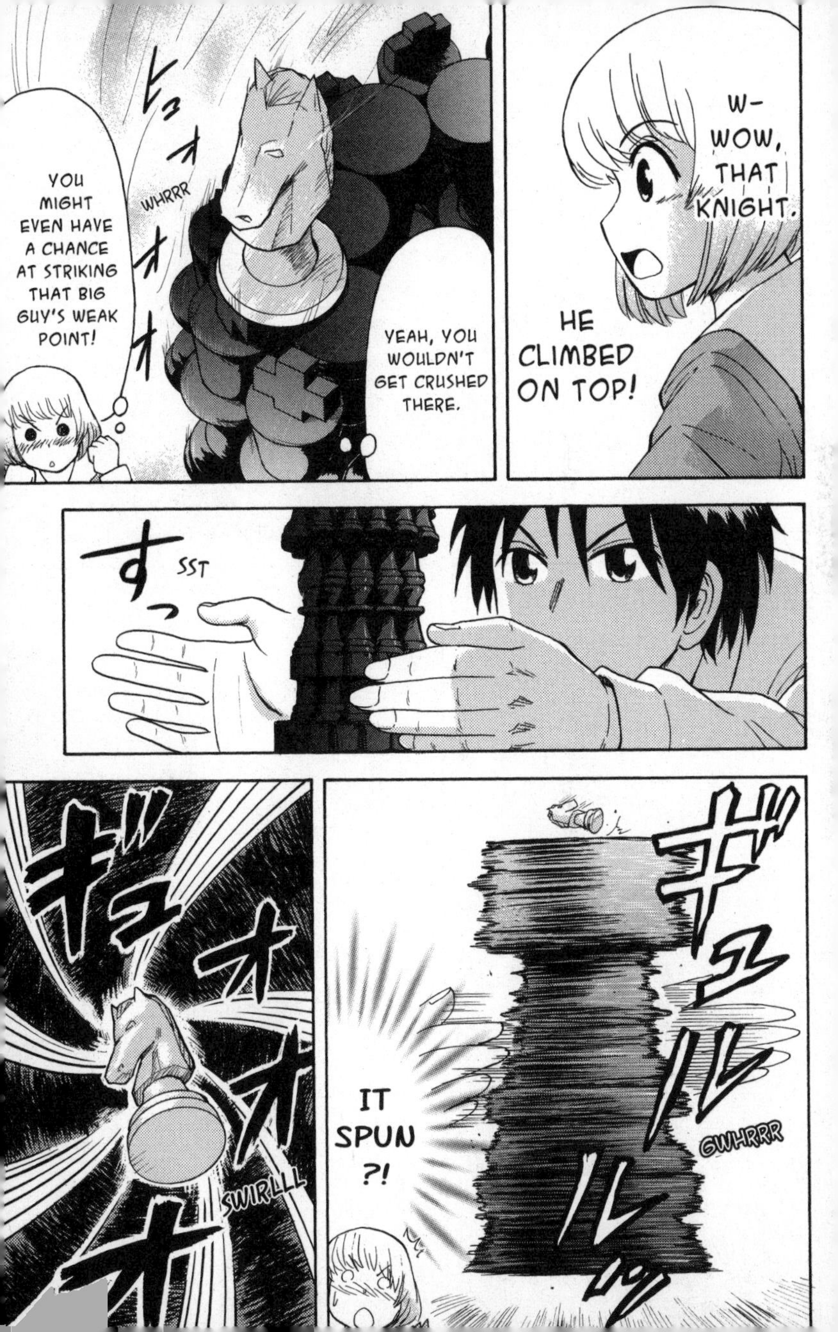
W-WOW, THAT KNIGHT.
HE CLIMBED ON TOP!
YEAH, YOU WOULDN'T GET CRUSHED THERE.
YOU MIGHT EVEN HAVE A CHANCE AT STRIKING THAT BIG GUY'S WEAK POINT!
WHRRR
SST
GWHRRR
IT SPUN ?!
SWIRLLL

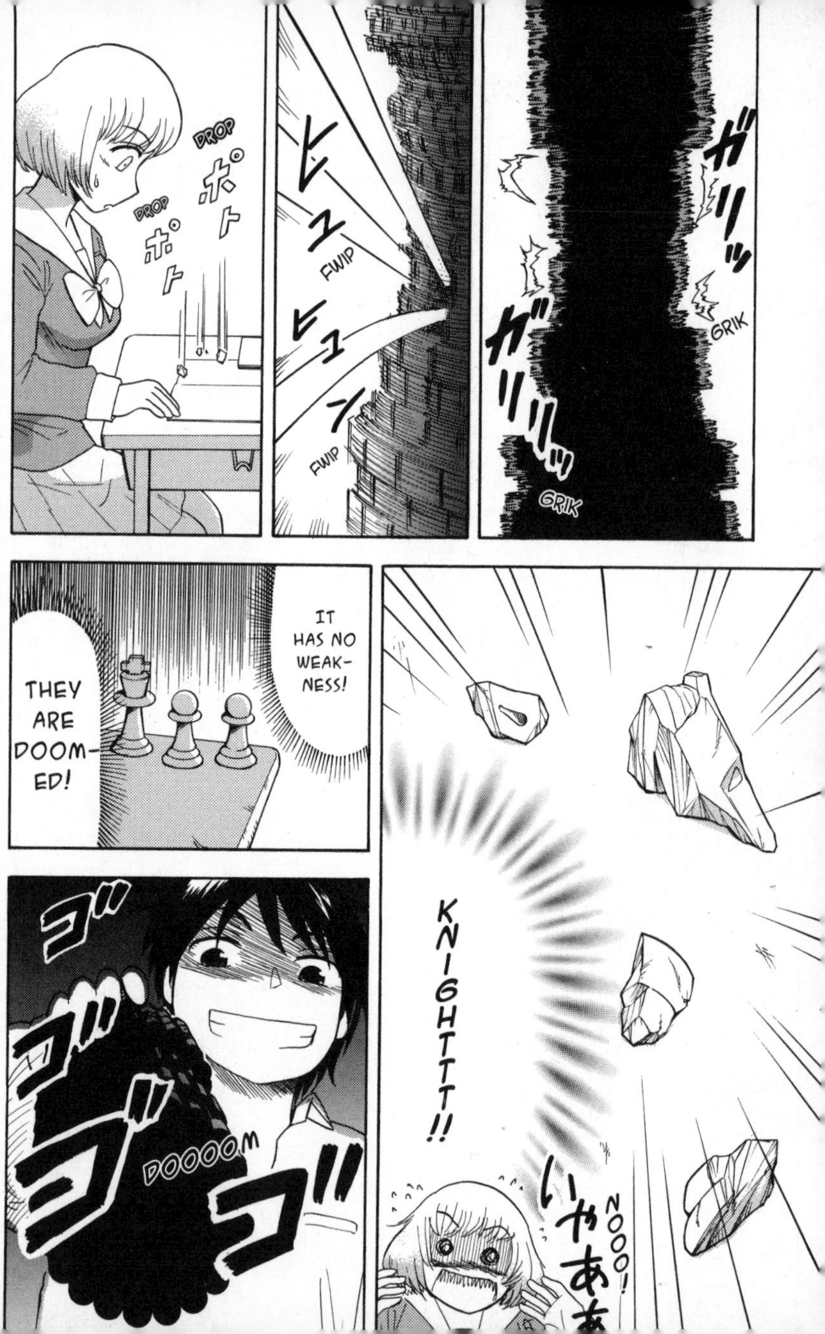

ガリッ
GRIK
ガリリッ
GRIK
ヒュ
FWIP
ヒュン
FWIP
DROP
ポト
DROP
ポト
KNIGHTTTT!!
いやあぁ
NOOOO!
IT HAS NO WEAK-NESS!
THEY ARE DOOM-ED!
ゴゴゴゴ
DOOOOOM

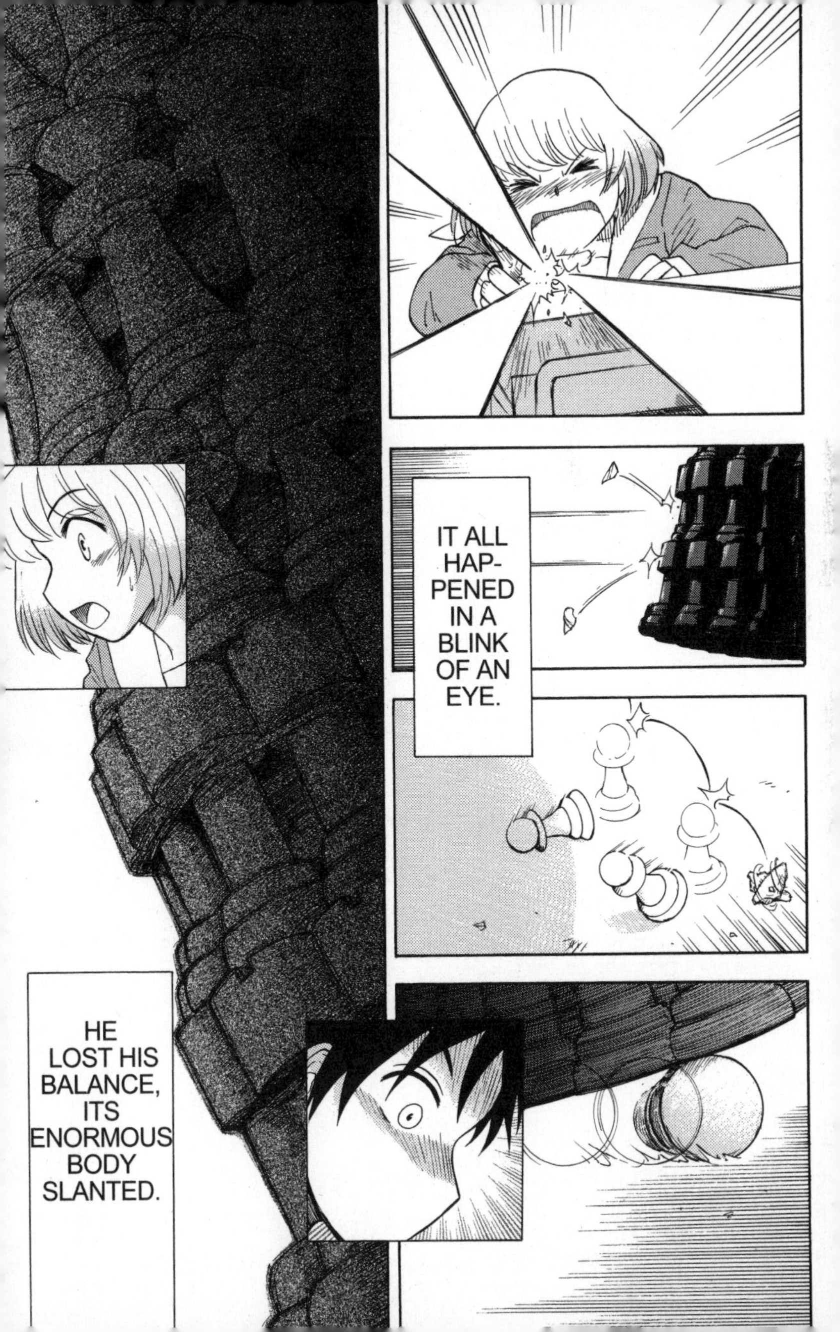
IT ALL HAP-PENED IN A BLINK OF AN EYE.
HE LOST HIS BALANCE, ITS ENORMOUS BODY SLANTED.

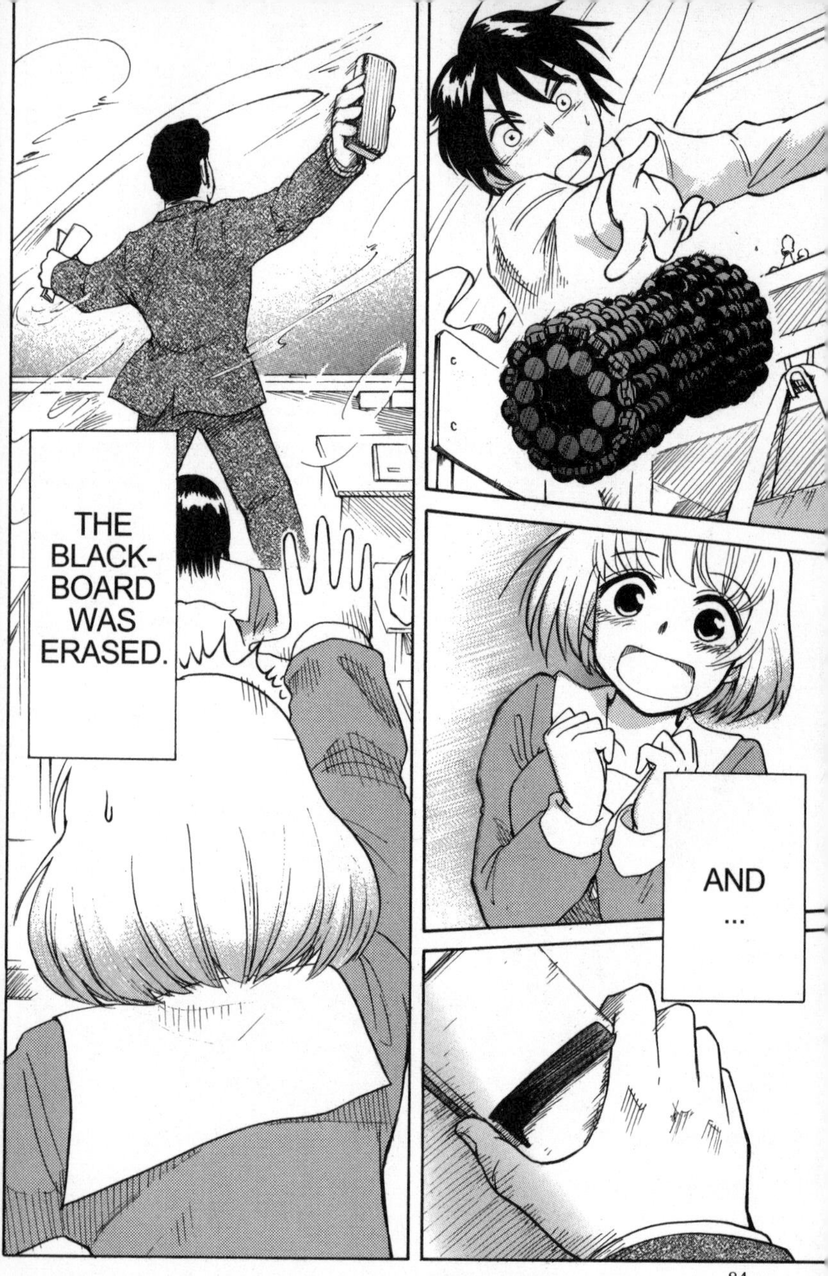
AND ...
THE BLACK-BOARD WAS ERASED.

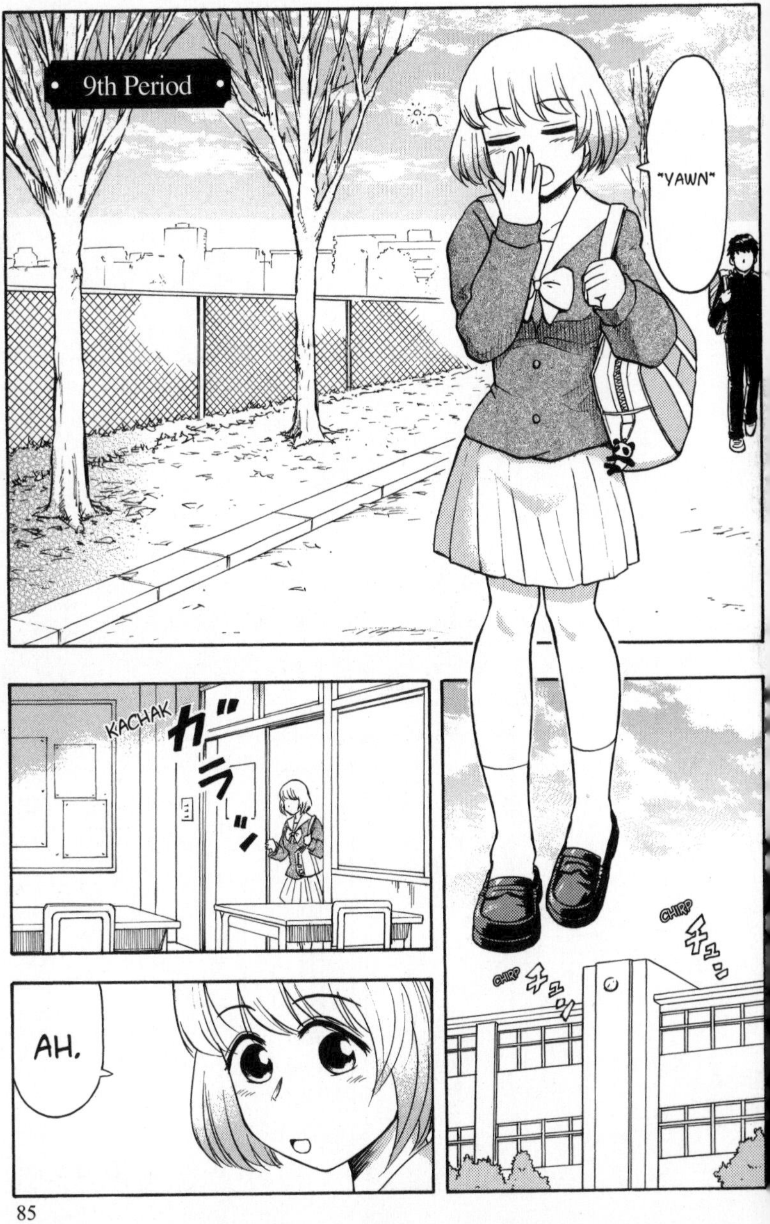

9th Period
YAWN
CHIRP
チュン
CHIRP
チュン
KACHAK
ガラッ
AH.

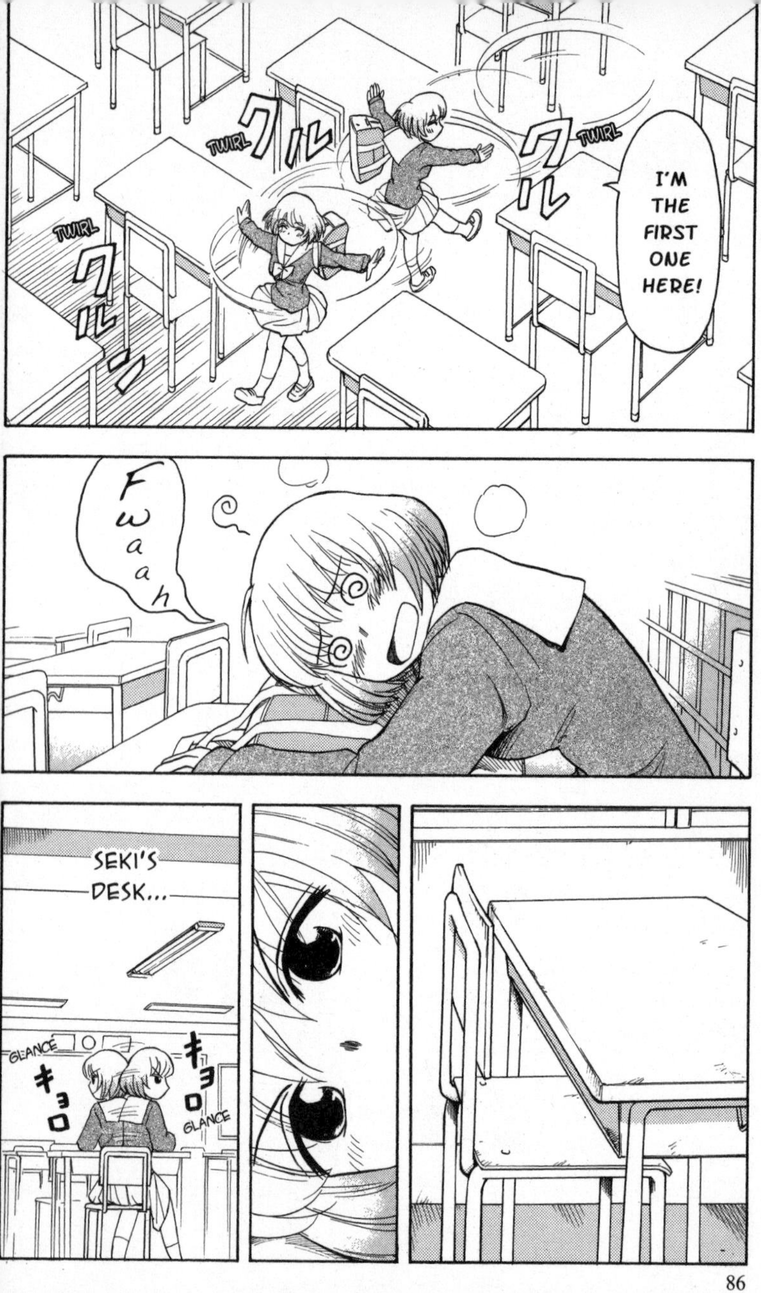
I'M THE FIRST ONE HERE!
TWIRL
クル
TWIRL
クル
TWIRL
クルン
Fwaah
SEKI'S DESK...
GLANCE
キョロ
GLANCE
キョロ

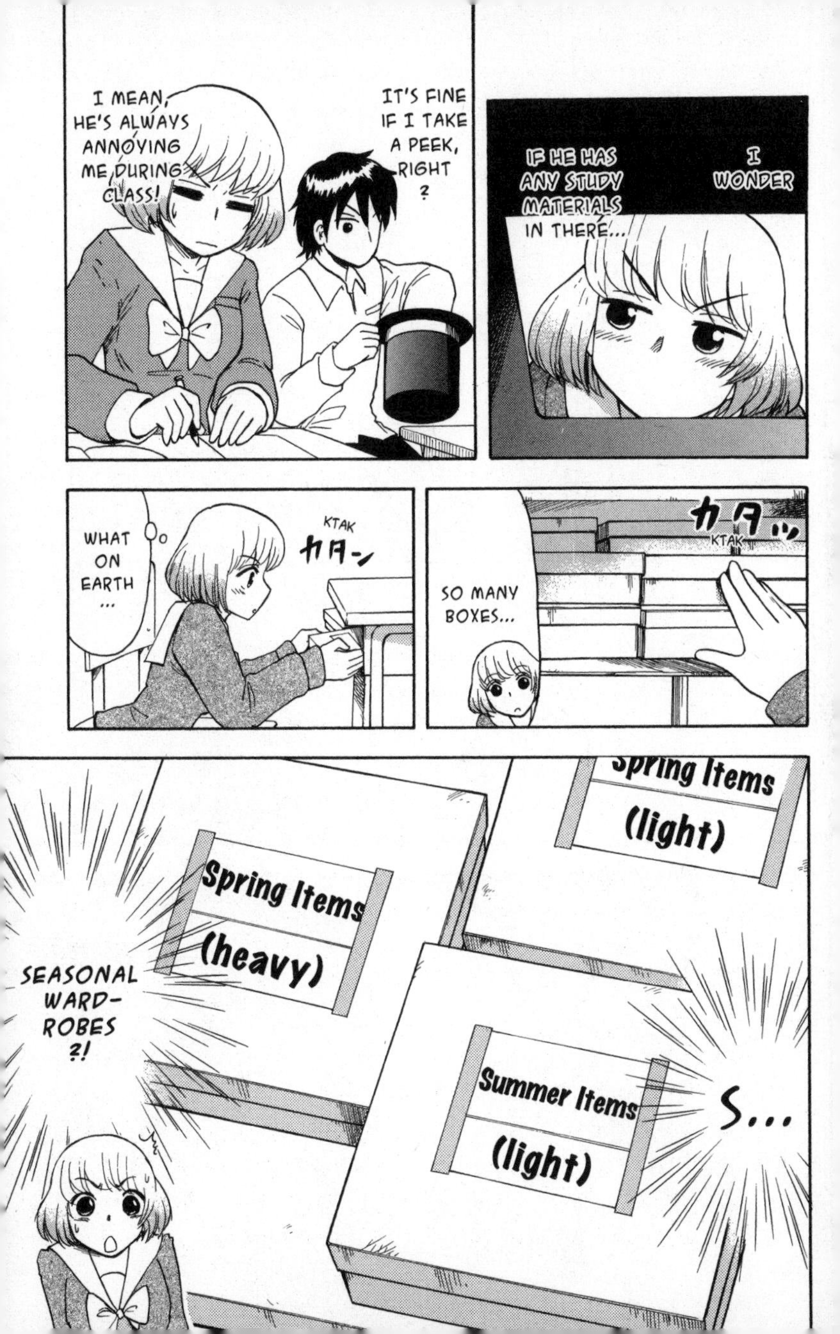

I WONDER
IF HE HAS ANY STUDY MATERIALS IN THERE...
IT'S FINE IF I TAKE A PEEK, RIGHT?
I MEAN, HE'S ALWAYS ANNOYING ME DURING CLASS!
カタッ
KTAK
SO MANY BOXES...
KTAK
カターン
WHAT ON EARTH ...
Spring Items
(light)
Spring Items
(heavy)
Summer Items
(light)
S...
SEASONAL WARD-ROBES ?!

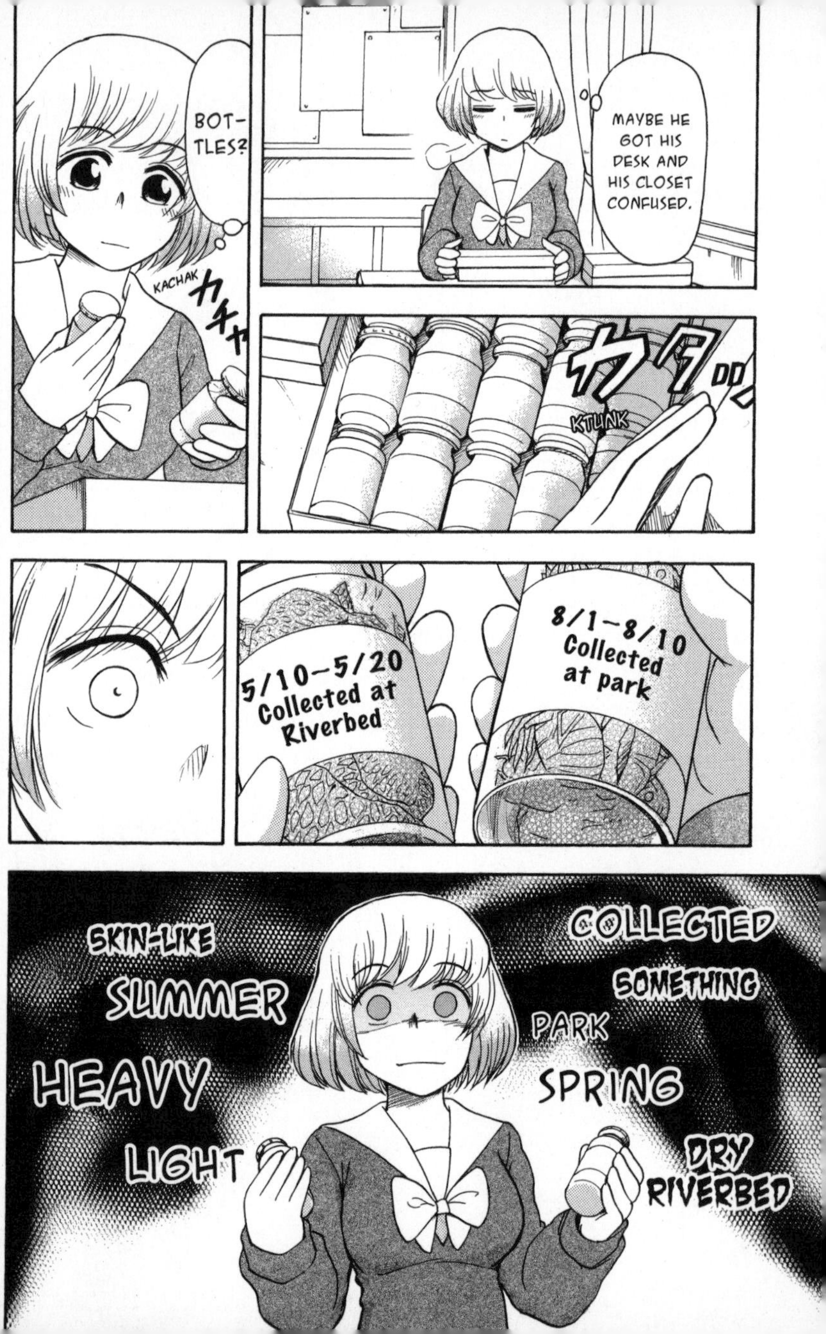
MAYBE HE GOT HIS DESK AND HIS CLOSET CONFUSED.
KTUNK
BOT-TLES?
KACHAK
8/1~8/10 Collected at park
5/10~5/20 Collected at Riverbed
COLLECTED
SOMETHING
PARK
SPRING
DRY RIVERBED
SKIN-LIKE
SUMMER
HEAVY
LIGHT

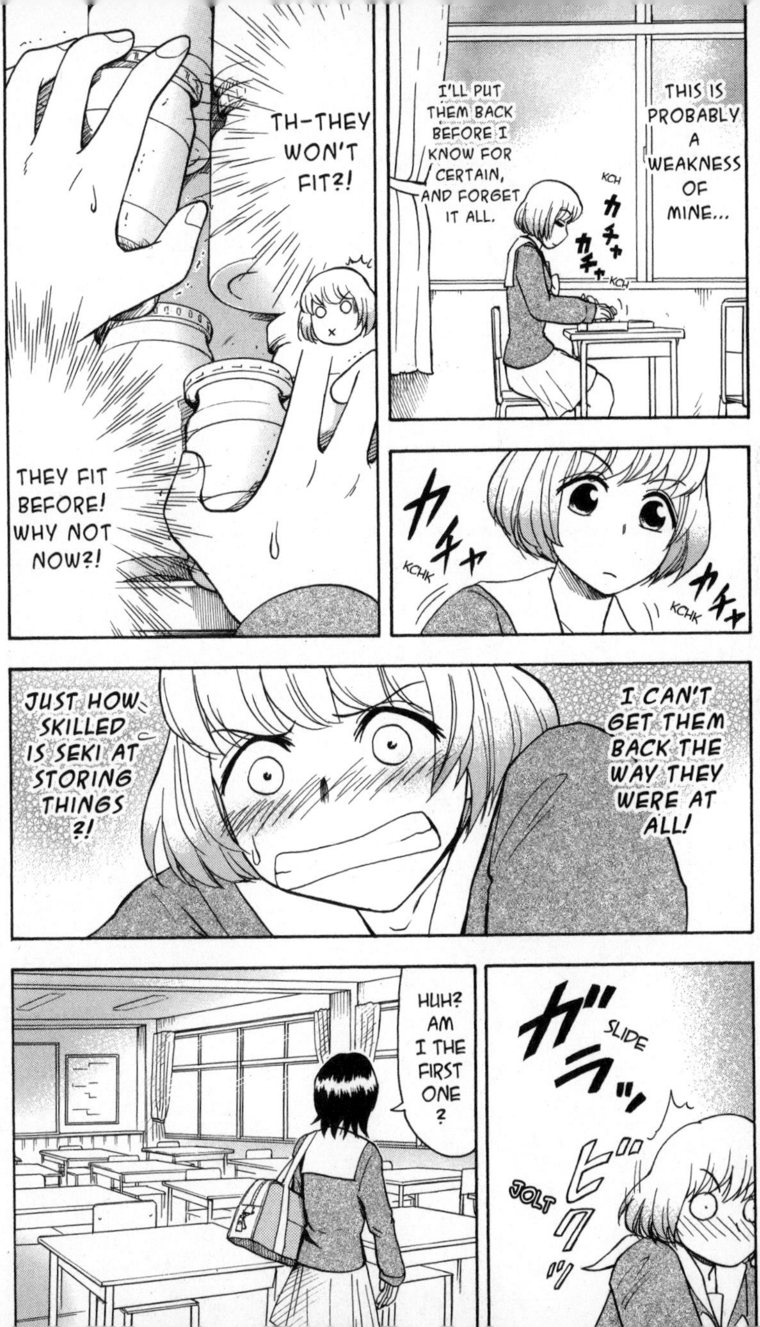
THIS IS PROBABLY A WEAKNESS OF MINE...
I'LL PUT THEM BACK BEFORE I KNOW FOR CERTAIN, AND FORGET IT ALL.
KCH
カチャ カチャ
KCH
カチャ
KCHK
カチャ
KCHK
TH-THEY WON'T FIT?!
THEY FIT BEFORE! WHY NOT NOW?!
I CAN'T GET THEM BACK THE WAY THEY WERE AT ALL!
JUST HOW SKILLED IS SEKI AT STORING THINGS?!
ガラッ
SLIDE
ビクッ
JOLT
HUH? AM I THE FIRST ONE?

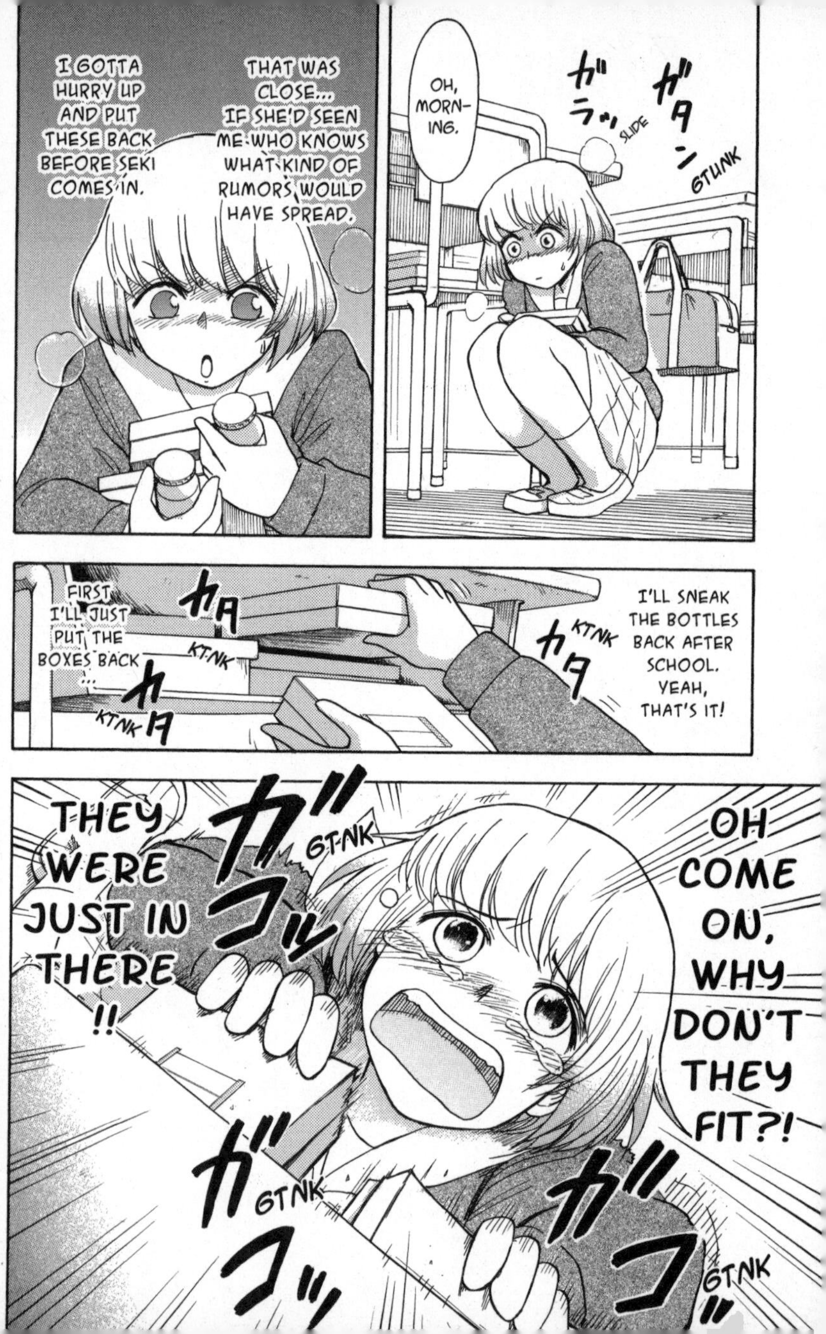
OH, MORNING.
SLIDE
GTUNK
THAT WAS CLOSE... IF SHE'D SEEN ME WHO KNOWS WHAT KIND OF RUMORS WOULD HAVE SPREAD.
I GOTTA HURRY UP AND PUT THESE BACK BEFORE SEKI COMES IN.
I'LL SNEAK THE BOTTLES BACK AFTER SCHOOL. YEAH, THAT'S IT!
KTNK
FIRST I'LL JUST PUT THE BOXES BACK ...
KTNK
KTNK
OH COME ON, WHY DON'T THEY FIT?!
GTNK
THEY WERE JUST IN THERE !!
GTNK
GTNK

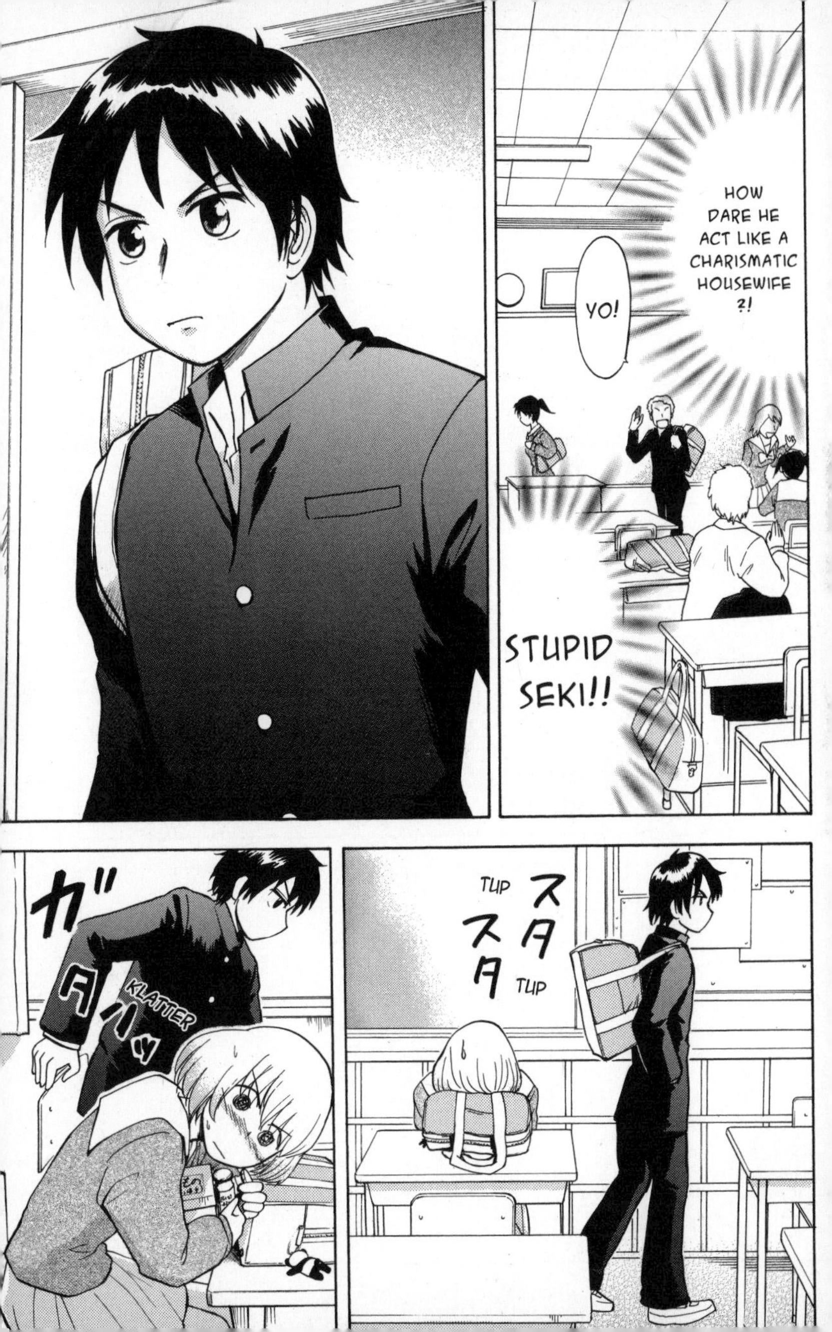
HOW DARE HE ACT LIKE A CHARISMATIC HOUSEWIFE ?!
YO!
STUPID SEKI!!
スタスタ
TUP
TUP
ガタッ
KLATTER

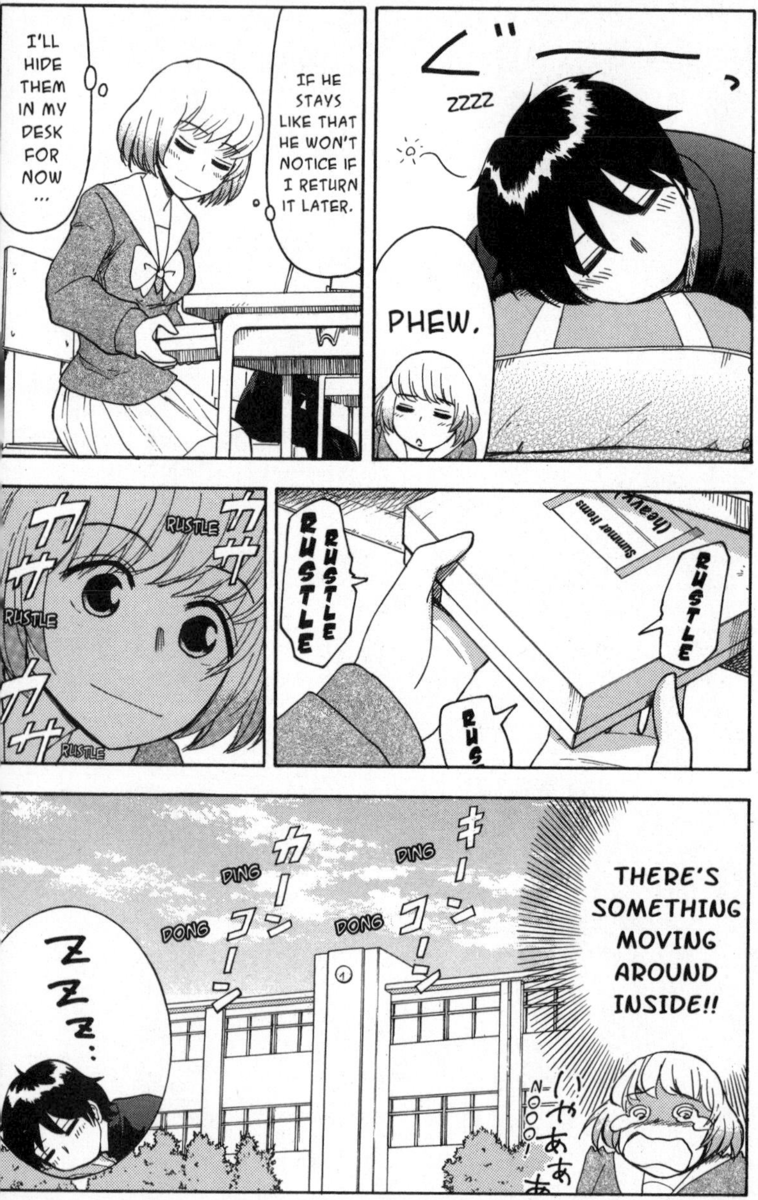
ZZZZ
PHEW.
IF HE STAYS LIKE THAT HE WON'T NOTICE IF I RETURN IT LATER.
I'LL HIDE THEM IN MY DESK FOR NOW ...
RUSTLE
Summer Items (heavy)
RUSTLE RUSTLE
RUS-
カサ
RUSTLE
カサ
RUSTLE
カサ
RUSTLE
THERE'S SOMETHING MOVING AROUND INSIDE!!
N-NOOOO!
いやあああ
DING
キーンコーン
DONG
DING
カーンコーン
DONG
Z Z Z..

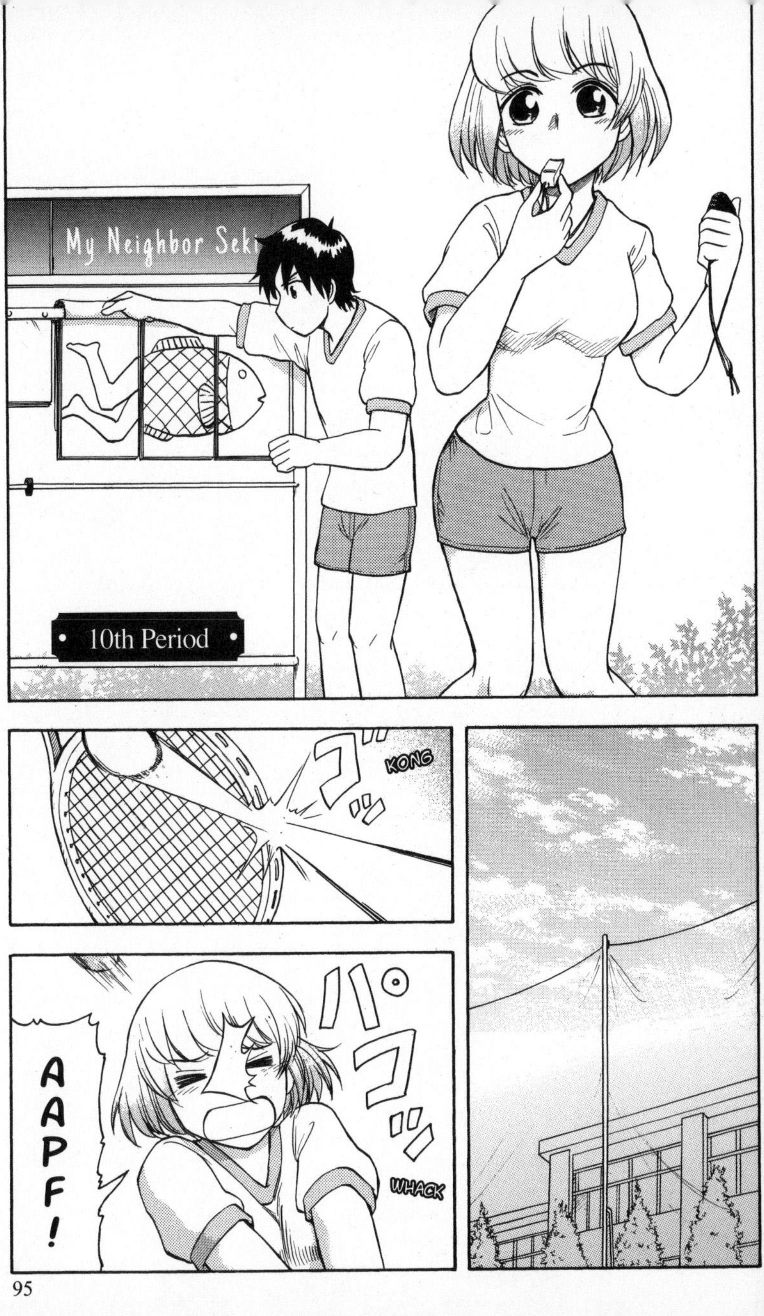
My Neighbor Seki
10th Period
ゴッ
KONG
パコッ
WHACK
AAPF!

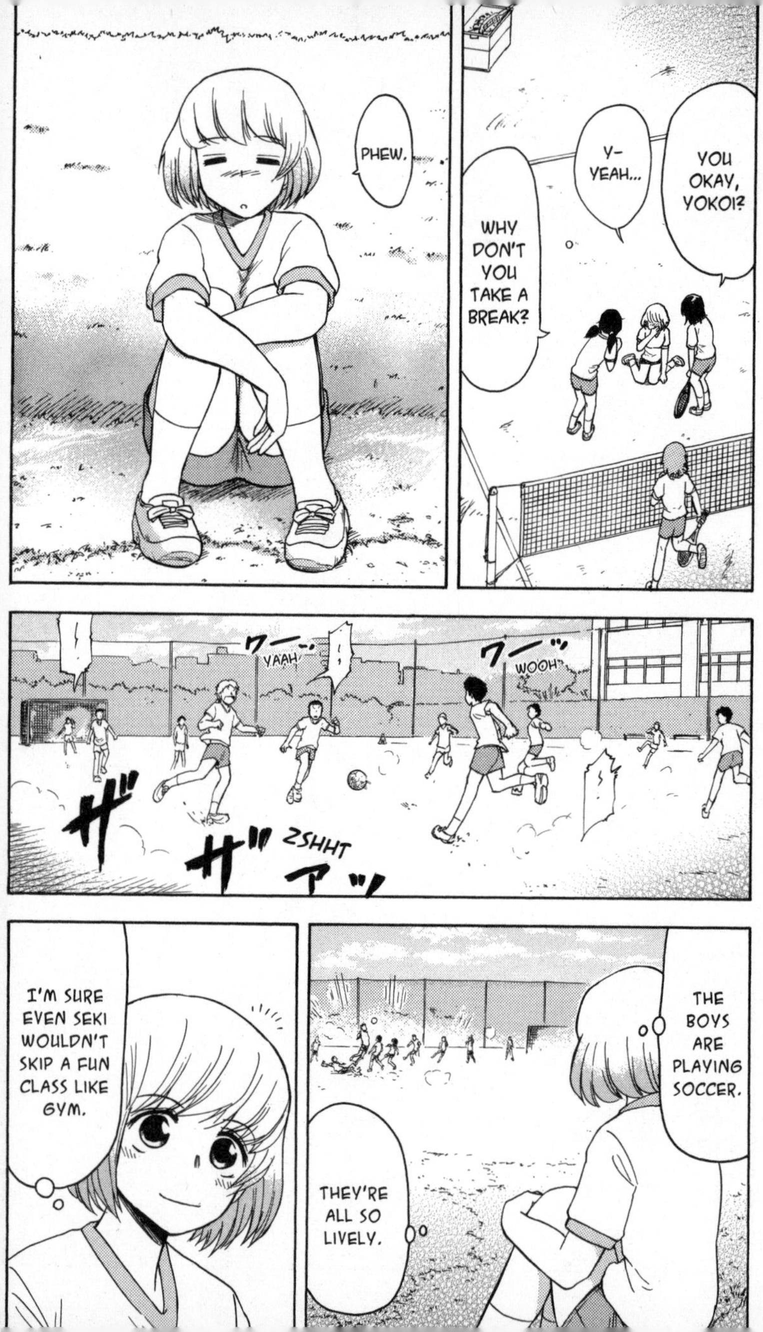
YOU OKAY, YOKOI?
Y-YEAH...
WHY DON'T YOU TAKE A BREAK?
PHEW.
ワーッ
WOOH
ワー
YAAH
ザザアッ
ZSHHT
THE BOYS ARE PLAYING SOCCER.
THEY'RE ALL SO LIVELY.
I'M SURE EVEN SEKI WOULDN'T SKIP A FUN CLASS LIKE GYM.

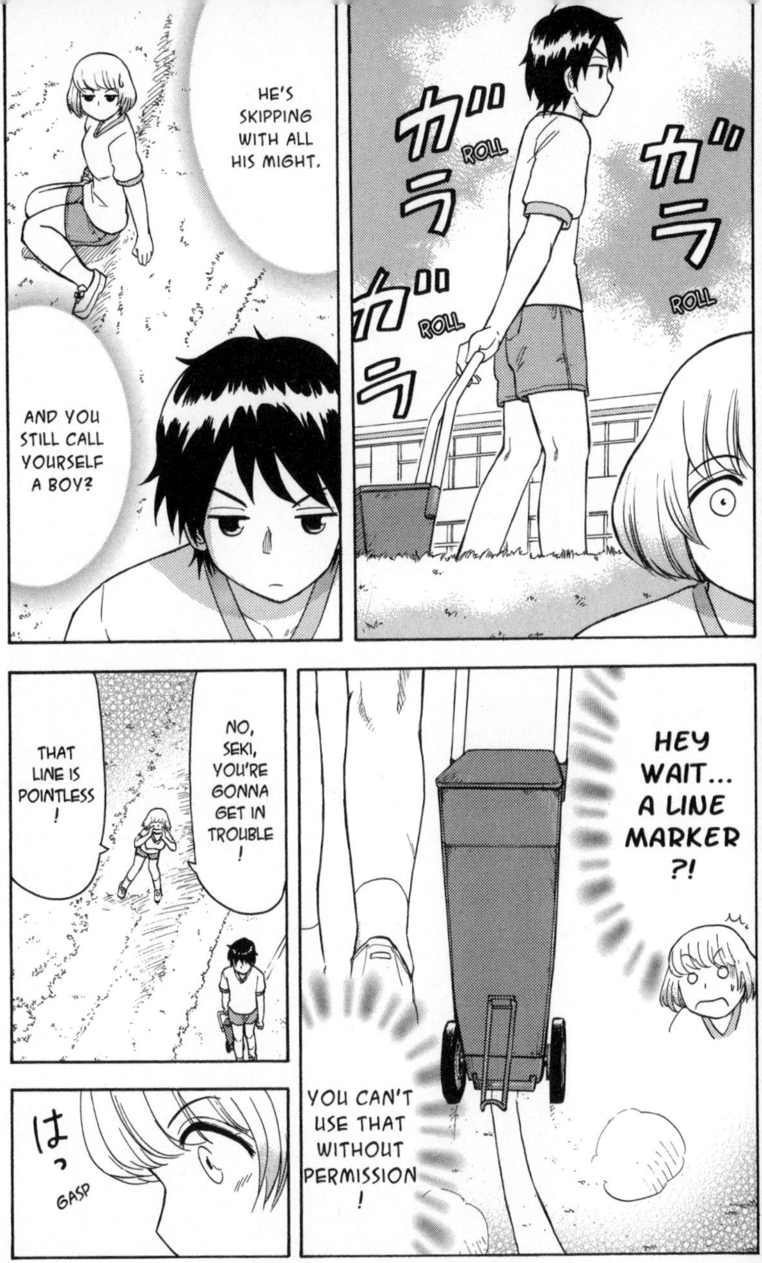

ガラ
ROLL
ガラ
ROLL
ガラ
ROLL
HE'S SKIPPING WITH ALL HIS MIGHT.
AND YOU STILL CALL YOURSELF A BOY?
HEY WAIT... A LINE MARKER ?!
YOU CAN'T USE THAT WITHOUT PERMISSION !
NO, SEKI, YOU'RE GONNA GET IN TROUBLE !
THAT LINE IS POINTLESS !
はっ
GASP

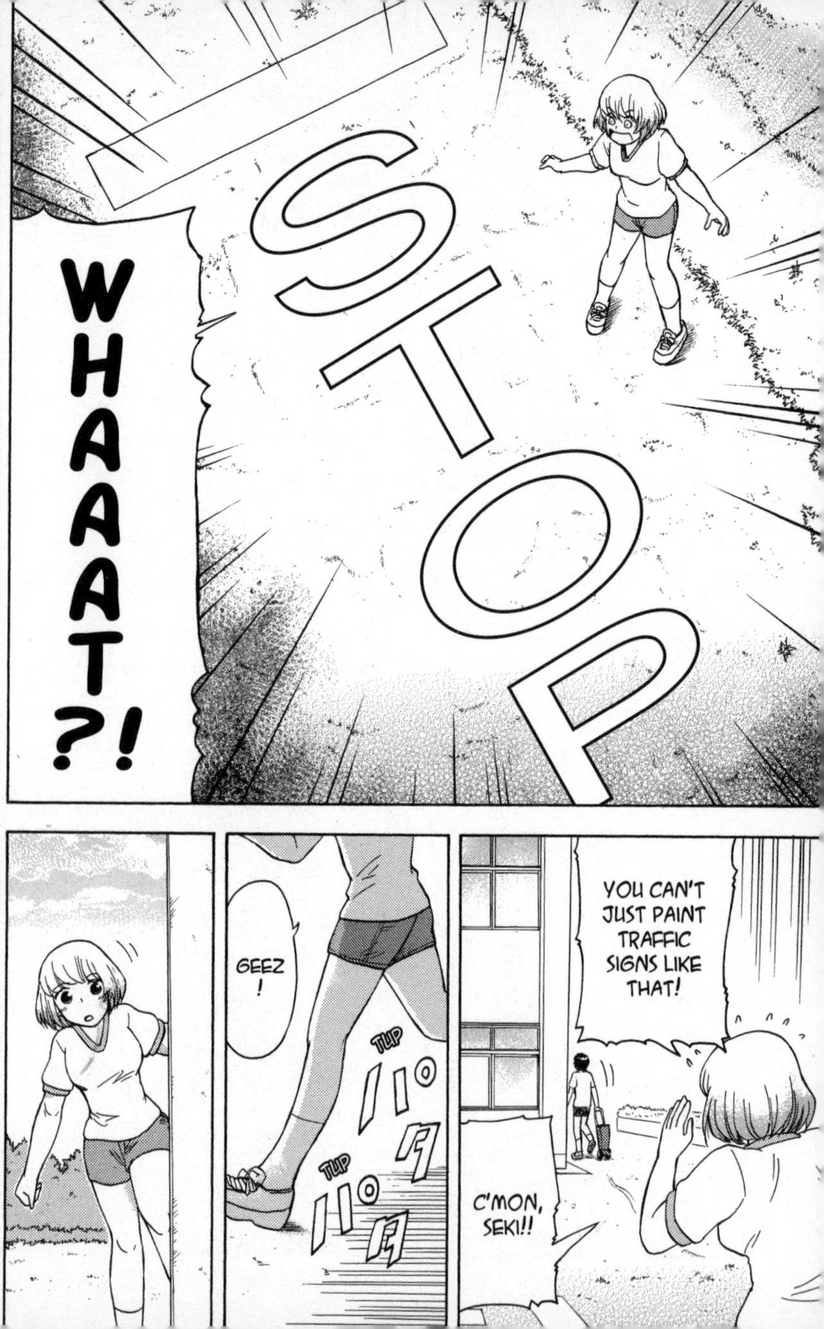
STOP
WHAAAT?!
YOU CAN'T JUST PAINT TRAFFIC SIGNS LIKE THAT!
C'MON, SEKI!!
GEEZ!
TUP
TUP

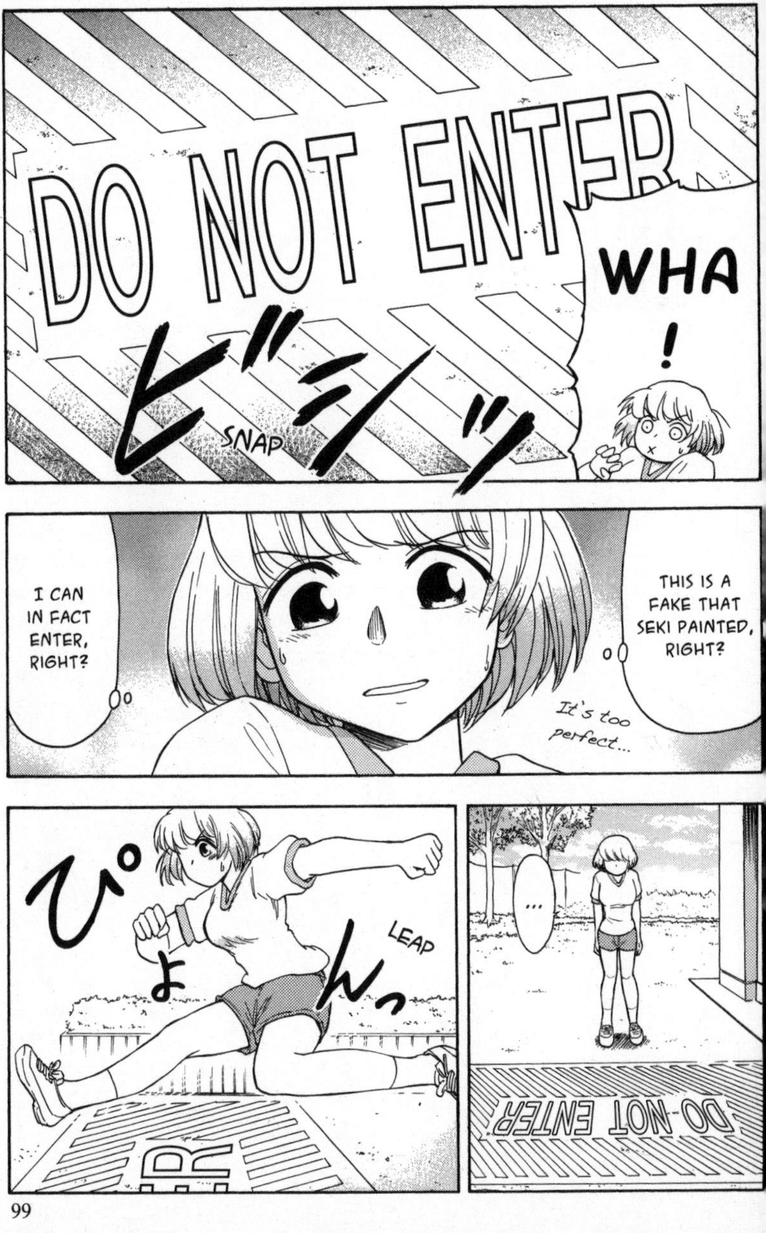
DO NOT ENTER
WHA
!
ビシッ
SNAP
THIS IS A FAKE THAT SEKI PAINTED, RIGHT?
It's too perfect...
I CAN IN FACT ENTER, RIGHT?
...
DO NOT ENTER
ぴょんっ
LEAP

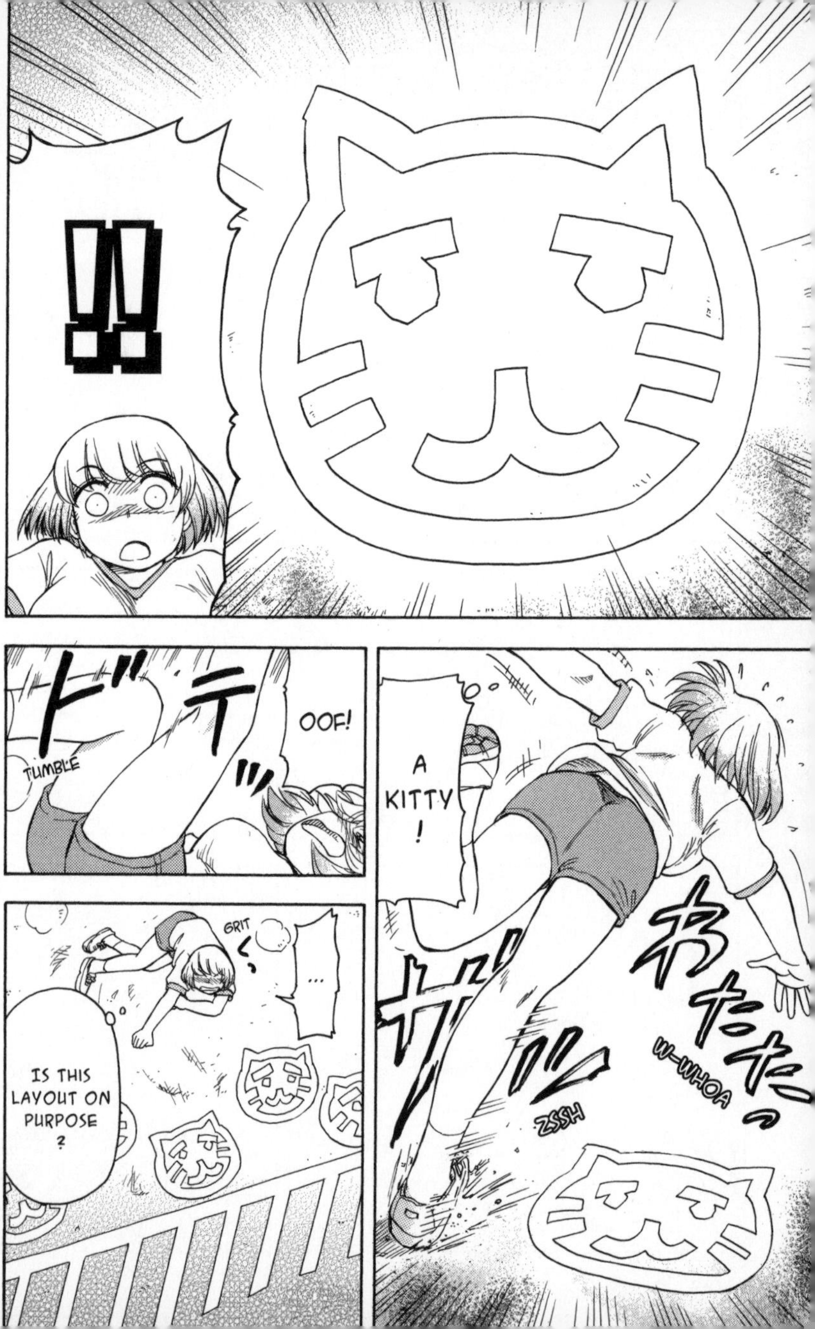
!!
A KITTY!
わたたっ
W-WHOA
ザッ
ZSSH
ドテ
TUMBLE
OOF!
GRIT
...
IS THIS LAYOUT ON PURPOSE?

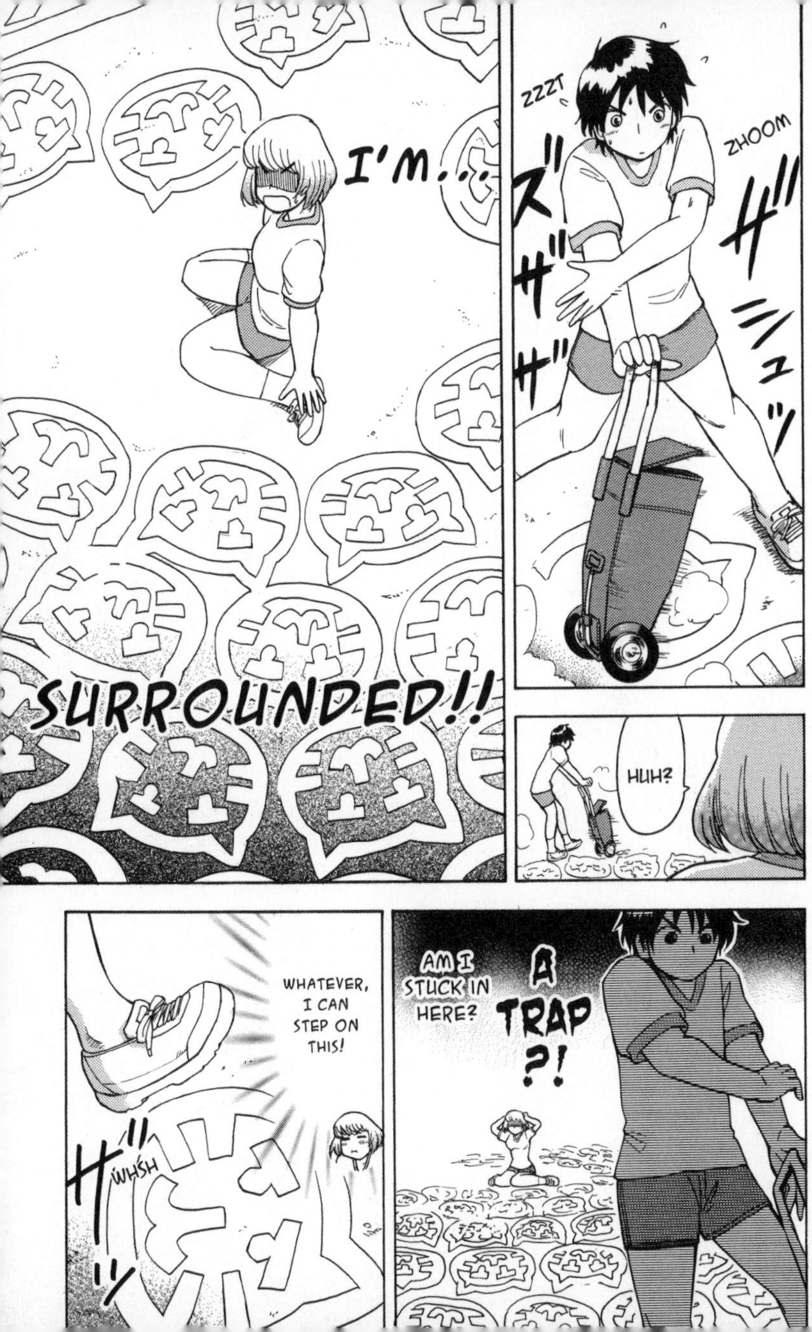
ZZZT
ZHOOM
ズザザ
ザシュッ
HUH?
I'M...
SURROUNDED!!
AM I STUCK IN HERE?
A TRAP ?!
WHATEVER, I CAN STEP ON THIS!
WHSH
ザッ

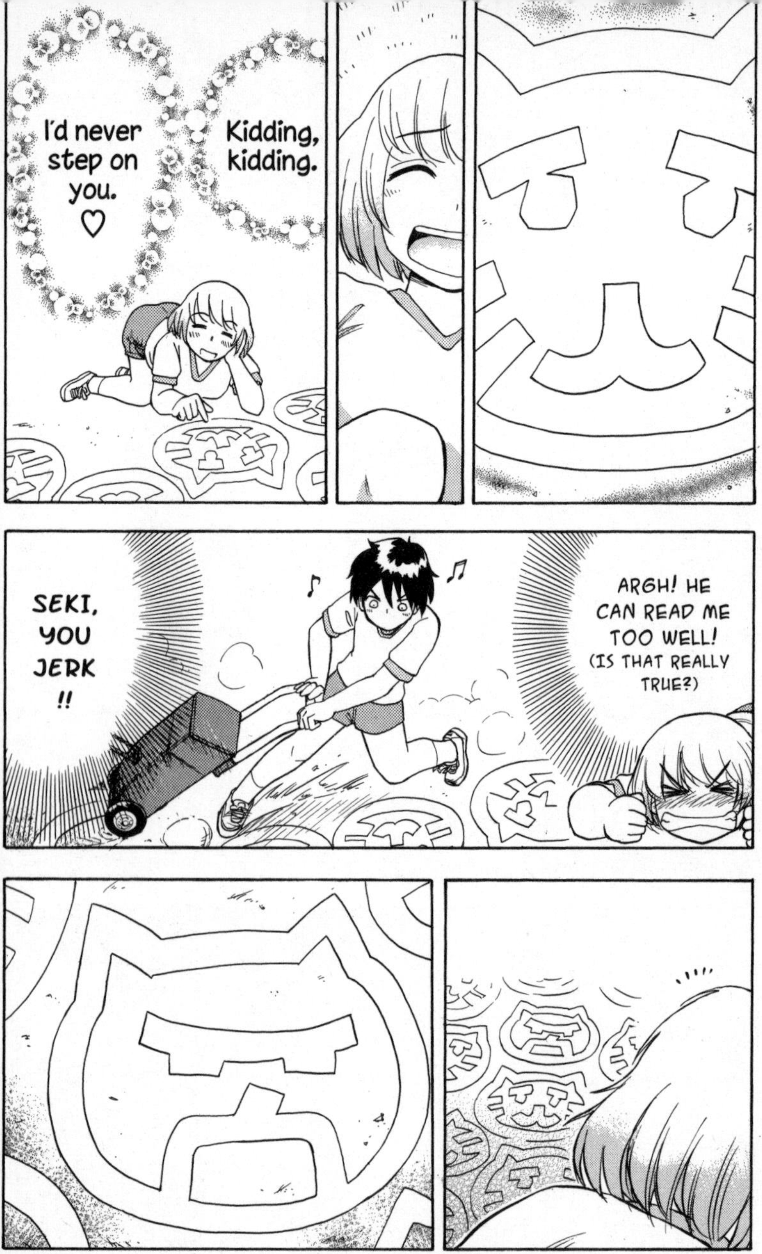
Kidding, kidding.
I'd never step on you. ♡
ARGH! HE CAN READ ME TOO WELL!
(IS THAT REALLY TRUE?)
SEKI, YOU JERK !!

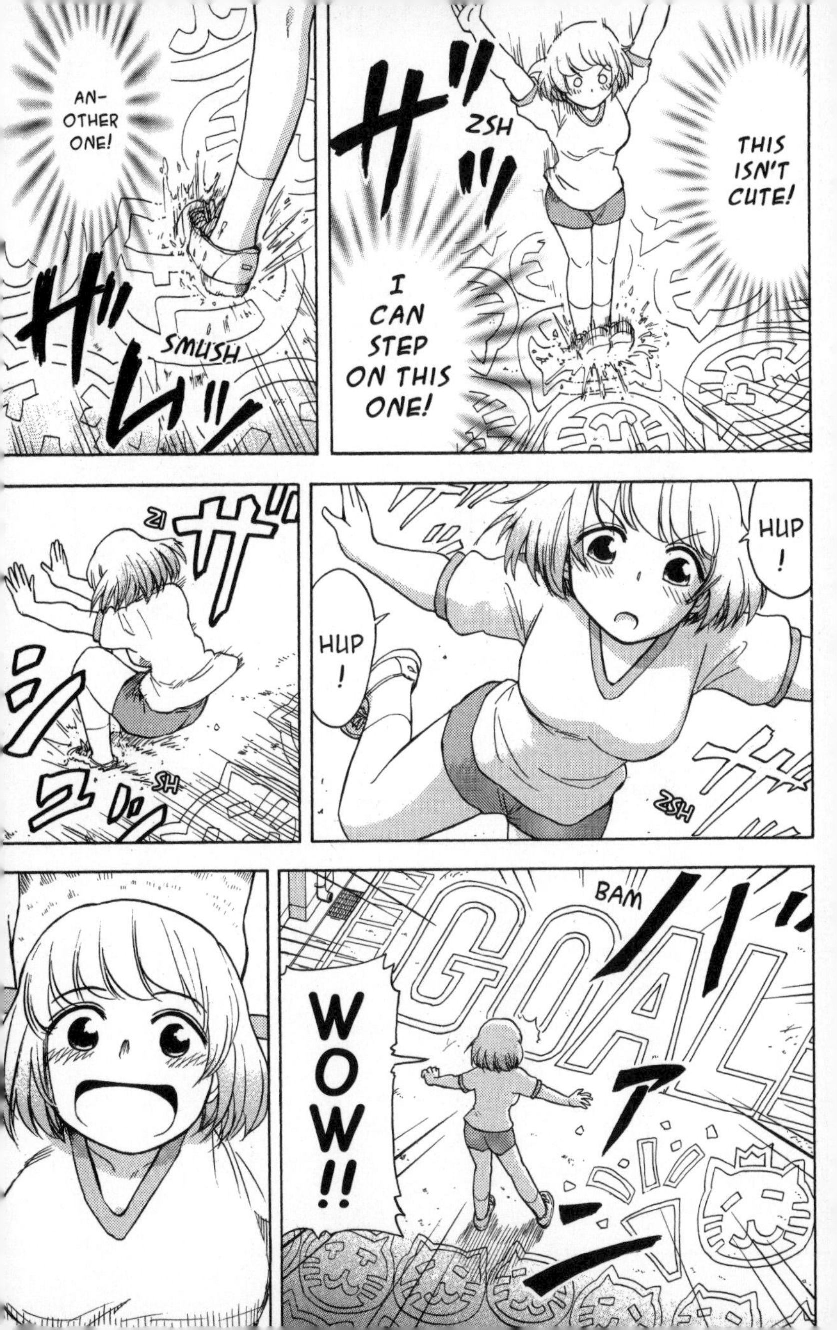
THIS ISN'T CUTE!
ZSH
I CAN STEP ON THIS ONE!
AN-OTHER ONE!
SMUSH
HUP!
HUP!
ZSH
ZSH
SH
BAM
GOAL
WOW!!

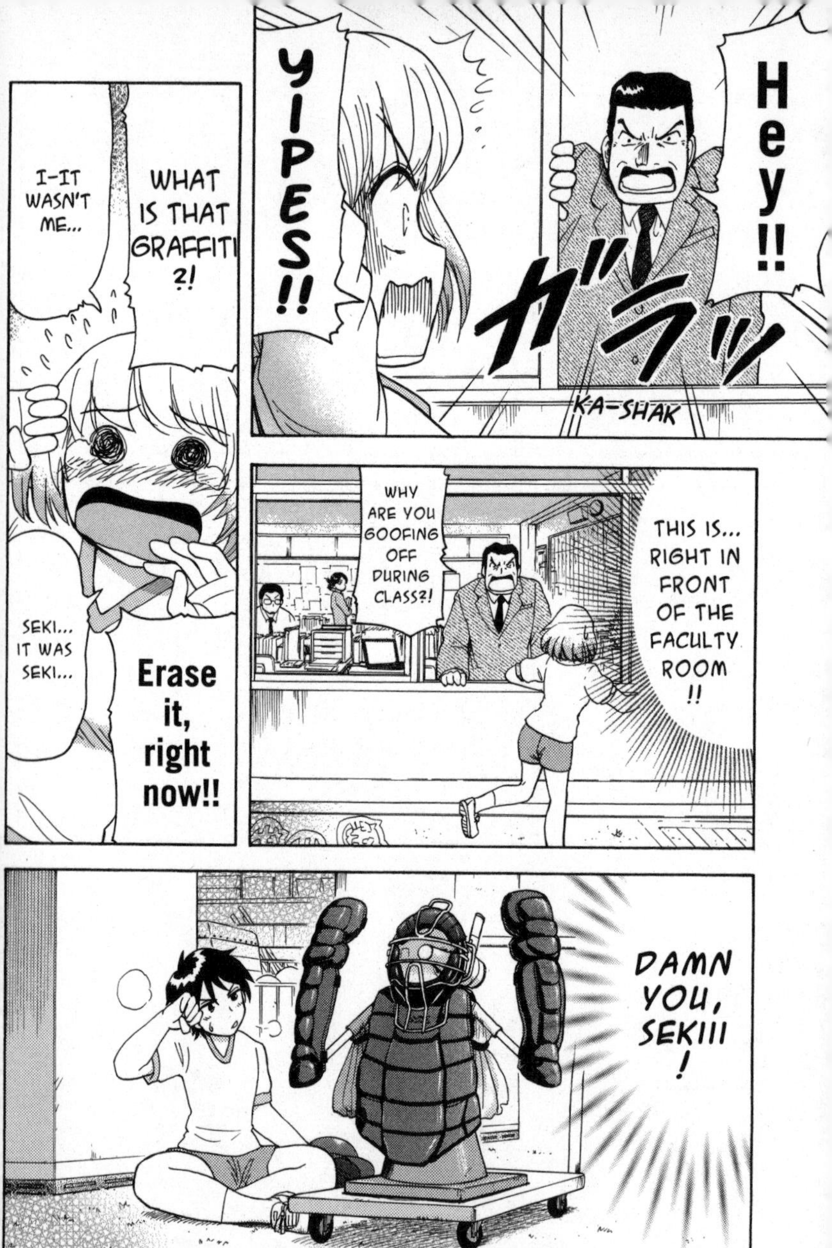
Hey!!
ガラッ
KA-SHAK
YIPES!!
THIS IS... RIGHT IN FRONT OF THE FACULTY ROOM!!
WHY ARE YOU GOOFING OFF DURING CLASS?!
WHAT IS THAT GRAFFITI?!
I-IT WASN'T ME...
Erase it, right now!!
SEKI... IT WAS SEKI...
DAMN YOU, SEKIII!

11th Period

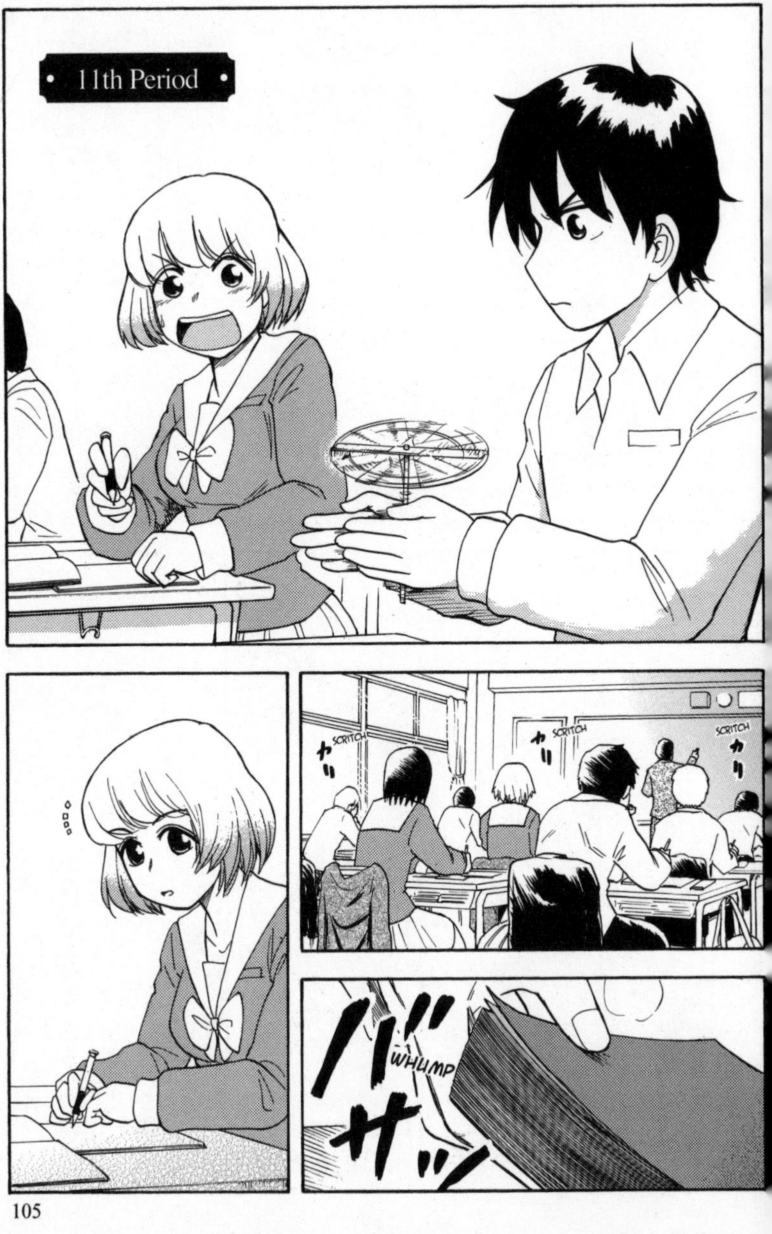
SCRITCH
カリ
SCRITCH
カリ
SCRITCH
カリ
バサッ
WHUMP

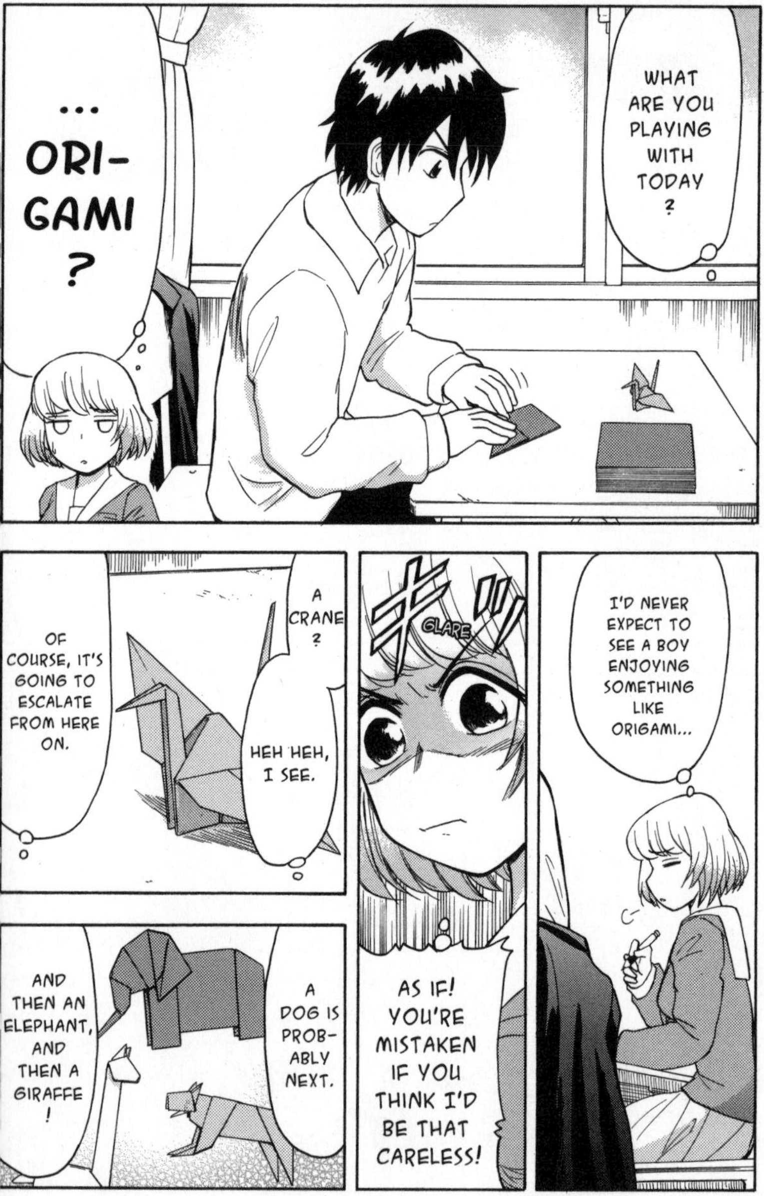
WHAT ARE YOU PLAYING WITH TODAY?
... ORI-GAMI?
I'D NEVER EXPECT TO SEE A BOY ENJOYING SOMETHING LIKE ORIGAMI...
GLARE
AS IF! YOU'RE MISTAKEN IF YOU THINK I'D BE THAT CARELESS!
A CRANE?
HEH HEH, I SEE.
OF COURSE, IT'S GOING TO ESCALATE FROM HERE ON.
A DOG IS PROB-ABLY NEXT.
AND THEN AN ELEPHANT, AND THEN A GIRAFFE!

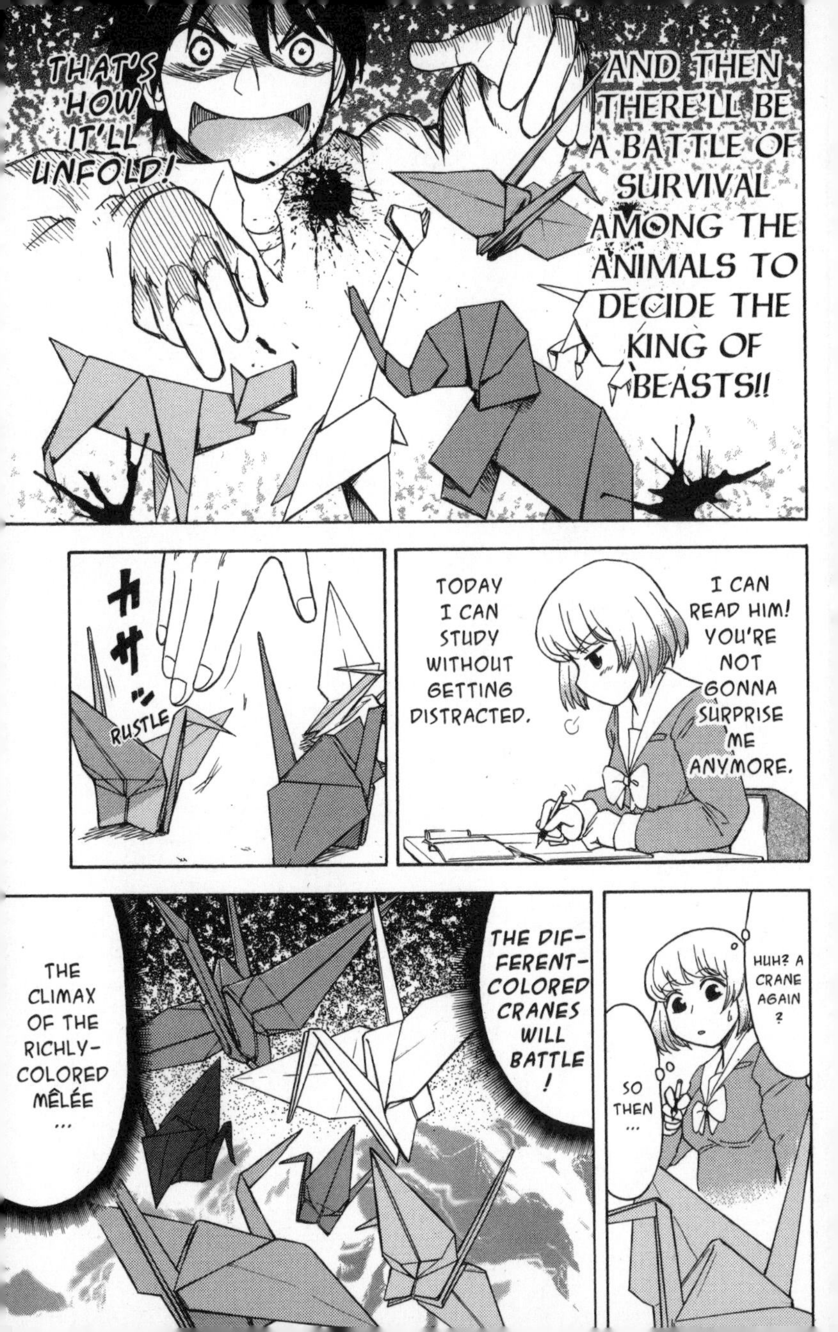
AND THEN THERE'LL BE A BATTLE OF SURVIVAL AMONG THE ANIMALS TO DECIDE THE KING OF BEASTS!!
THAT'S HOW IT'LL UNFOLD!
I CAN READ HIM! YOU'RE NOT GONNA SURPRISE ME ANYMORE.
TODAY I CAN STUDY WITHOUT GETTING DISTRACTED.
カサッ
RUSTLE
HUH? A CRANE AGAIN?
SO THEN ...
THE DIF-FERENT-COLORED CRANES WILL BATTLE!
THE CLIMAX OF THE RICHLY-COLORED MÊLÉE ...

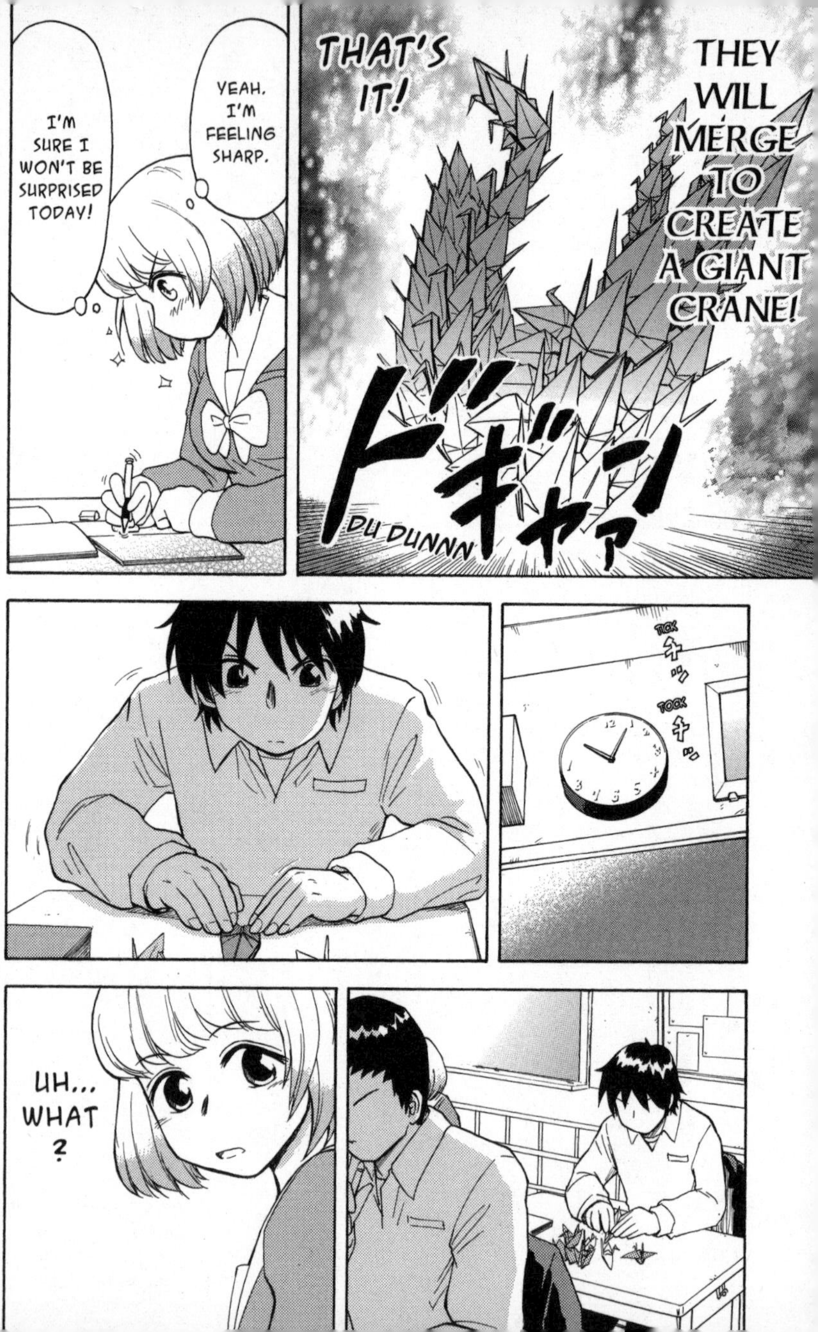
THEY WILL MERGE TO CREATE A GIANT CRANE!
THAT'S IT!
ドギャア
DU DUNNN
YEAH. I'M FEELING SHARP.
I'M SURE I WON'T BE SURPRISED TODAY!
TICK
チッ
TOCK
チッ
UH... WHAT?

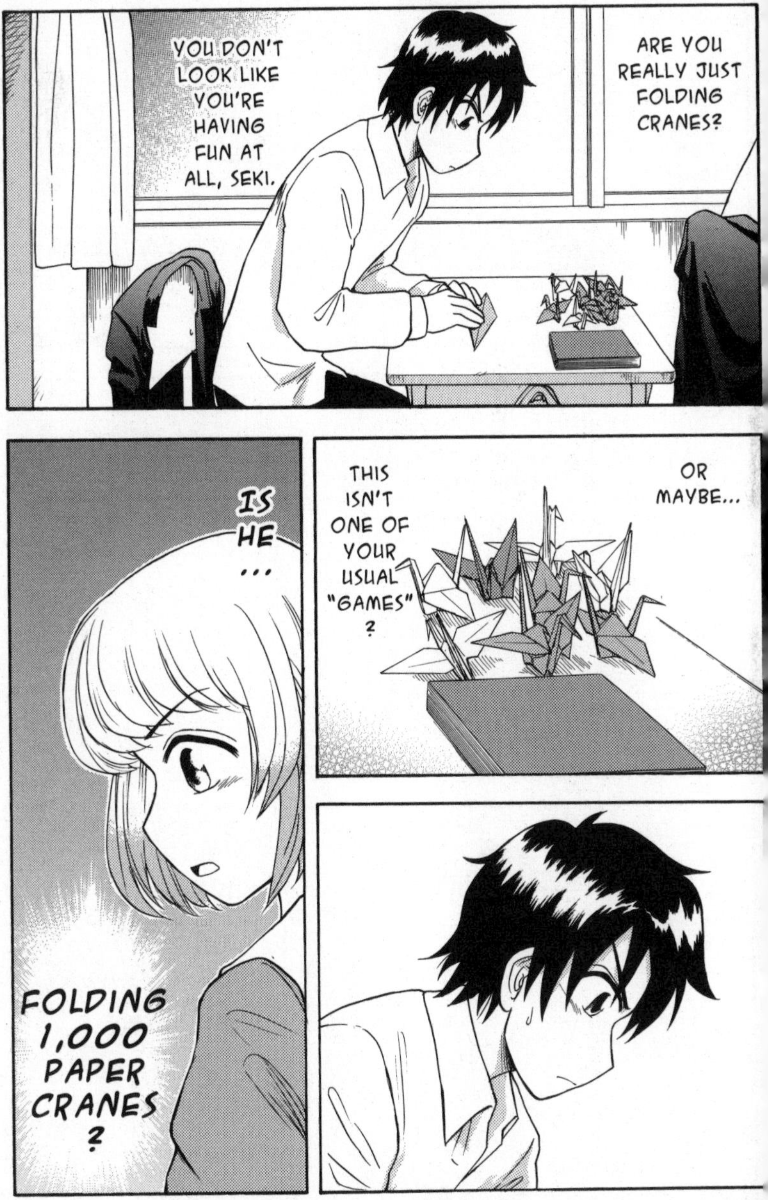
ARE YOU REALLY JUST FOLDING CRANES?
YOU DON'T LOOK LIKE YOU'RE HAVING FUN AT ALL, SEKI.
OR MAYBE...
THIS ISN'T ONE OF YOUR USUAL "GAMES"?
IS HE...
FOLDING 1,000 PAPER CRANES?

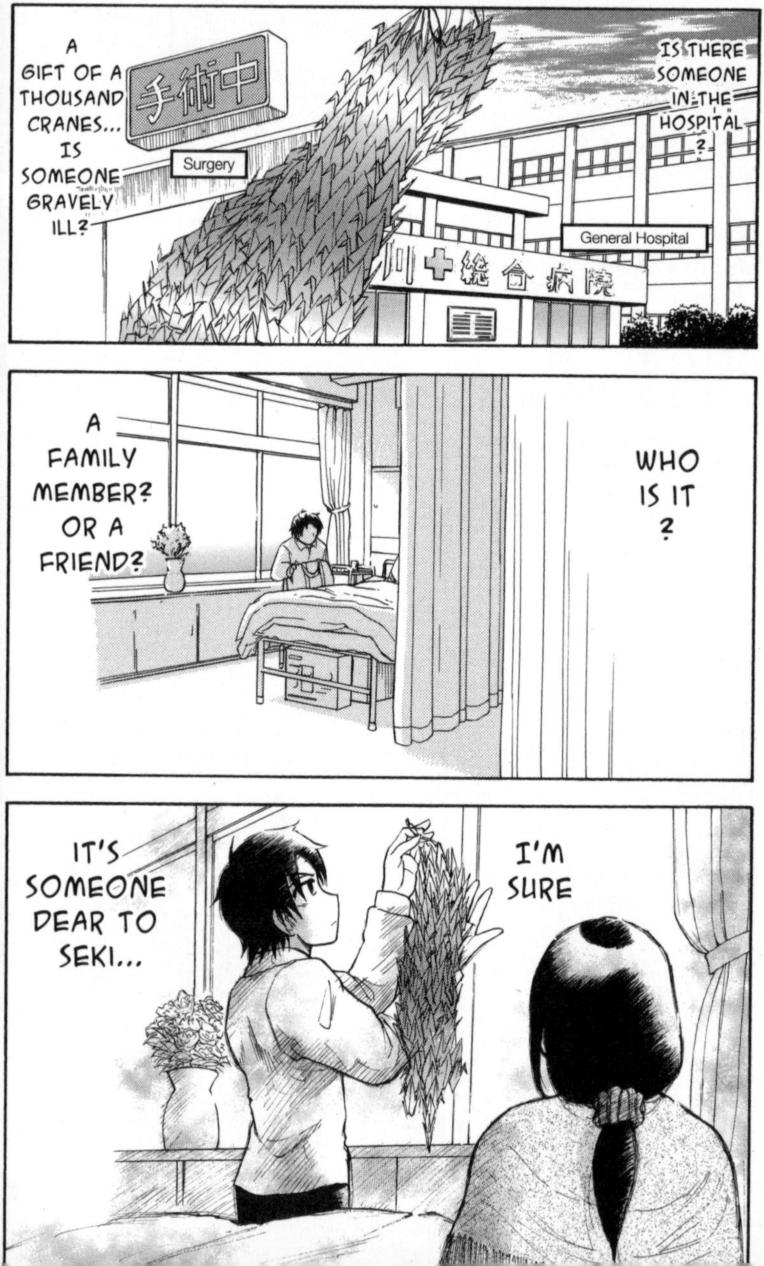
IS THERE SOMEONE IN THE HOSPITAL?
General Hospital
総合病院
手術中
Surgery
A GIFT OF A THOUSAND CRANES... IS SOMEONE GRAVELY ILL?
WHO IS IT?
A FAMILY MEMBER? OR A FRIEND?
I'M SURE
IT'S SOMEONE DEAR TO SEKI...

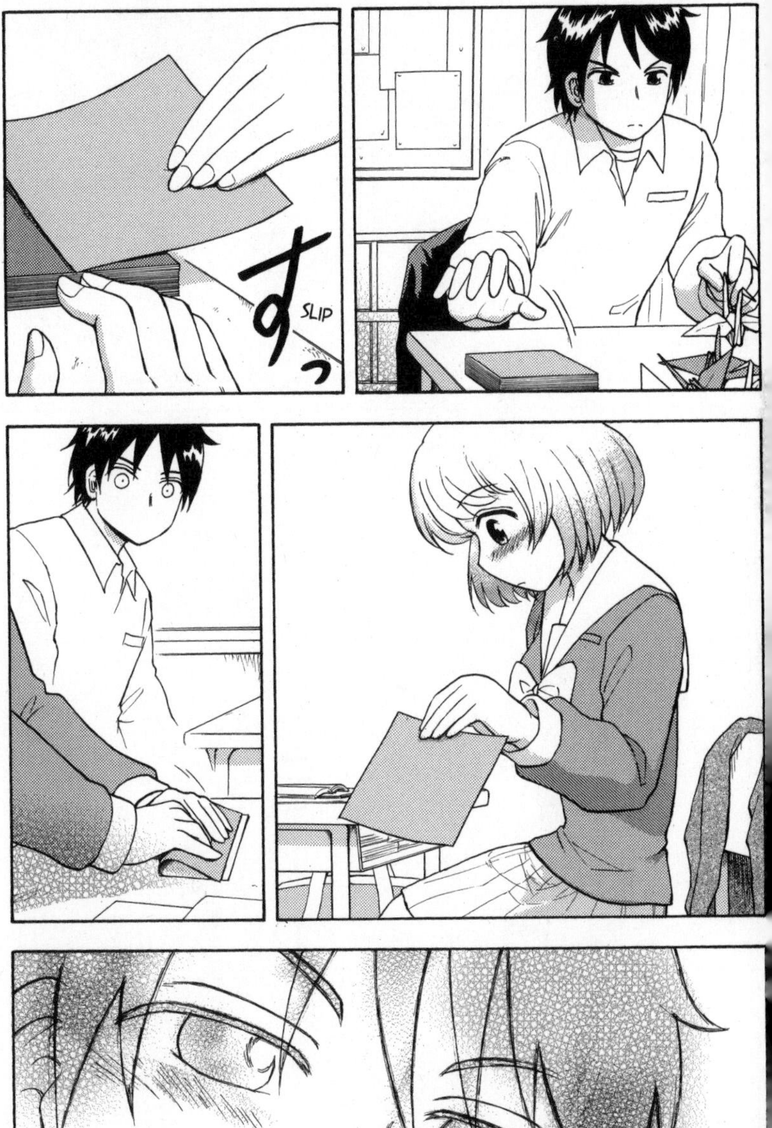
すっ
SLIP

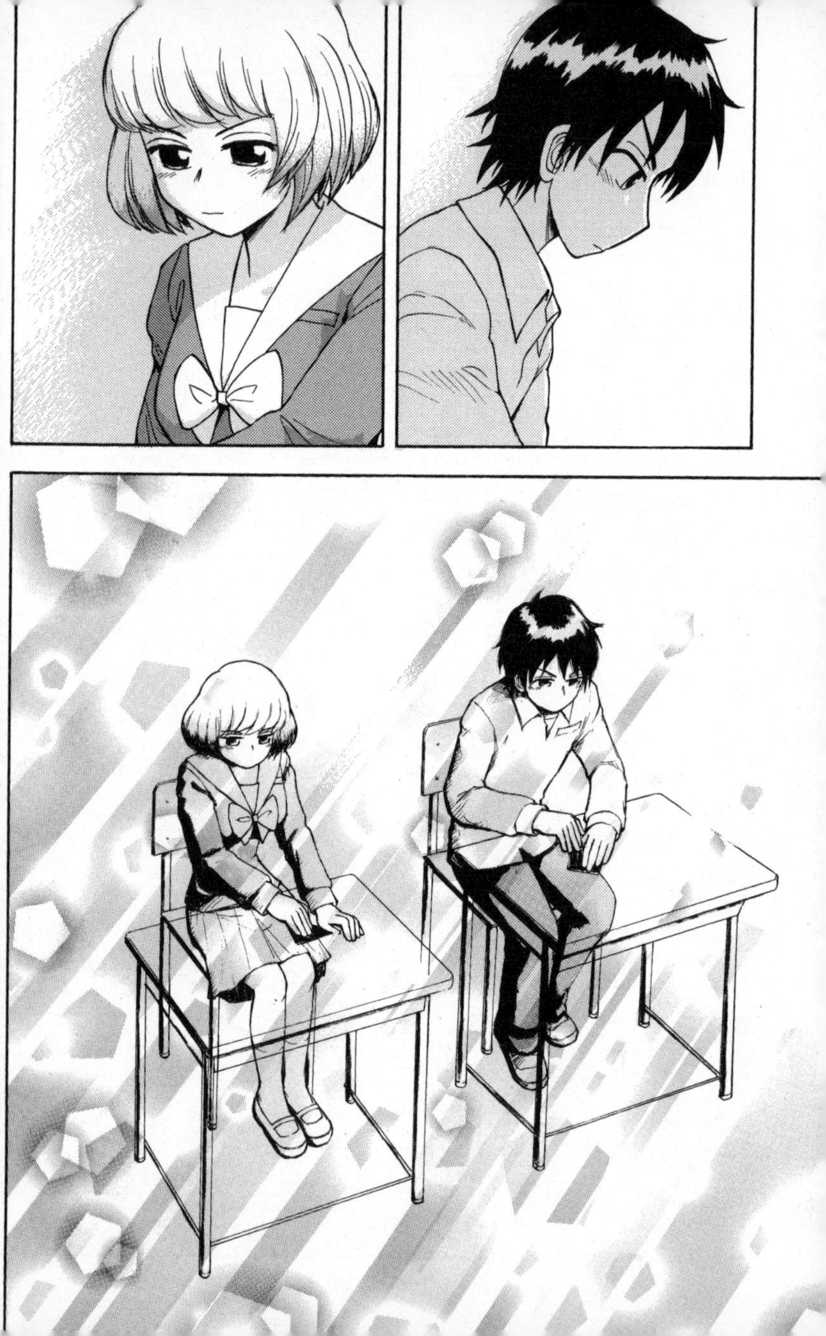

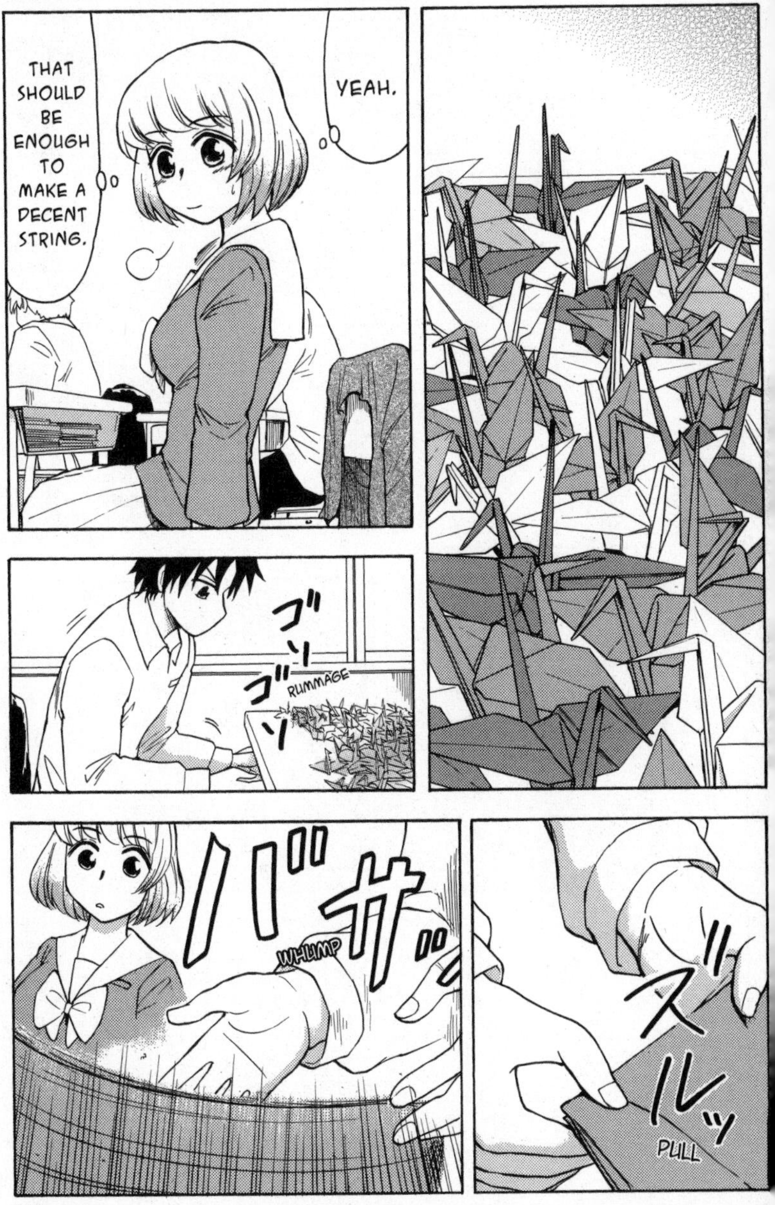
YEAH.
THAT SHOULD BE ENOUGH TO MAKE A DECENT STRING.
ゴソゴソ
RUMMAGE
ズルッ
PULL
バサッ
WHUMP

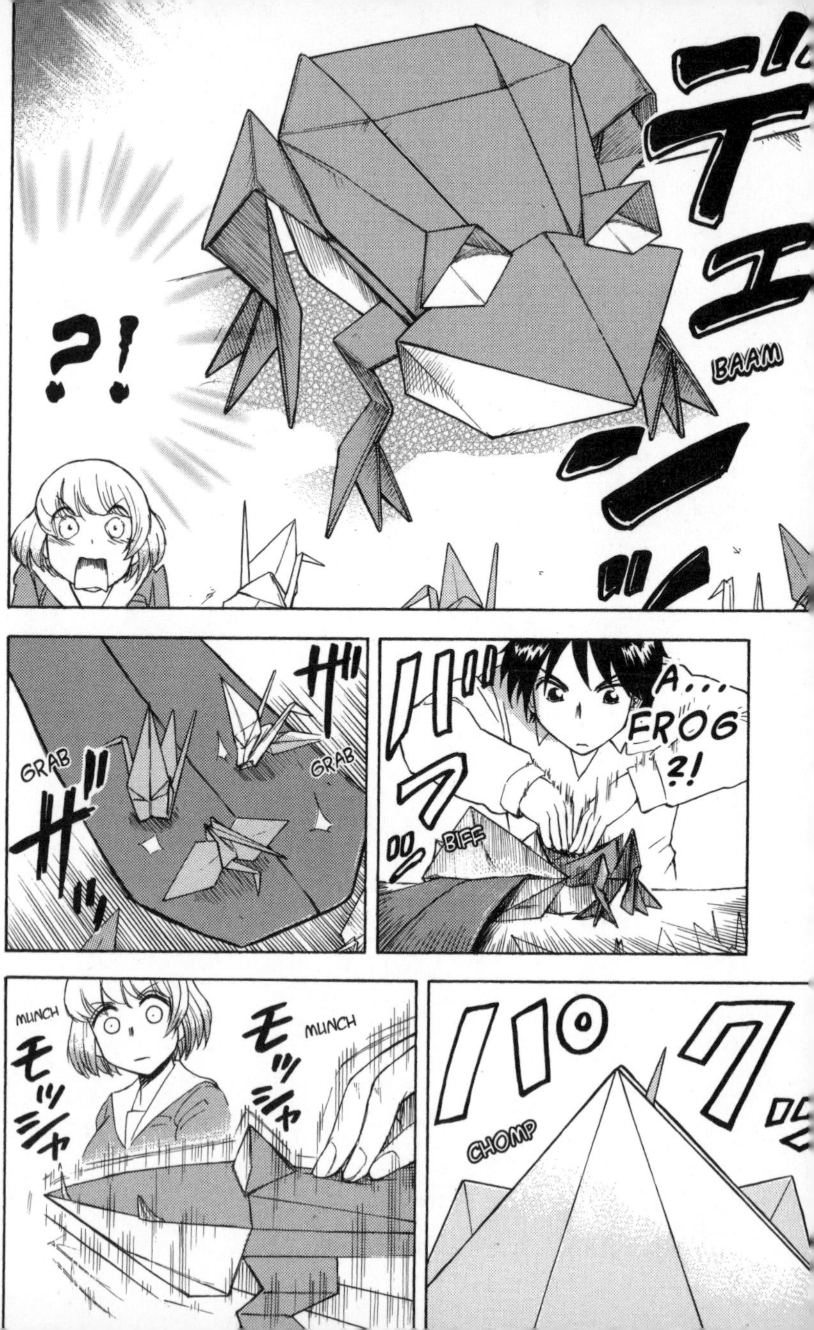
BAAM
?!
A... FROG?!
BIFF
GRAB
GRAB
CHOMP
MUNCH
MUNCH
モッシャ
モッシャ

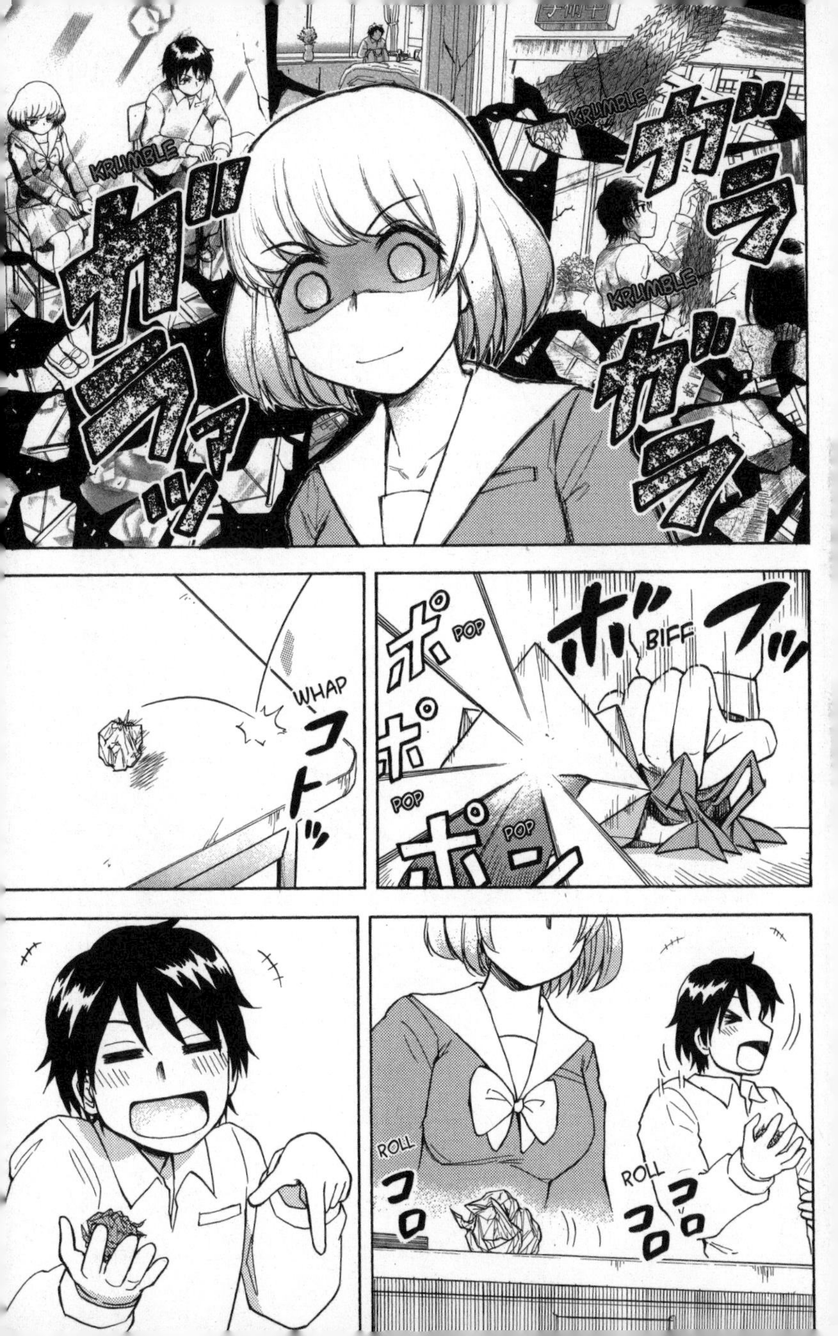
KRUMBLE
ガラ
KRUMBLE
ガラ
KRUMBLE
BIFF
ボフッ
POP
POP
POP
ポポポーン
WHAP
コトッ
ROLL
コロコロ
ROLL
コロ

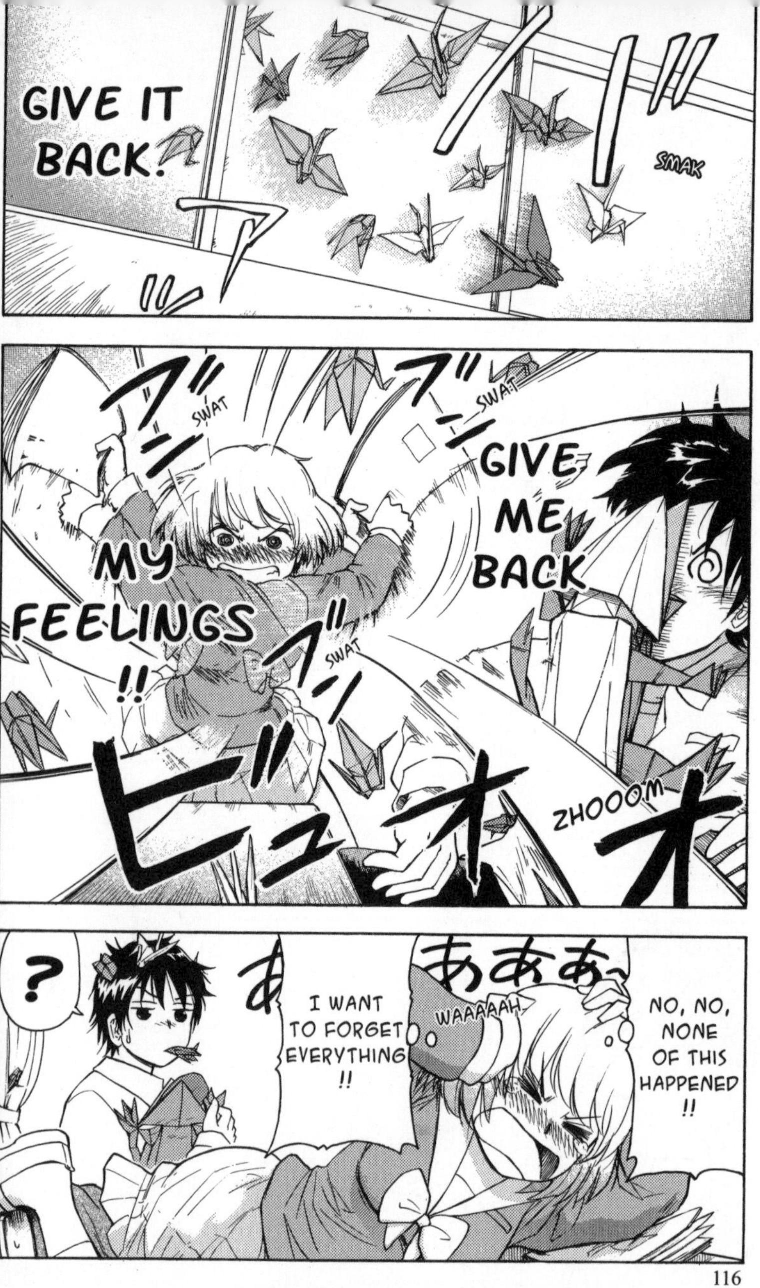
SMAK
GIVE IT BACK.
SWAT
SWAT
GIVE ME BACK
MY FEELINGS !!
SWAT
ビュオ
ZHOOOM
NO, NO, NONE OF THIS HAPPENED !!
WAAAAAH
あああああ~
I WANT TO FORGET EVERYTHING !!
?

12th Period

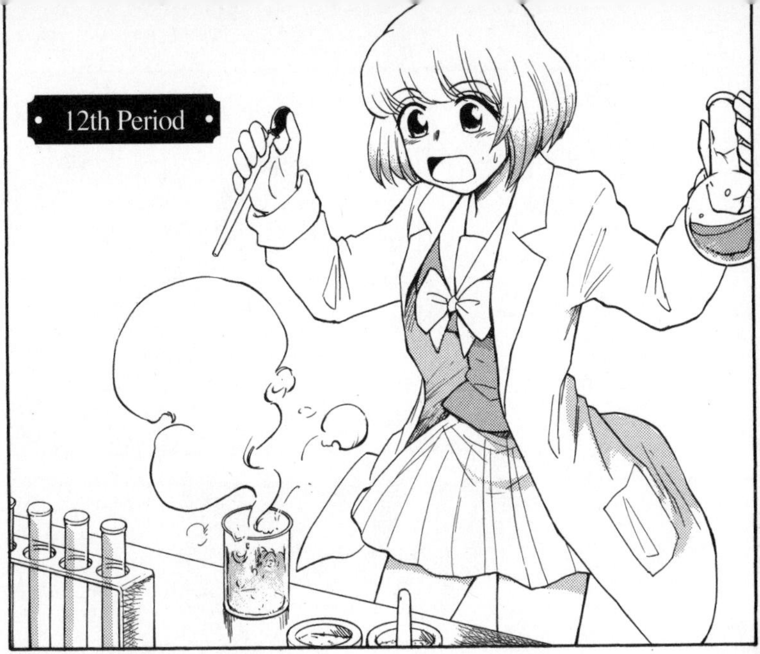

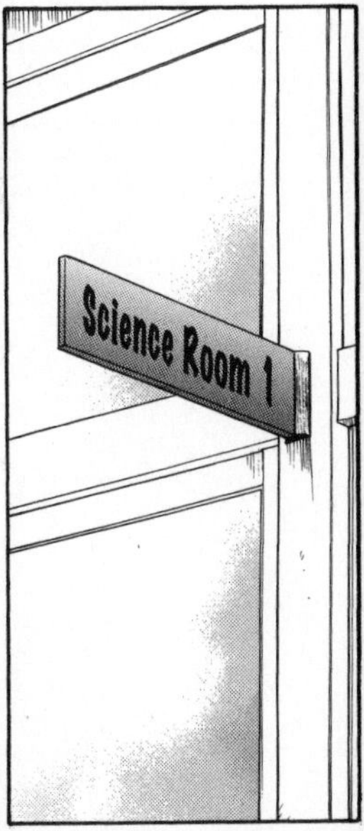
Science Room 1

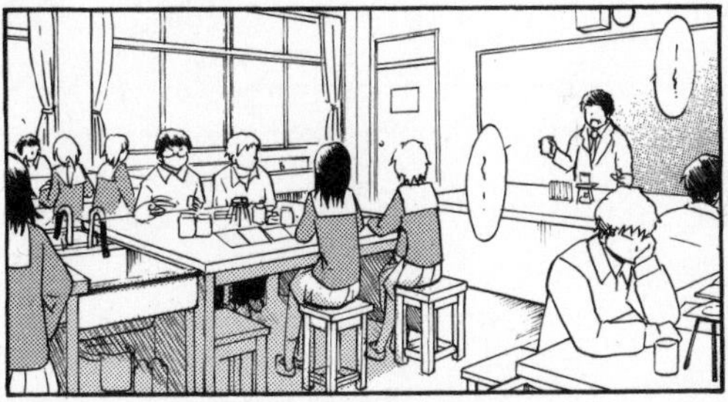
!
?

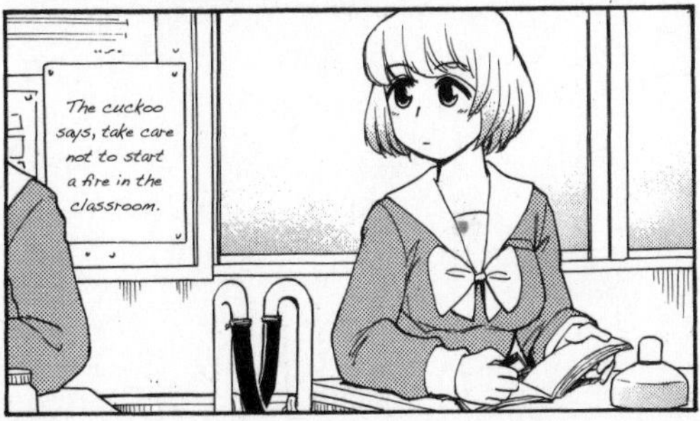
The cuckoo says, take care not to start a fire in the classroom.

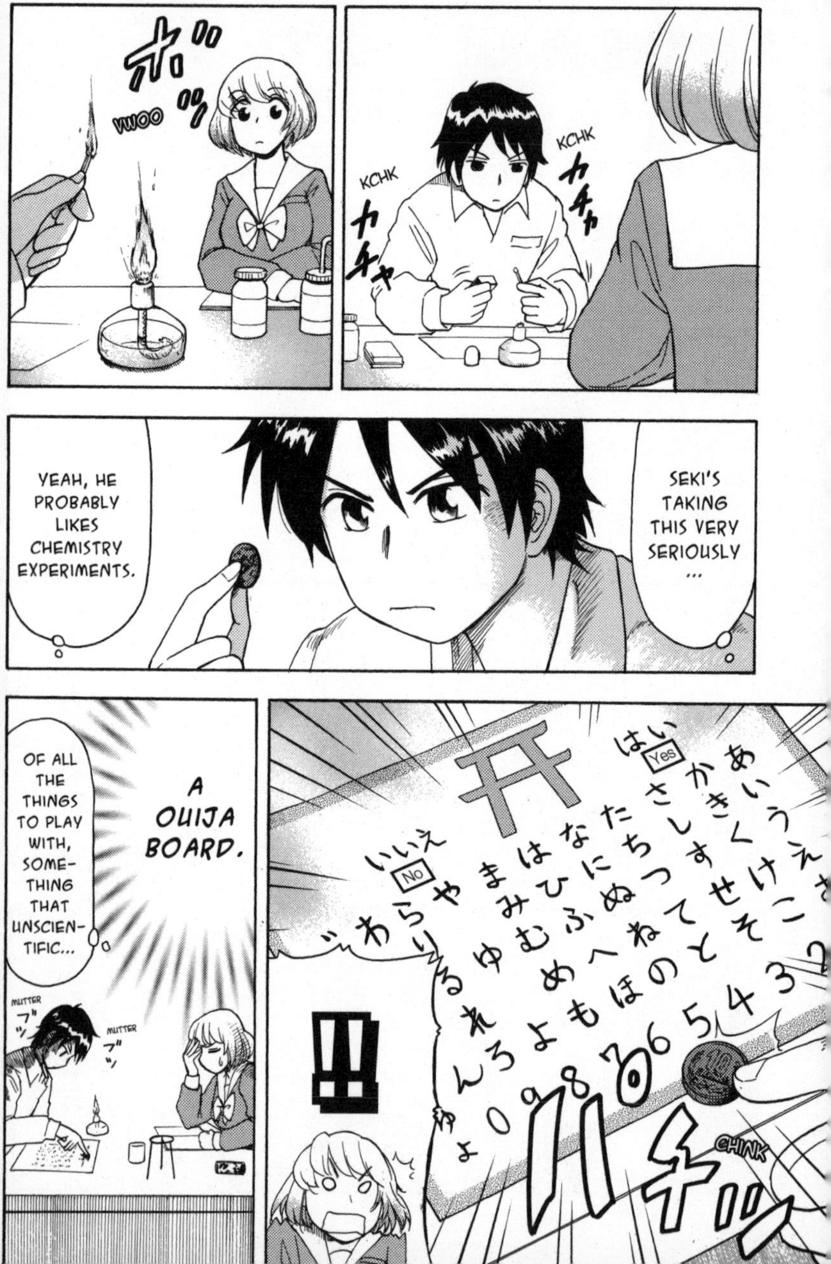
KCHK
KCHK
VWOO
SEKI'S TAKING THIS VERY SERIOUSLY ...
YEAH, HE PROBABLY LIKES CHEMISTRY EXPERIMENTS.
はい Yes
いいえ No
!!
CHINK
A OUIJA BOARD.
OF ALL THE THINGS TO PLAY WITH, SOMETHING THAT UNSCIENTIFIC...
MUTTER
MUTTER

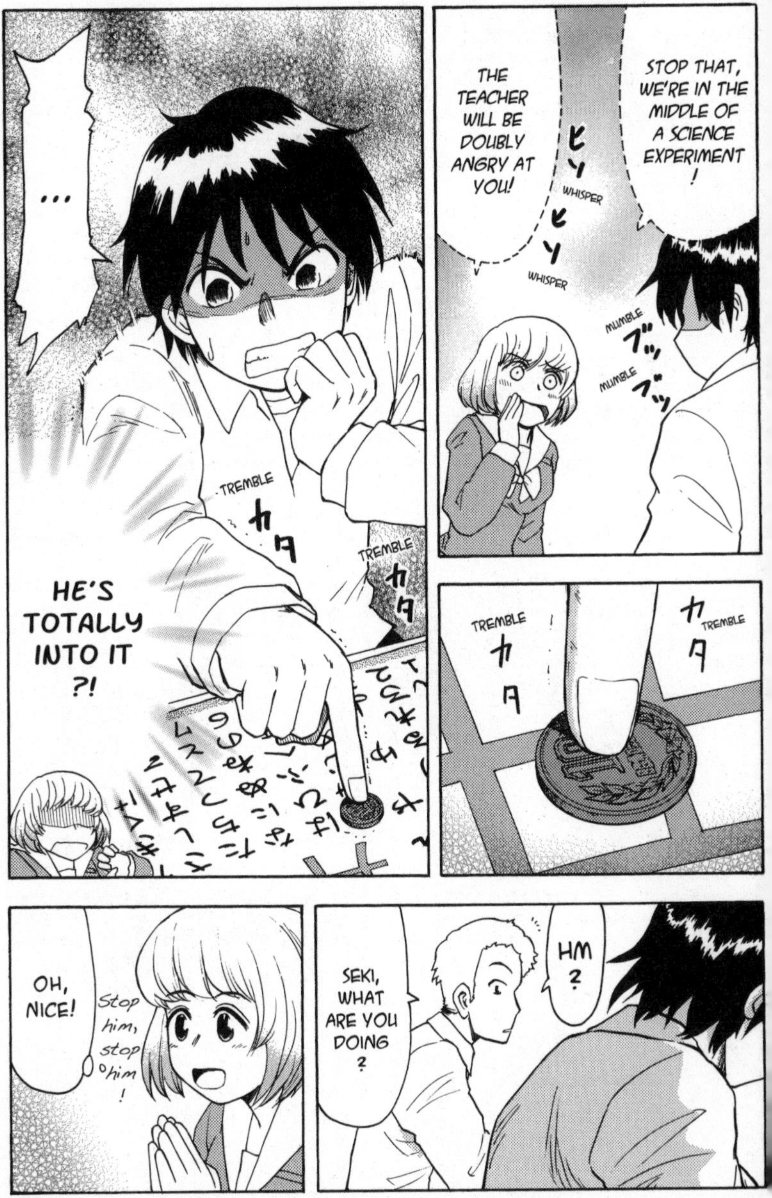
STOP THAT, WE'RE IN THE MIDDLE OF A SCIENCE EXPERIMENT!
THE TEACHER WILL BE DOUBLY ANGRY AT YOU!
ヒソ
WHISPER
ヒソ
WHISPER
MUMBLE
ブツ
MUMBLE
ブツ
カタ
TREMBLE
TREMBLE
カタ
...
TREMBLE
カタ
TREMBLE
カタ
HE'S TOTALLY INTO IT?!
HM?
SEKI, WHAT ARE YOU DOING?
OH, NICE!
Stop him, stop him!

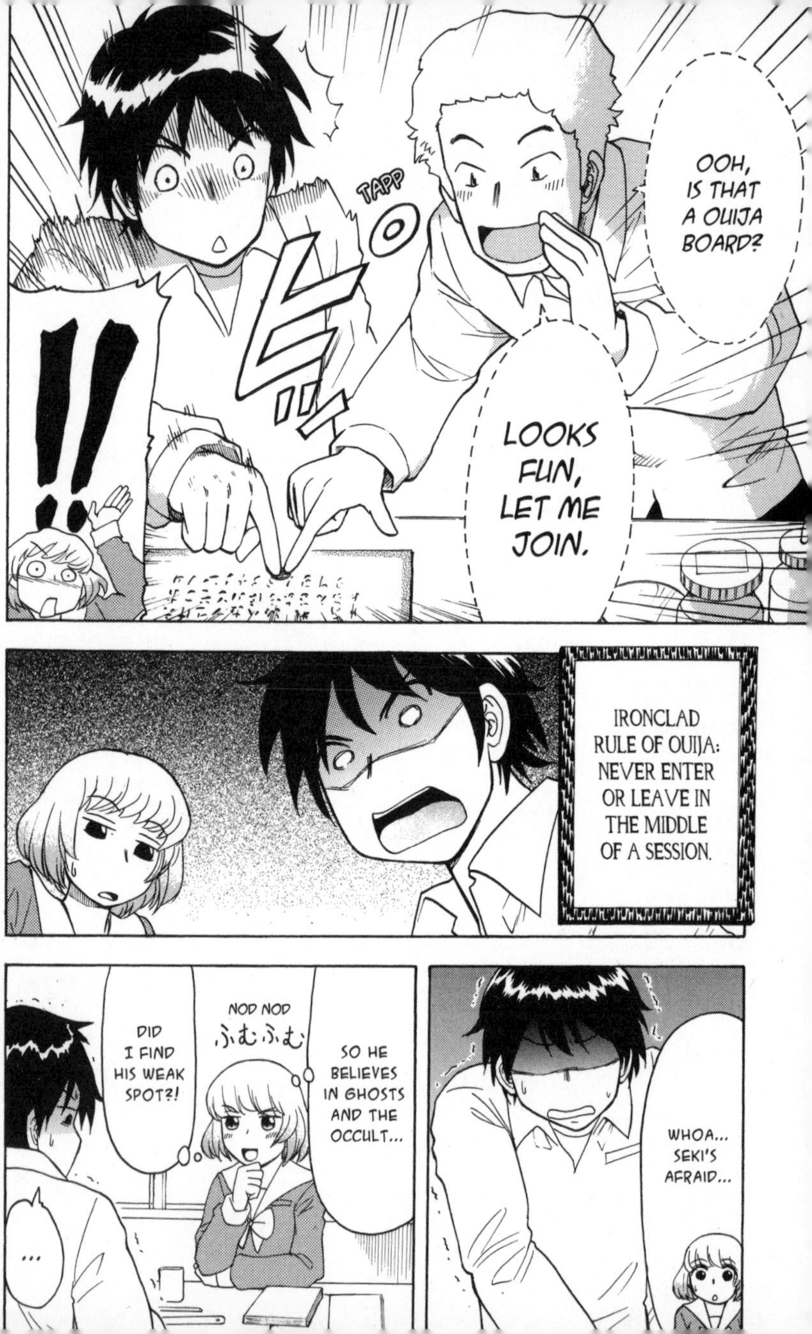
OOH, IS THAT A OUIJA BOARD?
TAPP
LOOKS FUN, LET ME JOIN.
IRONCLAD RULE OF OUIJA: NEVER ENTER OR LEAVE IN THE MIDDLE OF A SESSION.
WHOA... SEKI'S AFRAID...
SO HE BELIEVES IN GHOSTS AND THE OCCULT...
NOD NOD
ふむふむ
DID I FIND HIS WEAK SPOT?!
...

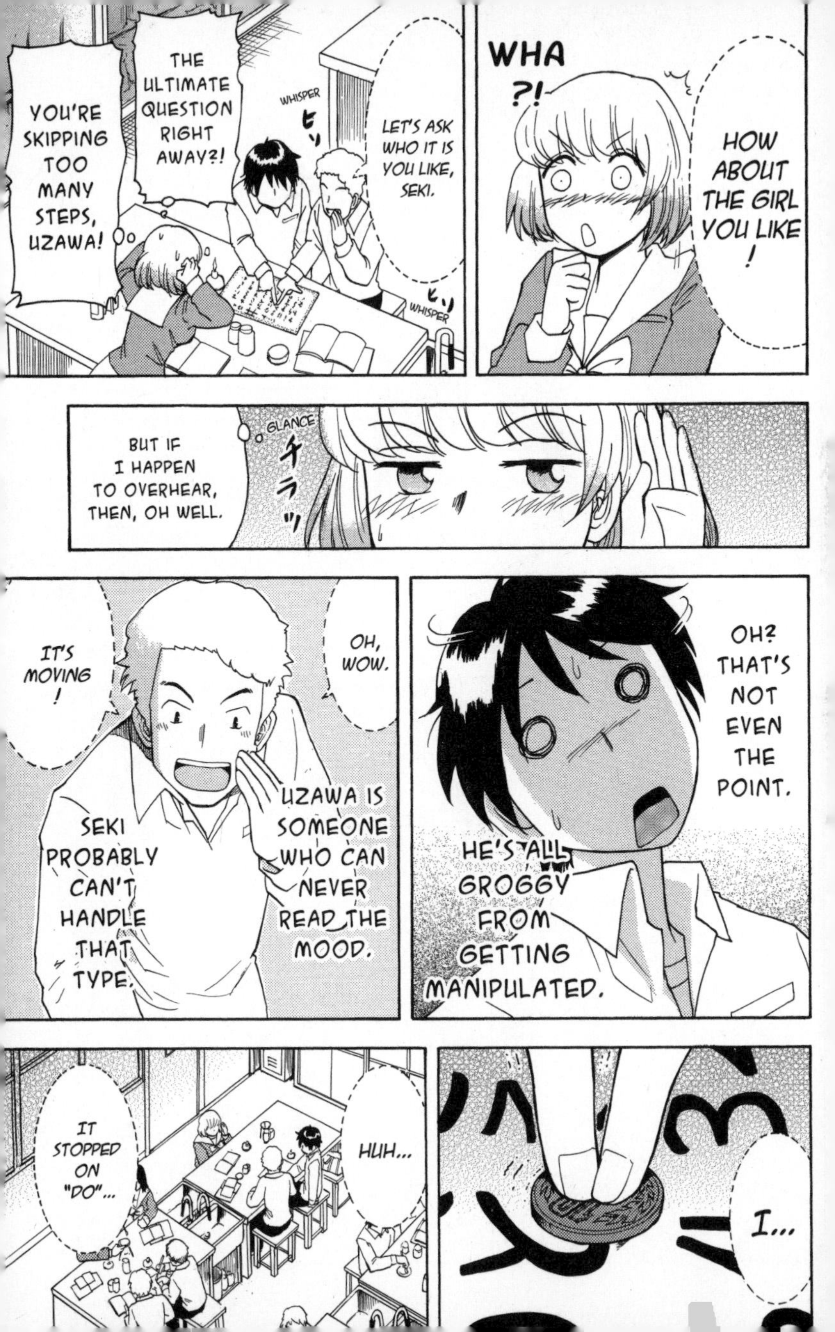
WHA ?!
HOW ABOUT THE GIRL YOU LIKE!
LET'S ASK WHO IT IS YOU LIKE, SEKI.
WHISPER
WHISPER
THE ULTIMATE QUESTION RIGHT AWAY?!
YOU'RE SKIPPING TOO MANY STEPS, UZAWA!
BUT IF I HAPPEN TO OVERHEAR, THEN, OH WELL.
GLANCE
OH? THAT'S NOT EVEN THE POINT.
HE'S ALL GROGGY FROM GETTING MANIPULATED.
OH, WOW.
IT'S MOVING!
UZAWA IS SOMEONE WHO CAN NEVER READ THE MOOD.
SEKI PROBABLY CAN'T HANDLE THAT TYPE.
I...
HUH...
IT STOPPED ON "DO"...

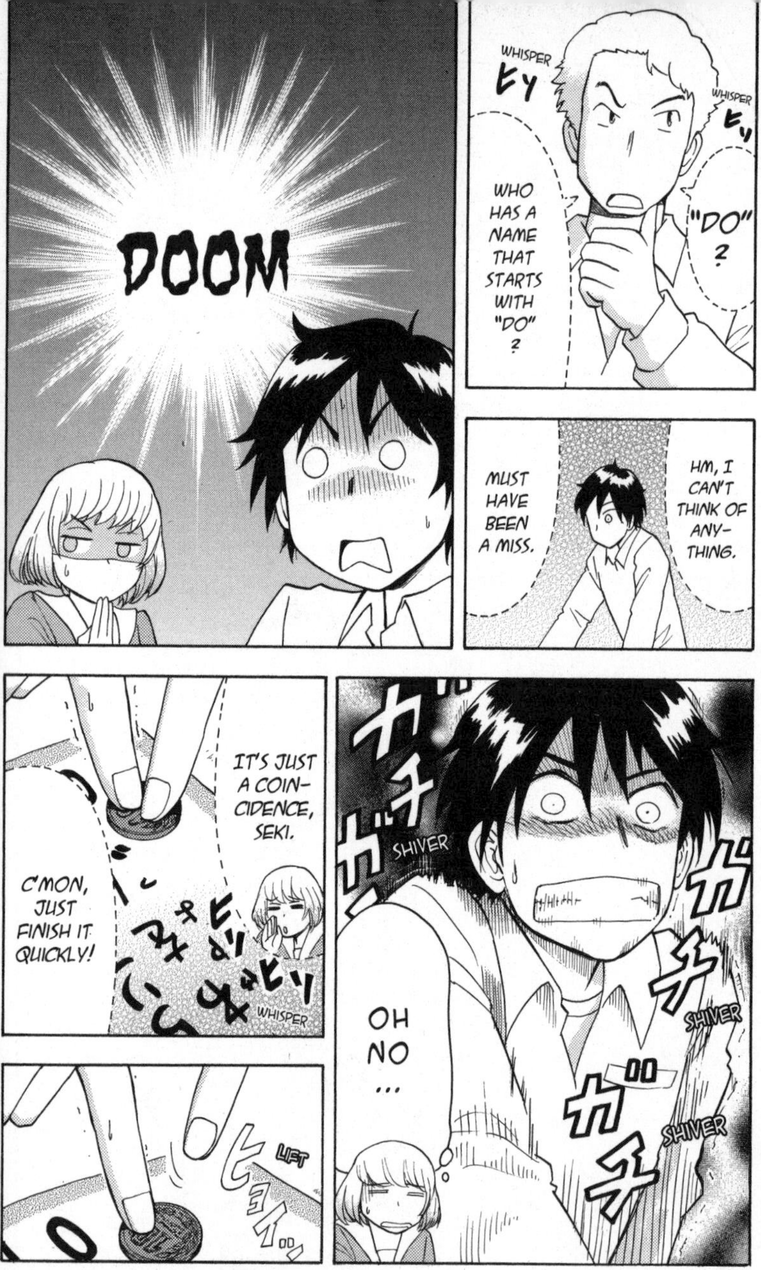
WHISPER
ヒッ
"DO" ?
WHISPER
ヒソ
WHO HAS A NAME THAT STARTS WITH "DO" ?
HM, I CAN'T THINK OF ANY-THING.
MUST HAVE BEEN A MISS.
DOOM
ガチ
SHIVER
ガチ
SHIVER
ガチ
SHIVER
OH NO ...
IT'S JUST A COIN-CIDENCE, SEKI.
C'MON, JUST FINISH IT QUICKLY!
ヒソ
ヒソ
WHISPER
LIFT
ヒョイ

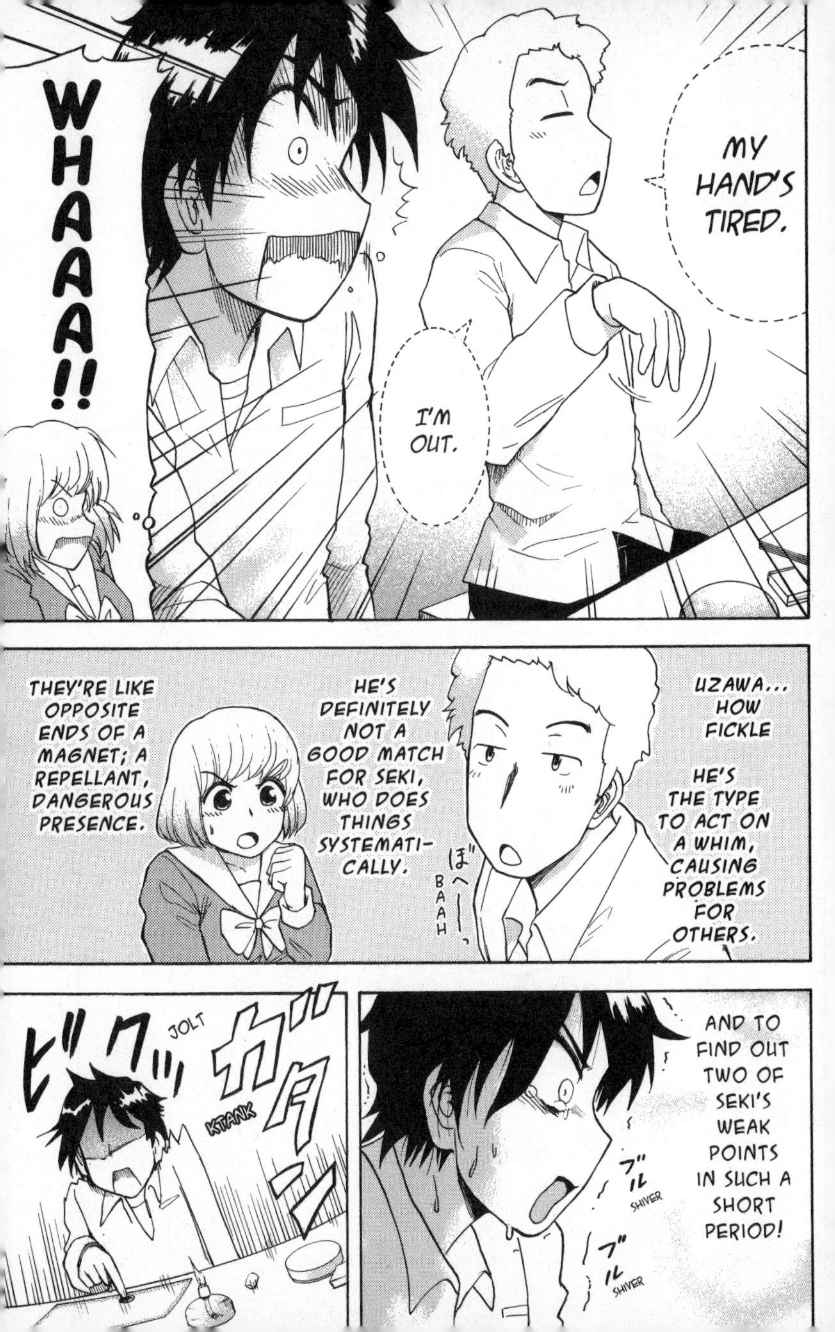
MY HAND'S TIRED.
I'M OUT.
WHAAAA!!
UZAWA... HOW FICKLE
HE'S THE TYPE TO ACT ON A WHIM, CAUSING PROBLEMS FOR OTHERS.
ぼへー
BAAH
HE'S DEFINITELY NOT A GOOD MATCH FOR SEKI, WHO DOES THINGS SYSTEMATI-CALLY.
THEY'RE LIKE OPPOSITE ENDS OF A MAGNET; A REPELLANT, DANGEROUS PRESENCE.
AND TO FIND OUT TWO OF SEKI'S WEAK POINTS IN SUCH A SHORT PERIOD!
ブル
SHIVER
ブル
SHIVER
ビクッ
JOLT
ガタ
KTANK

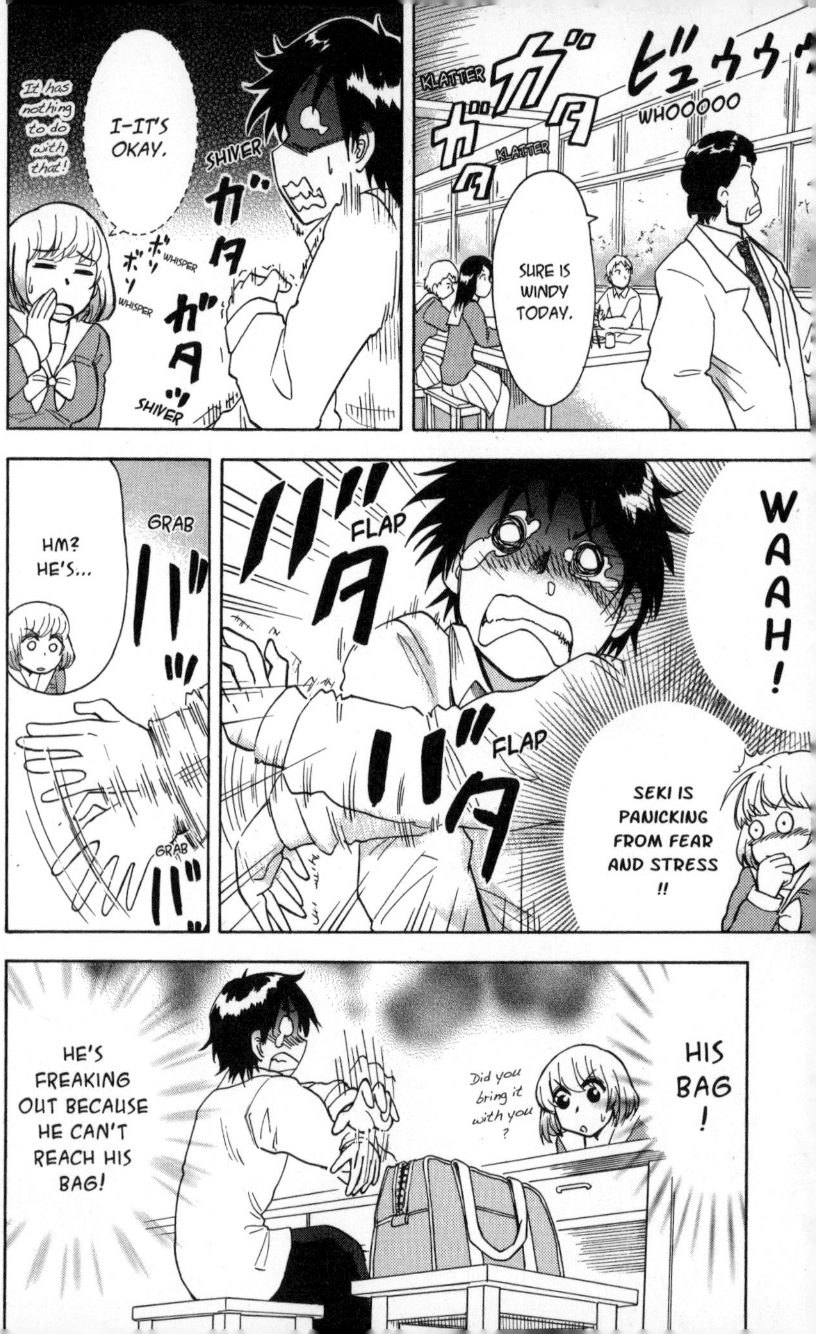
ビュウウウ
WHOOOOO
ガタ
KLATTER
ガタ
KLATTER
SURE IS WINDY TODAY.
I-IT'S OKAY.
It has nothing to do with that!
SHIVER
ガタ
ガタッ
SHIVER
WHISPER
WHISPER
WAAAH!
FLAP
FLAP
SEKI IS PANICKING FROM FEAR AND STRESS !!
HM? HE'S...
GRAB
GRAB
HIS BAG!
Did you bring it with you?
HE'S FREAKING OUT BECAUSE HE CAN'T REACH HIS BAG!

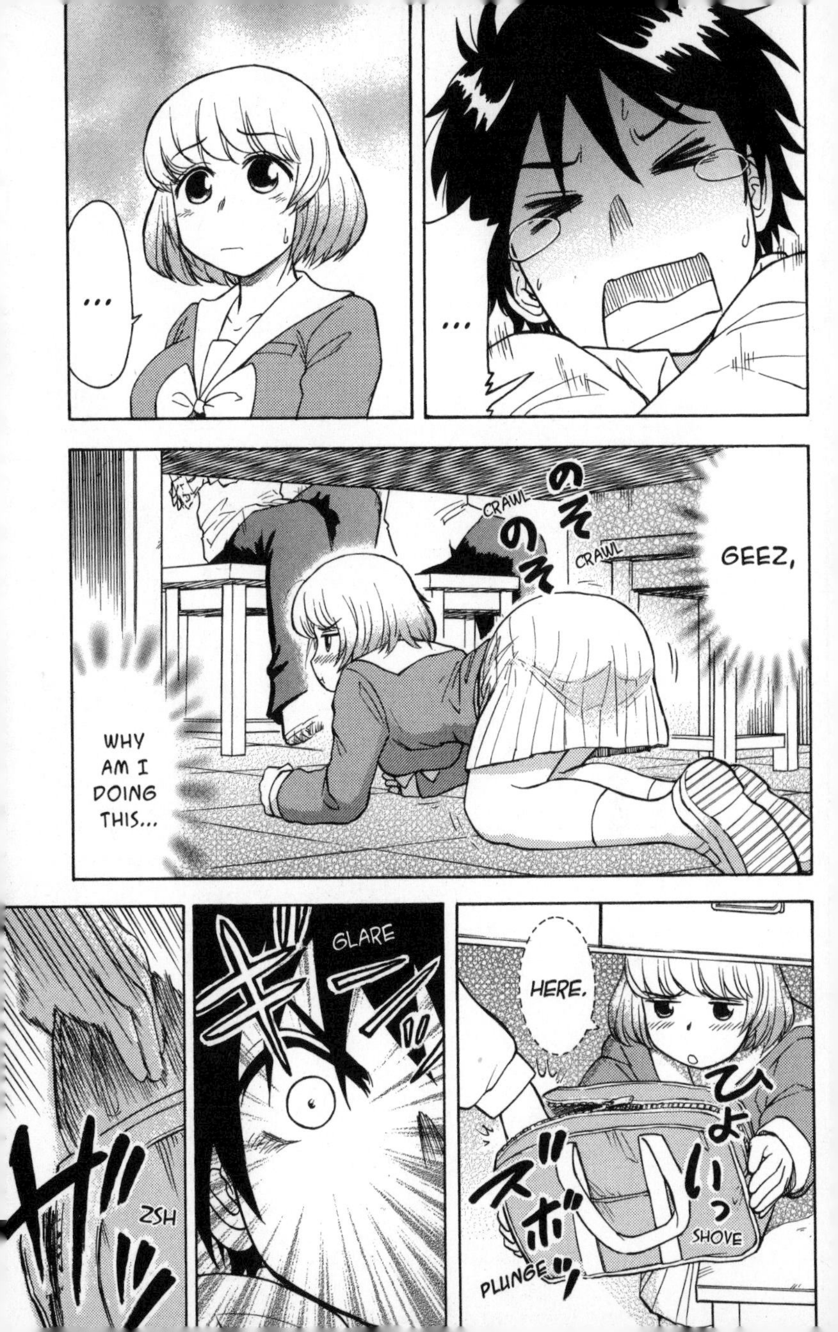
...
...
GEEZ,
のそのそ
CRAWL
CRAWL
WHY AM I DOING THIS...
HERE.
ひょいっ
SHOVE
ズボッ
PLUNGE
ギンッ
GLARE
ザッ
ZSH

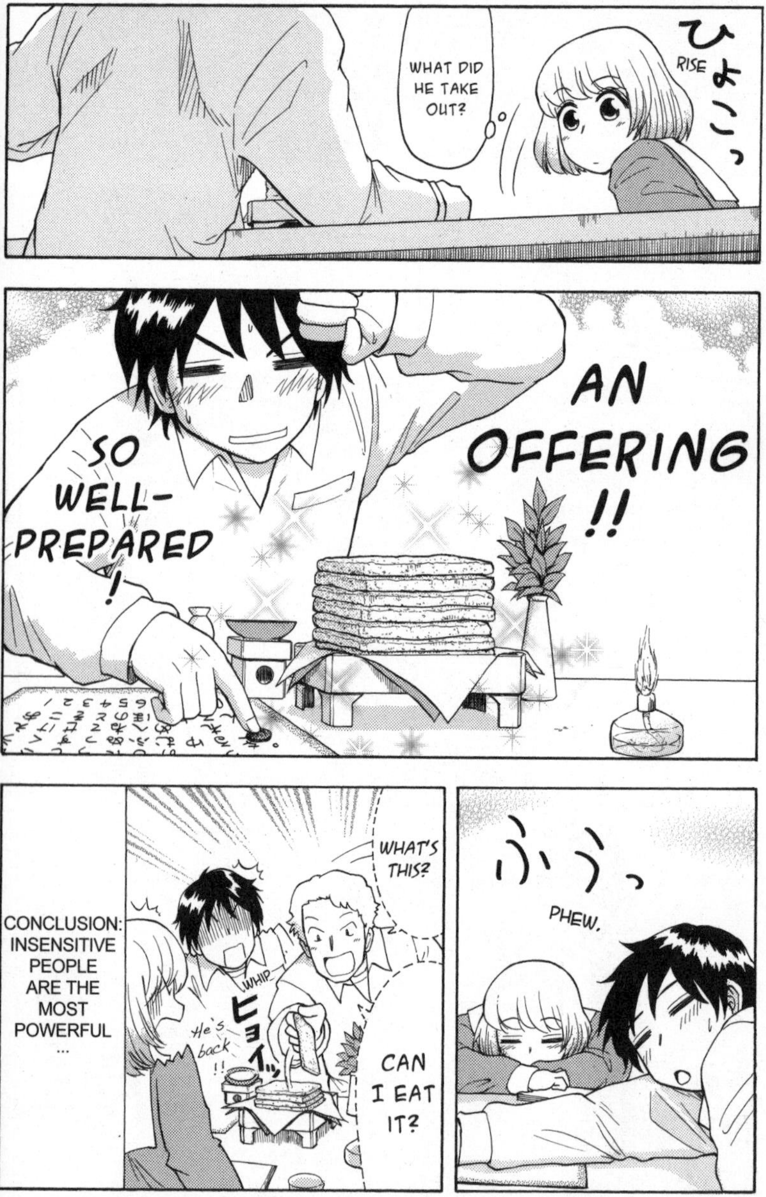

ひょこっ
RISE
WHAT DID HE TAKE OUT?
AN OFFERING!!
SO WELL-PREPARED!
ふうっ
PHEW.
WHAT'S THIS?
CAN I EAT IT?
WHIP
ヒョイッ
He's back!!
CONCLUSION: INSENSITIVE PEOPLE ARE THE MOST POWERFUL ...

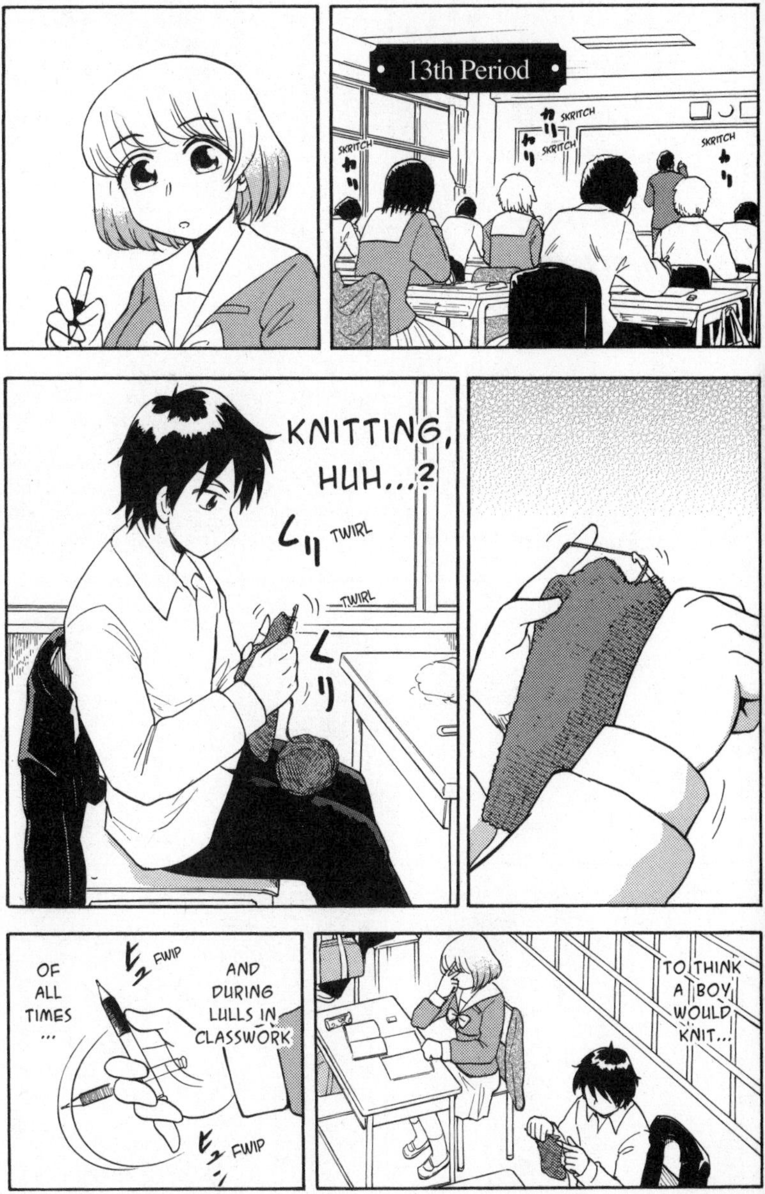
13th Period
SKRITCH
SKRITCH
SKRITCH
SKRITCH
KNITTING, HUH...?
TWIRL
TWIRL
TO THINK A BOY WOULD KNIT...
FWIP
AND DURING LULLS IN CLASSWORK
OF ALL TIMES...
FWIP

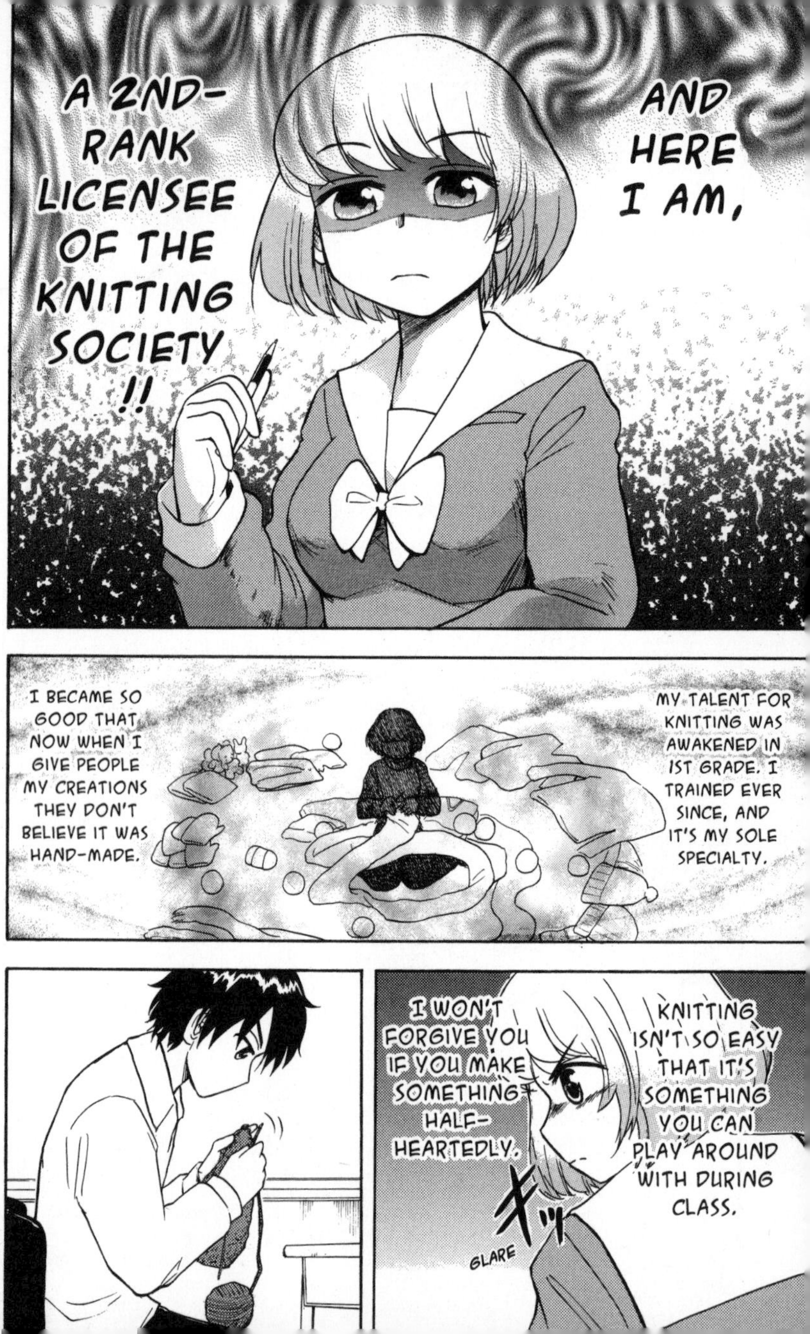
AND HERE I AM,
A 2ND-RANK LICENSEE OF THE KNITTING SOCIETY !!
MY TALENT FOR KNITTING WAS AWAKENED IN 1ST GRADE. I TRAINED EVER SINCE, AND IT'S MY SOLE SPECIALTY.
I BECAME SO GOOD THAT NOW WHEN I GIVE PEOPLE MY CREATIONS THEY DON'T BELIEVE IT WAS HAND-MADE.
KNITTING ISN'T SO EASY THAT IT'S SOMETHING YOU CAN PLAY AROUND WITH DURING CLASS.
I WON'T FORGIVE YOU IF YOU MAKE SOMETHING HALF-HEARTEDLY.
GLARE

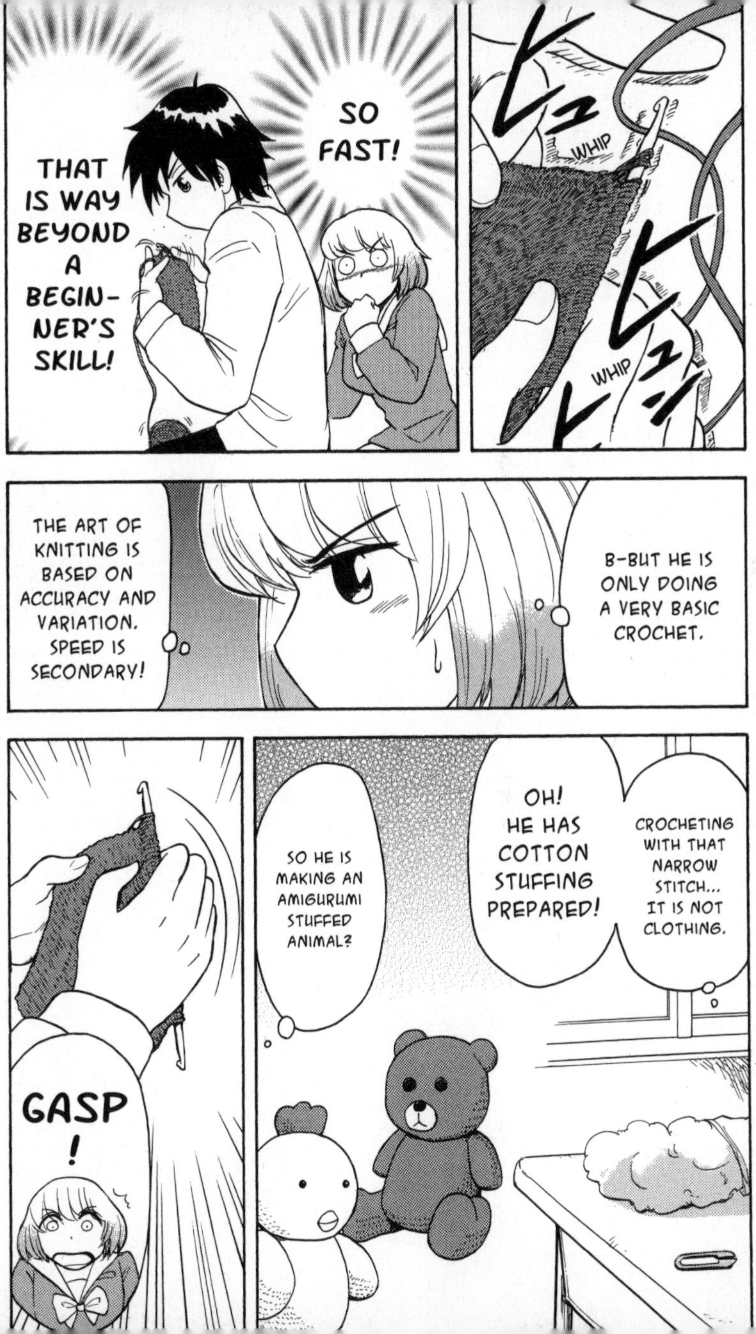
WHIP
WHIP
SO FAST!
THAT IS WAY BEYOND A BEGINNER'S SKILL!
B-BUT HE IS ONLY DOING A VERY BASIC CROCHET.
THE ART OF KNITTING IS BASED ON ACCURACY AND VARIATION. SPEED IS SECONDARY!
CROCHETING WITH THAT NARROW STITCH... IT IS NOT CLOTHING.
OH! HE HAS COTTON STUFFING PREPARED!
SO HE IS MAKING AN AMIGURUMI STUFFED ANIMAL?
GASP!

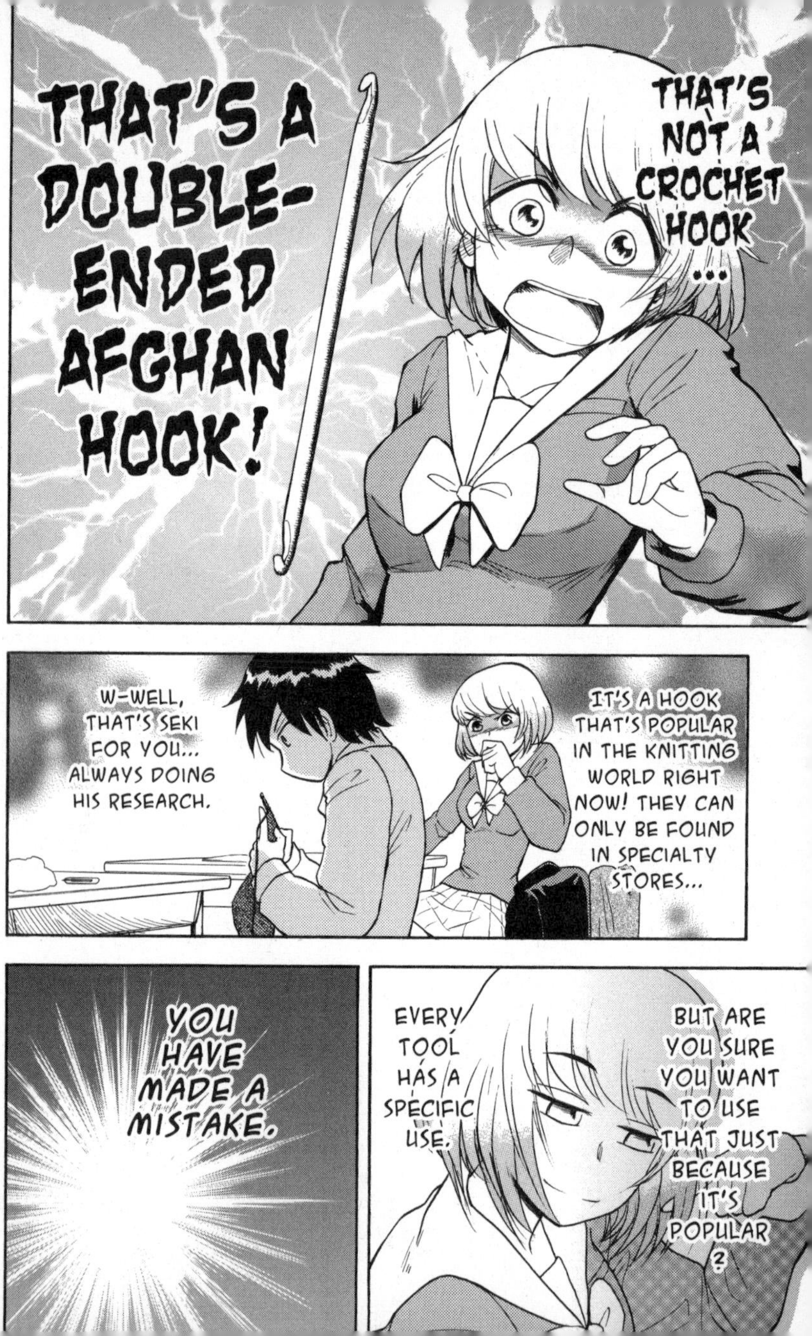
THAT'S NOT A CROCHET HOOK...
THAT'S A DOUBLE-ENDED AFGHAN HOOK!
IT'S A HOOK THAT'S POPULAR IN THE KNITTING WORLD RIGHT NOW! THEY CAN ONLY BE FOUND IN SPECIALTY STORES...
W-WELL, THAT'S SEKI FOR YOU... ALWAYS DOING HIS RESEARCH.
BUT ARE YOU SURE YOU WANT TO USE THAT JUST BECAUSE IT'S POPULAR?
EVERY TOOL HAS A SPECIFIC USE.
YOU HAVE MADE A MISTAKE.

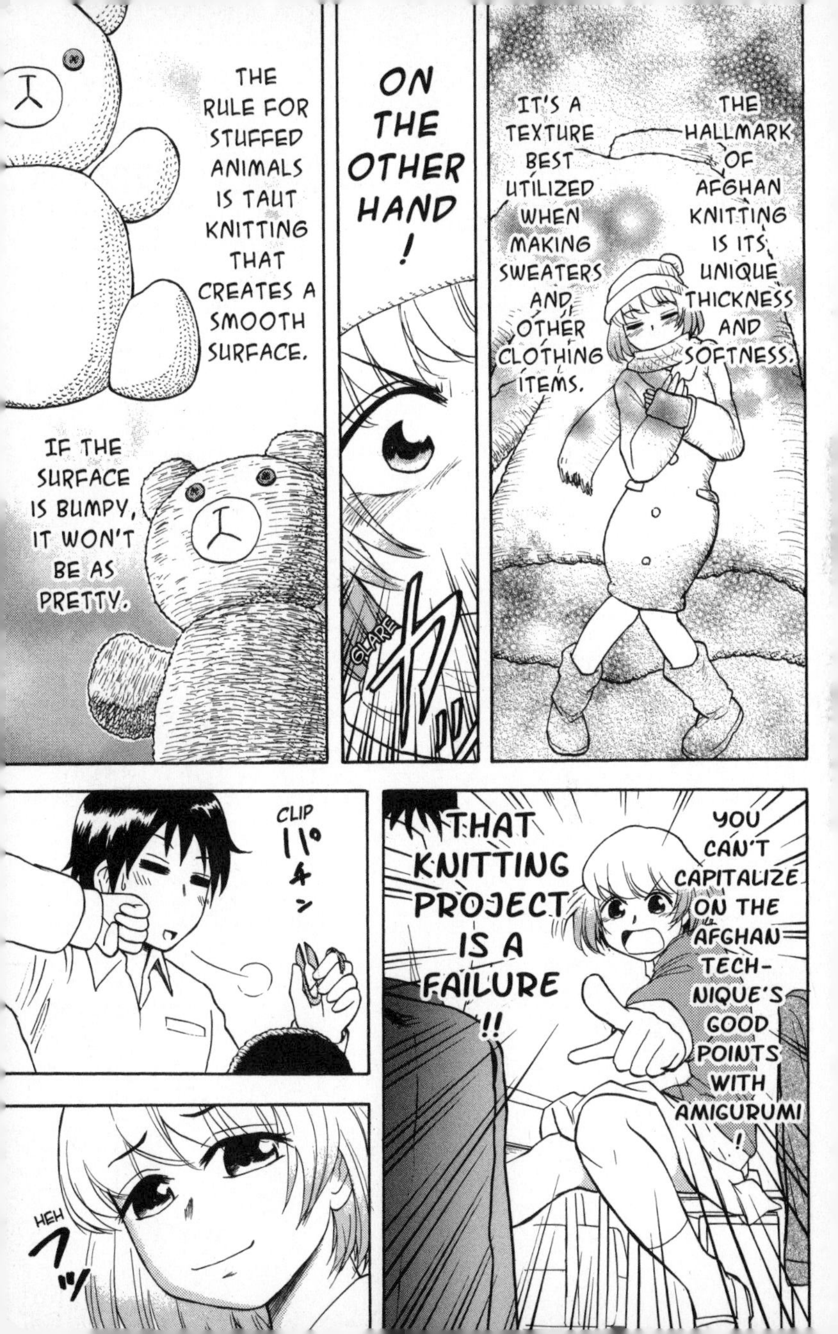
THE HALLMARK OF AFGHAN KNITTING IS ITS UNIQUE THICKNESS AND SOFTNESS.
IT'S A TEXTURE BEST UTILIZED WHEN MAKING SWEATERS AND OTHER CLOTHING ITEMS.
ON THE OTHER HAND!
GLARE
THE RULE FOR STUFFED ANIMALS IS TAUT KNITTING THAT CREATES A SMOOTH SURFACE.
IF THE SURFACE IS BUMPY, IT WON'T BE AS PRETTY.
YOU CAN'T CAPITALIZE ON THE AFGHAN TECH-NIQUE'S GOOD POINTS WITH AMIGURUMI!
THAT KNITTING PROJECT IS A FAILURE!!
CLIP
パチン
HEH
フッ

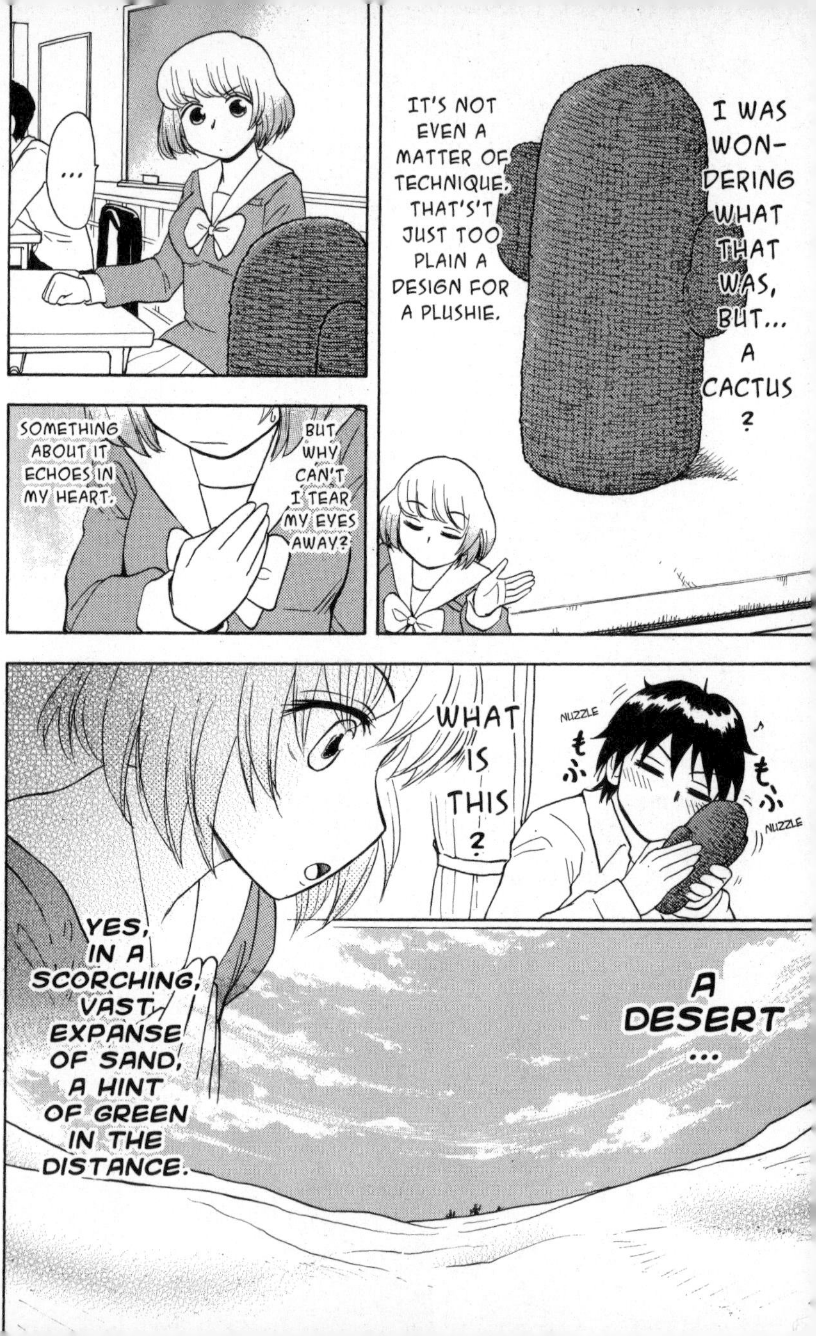

I WAS WONDERING WHAT THAT WAS, BUT... A CACTUS?
IT'S NOT EVEN A MATTER OF TECHNIQUE. THAT'S'T JUST TOO PLAIN A DESIGN FOR A PLUSHIE.
...
BUT WHY CAN'T I TEAR MY EYES AWAY?
SOMETHING ABOUT IT ECHOES IN MY HEART.
もふ
NUZZLE
もふ
NUZZLE
WHAT IS THIS?
A DESERT...
YES, IN A SCORCHING, VAST EXPANSE OF SAND, A HINT OF GREEN IN THE DISTANCE.

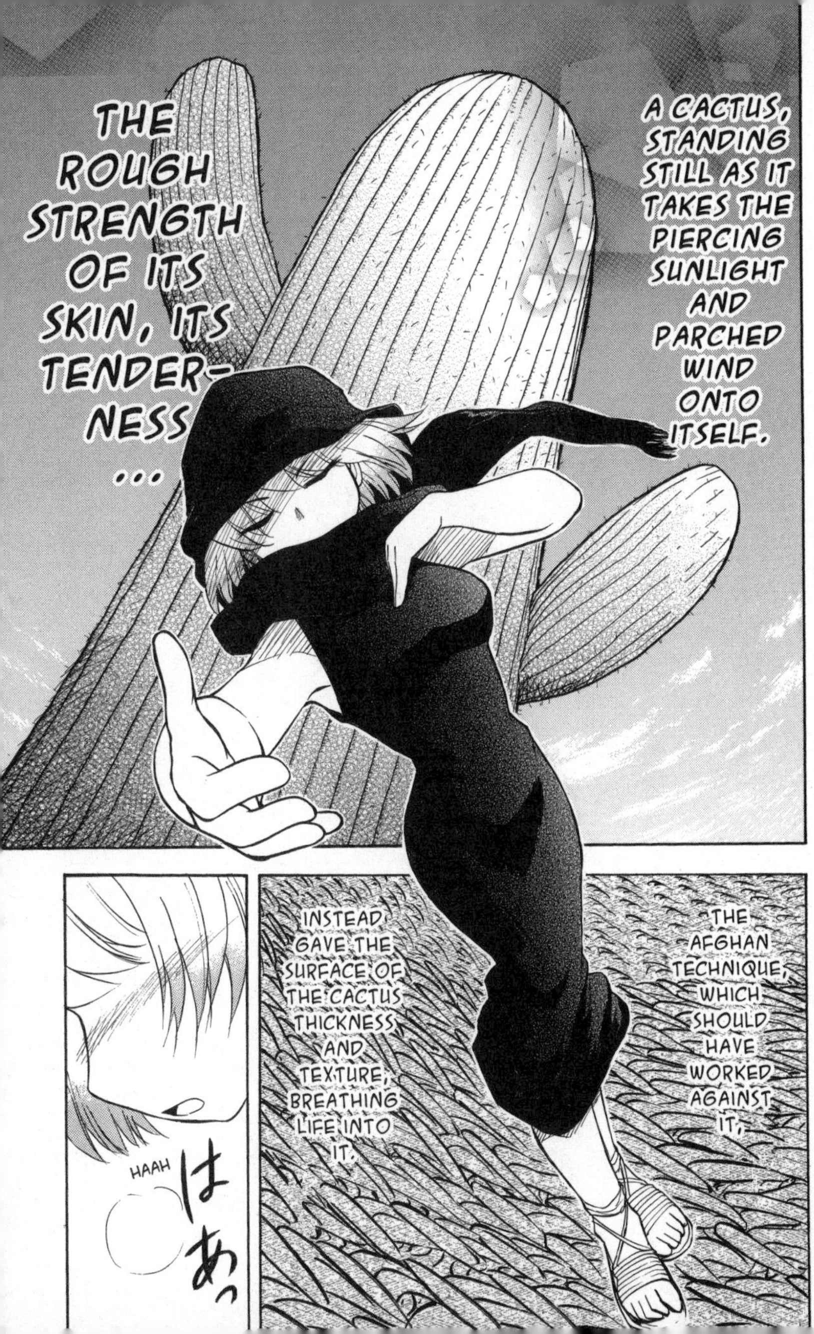
A CACTUS, STANDING STILL AS IT TAKES THE PIERCING SUNLIGHT AND PARCHED WIND ONTO ITSELF.
THE ROUGH STRENGTH OF ITS SKIN, ITS TENDER-NESS...
THE AFGHAN TECHNIQUE, WHICH SHOULD HAVE WORKED AGAINST IT,
INSTEAD GAVE THE SURFACE OF THE CACTUS THICKNESS AND TEXTURE, BREATHING LIFE INTO IT.
HAAH
はあっ

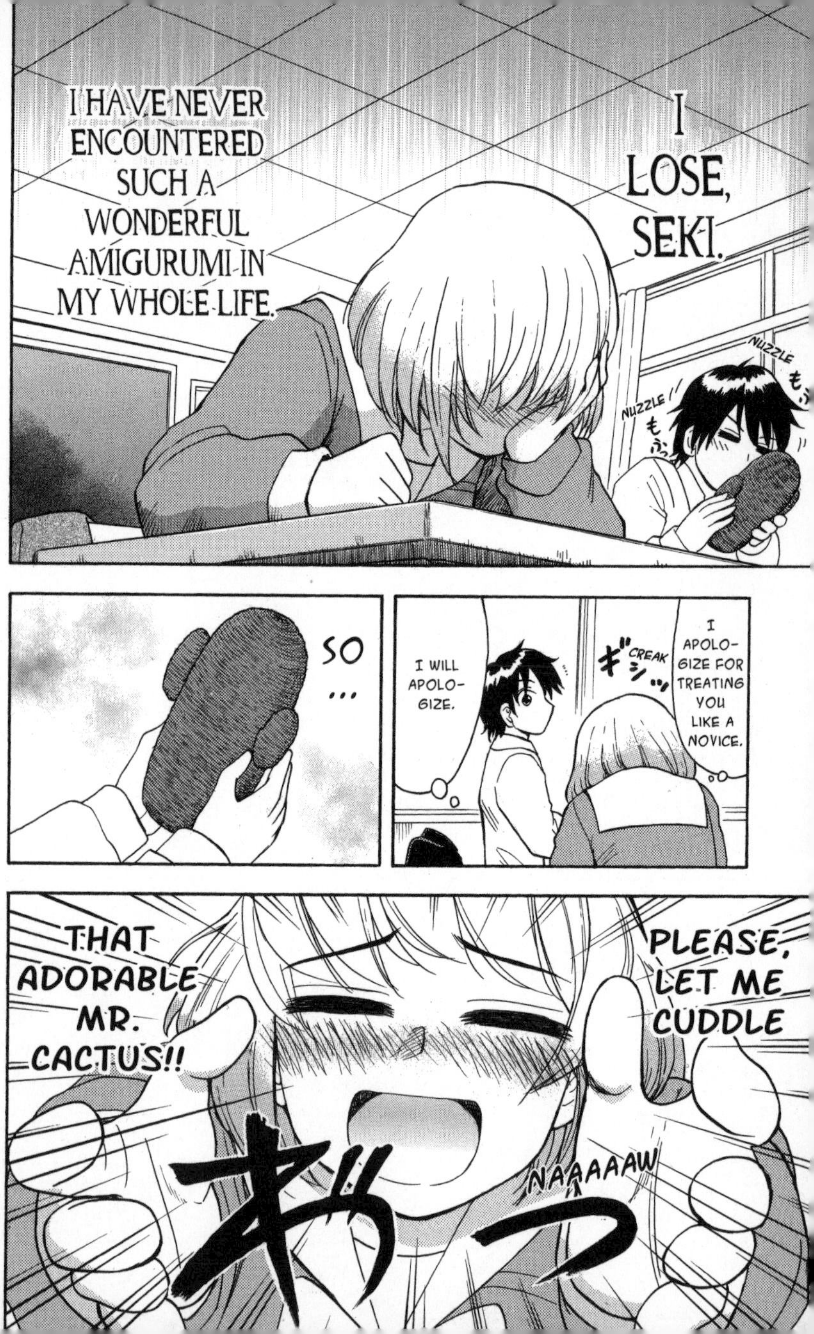
I LOSE, SEKI.
I HAVE NEVER ENCOUNTERED SUCH A WONDERFUL AMIGURUMI IN MY WHOLE LIFE.
NUZZLE
もふっ
NUZZLE
もふっ
I APOLOGIZE FOR TREATING YOU LIKE A NOVICE.
CREAK
ギシッ
I WILL APOLOGIZE.
SO ...
PLEASE, LET ME CUDDLE
THAT ADORABLE MR. CACTUS!!
NAAAAAW

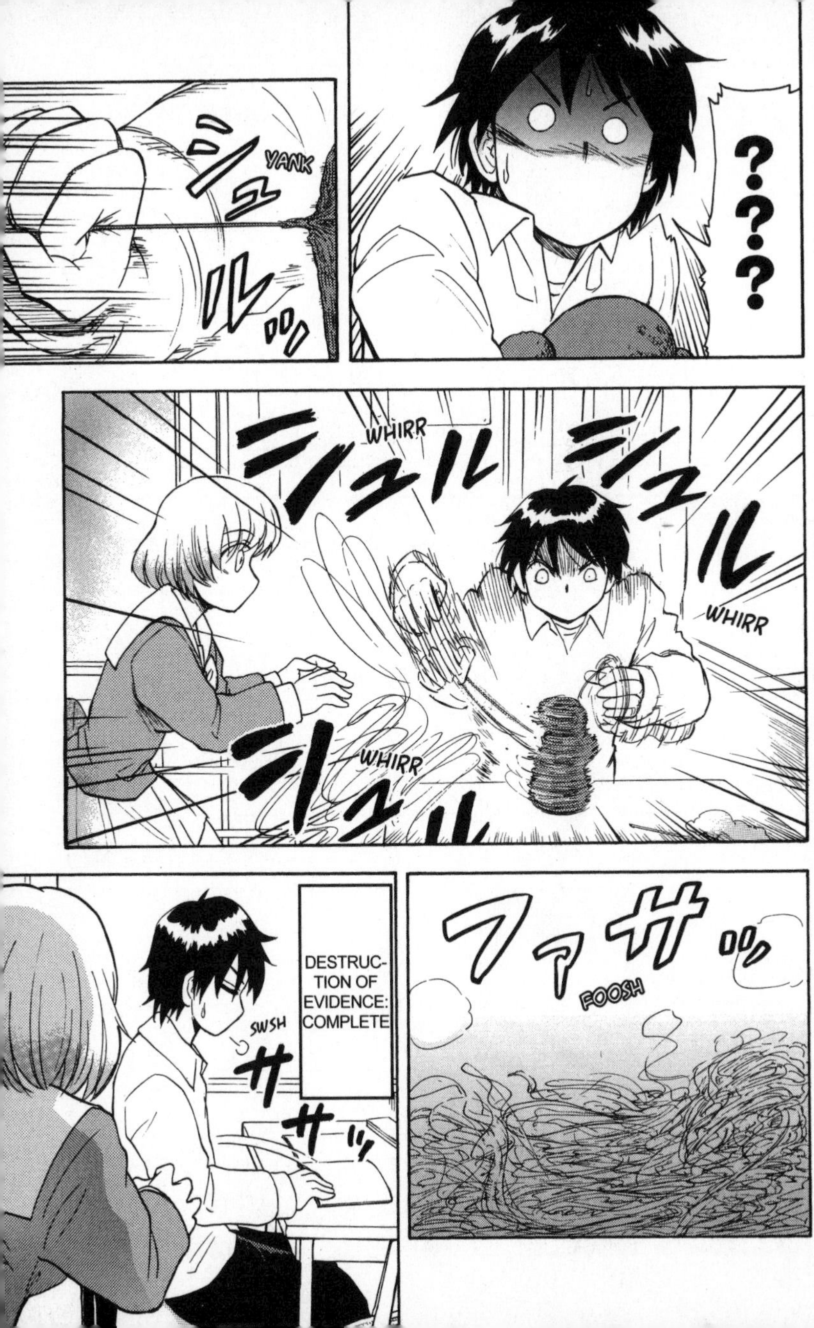

???
シュルッ
YANK
シュル シュル
WHIRR
WHIRR
シュル
WHIRR
ファサッ
FOOSH
DESTRUCTION OF EVIDENCE: COMPLETE
ササッ
SWSH

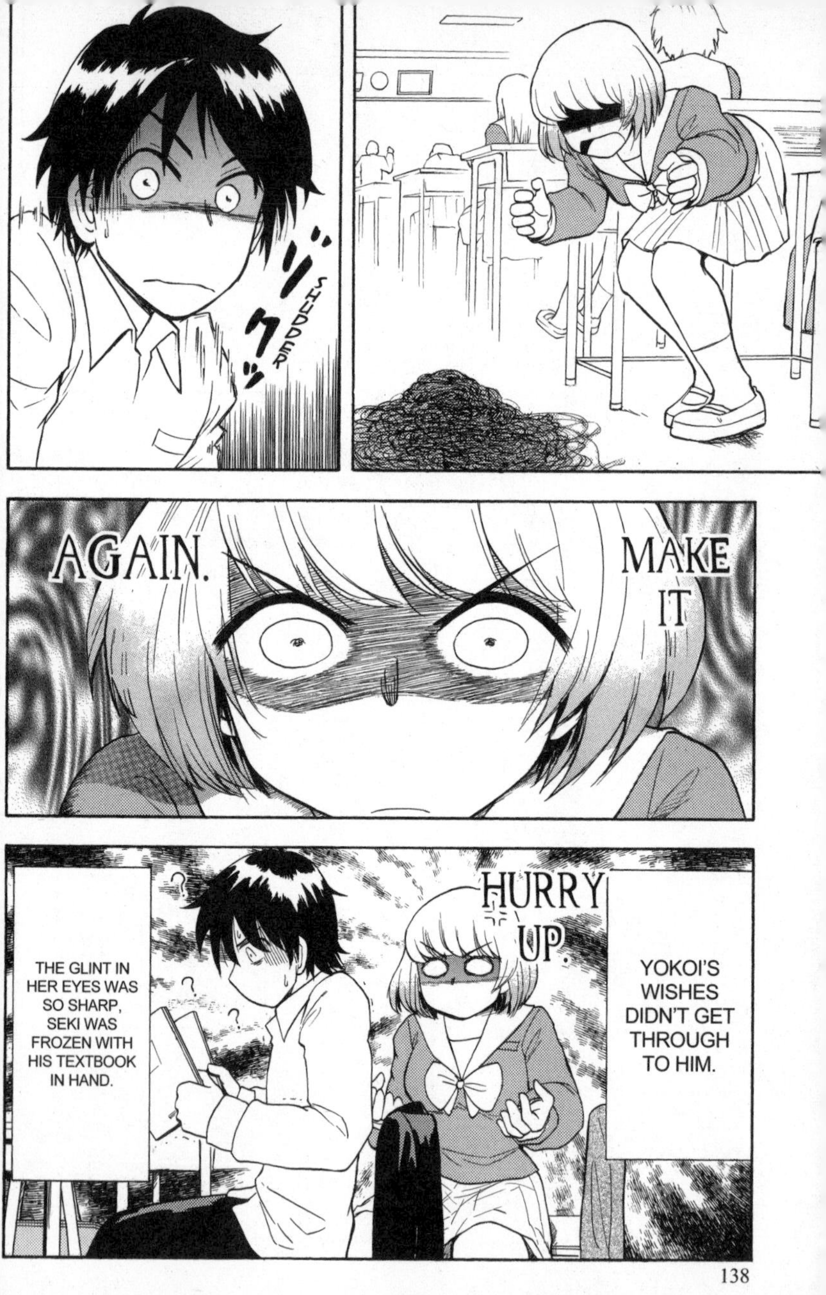
SHUDDER
MAKE IT
AGAIN.
YOKOI'S WISHES DIDN'T GET THROUGH TO HIM.
HURRY UP.
THE GLINT IN HER EYES WAS SO SHARP, SEKI WAS FROZEN WITH HIS TEXTBOOK IN HAND.

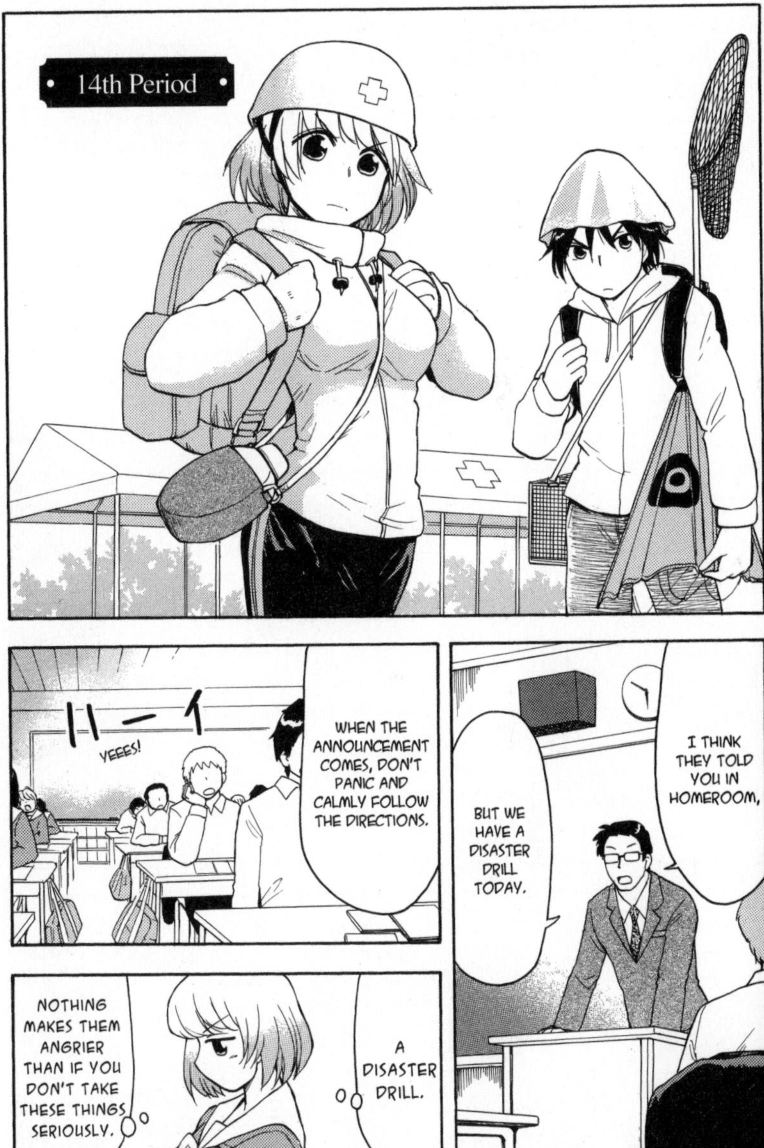
• 14th Period •
I THINK THEY TOLD YOU IN HOMEROOM,
BUT WE HAVE A DISASTER DRILL TODAY.
WHEN THE ANNOUNCEMENT COMES, DON'T PANIC AND CALMLY FOLLOW THE DIRECTIONS.
ハーイ
YEEES!
A DISASTER DRILL.
NOTHING MAKES THEM ANGRIER THAN IF YOU DON'T TAKE THESE THINGS SERIOUSLY.

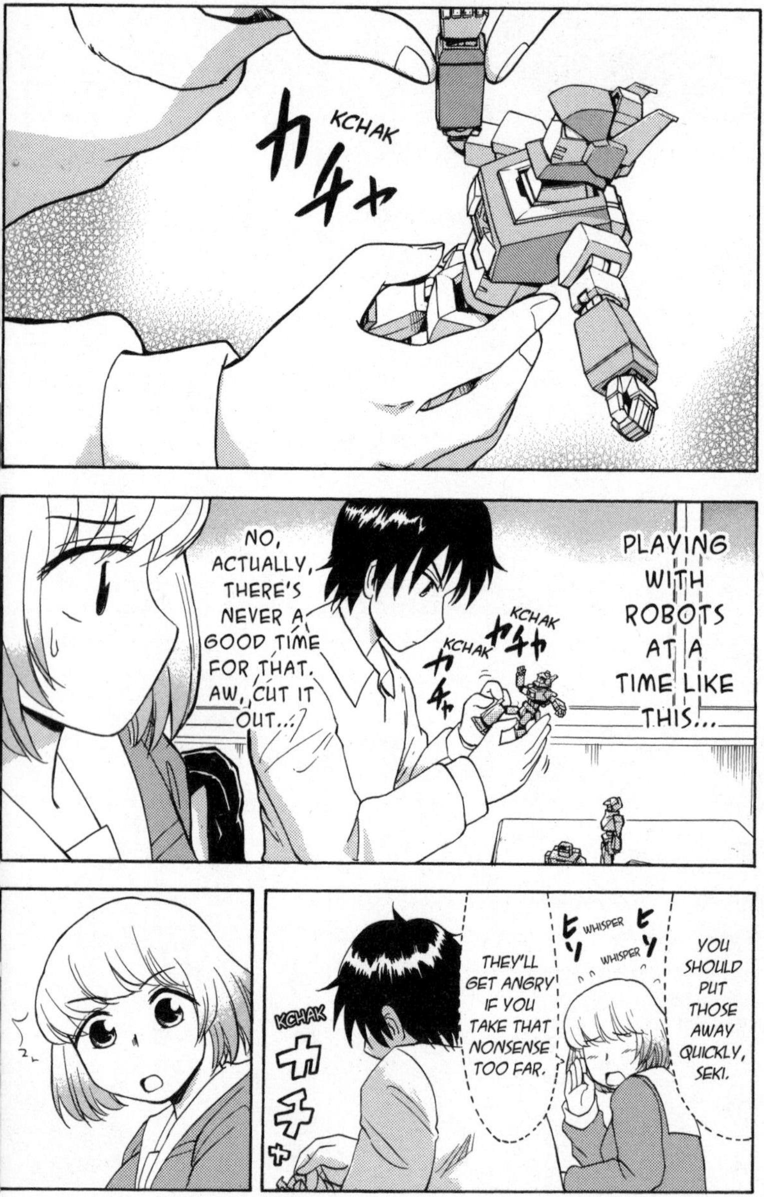
カチャ
KCHAK
PLAYING WITH ROBOTS AT A TIME LIKE THIS...
カチャ
KCHAK
カチャ
KCHAK
NO, ACTUALLY, THERE'S NEVER A GOOD TIME FOR THAT. AW, CUT IT OUT...
YOU SHOULD PUT THOSE AWAY QUICKLY, SEKI.
ヒソ
WHISPER
ヒソ
WHISPER
THEY'LL GET ANGRY IF YOU TAKE THAT NONSENSE TOO FAR.
カチャ
KCHAK

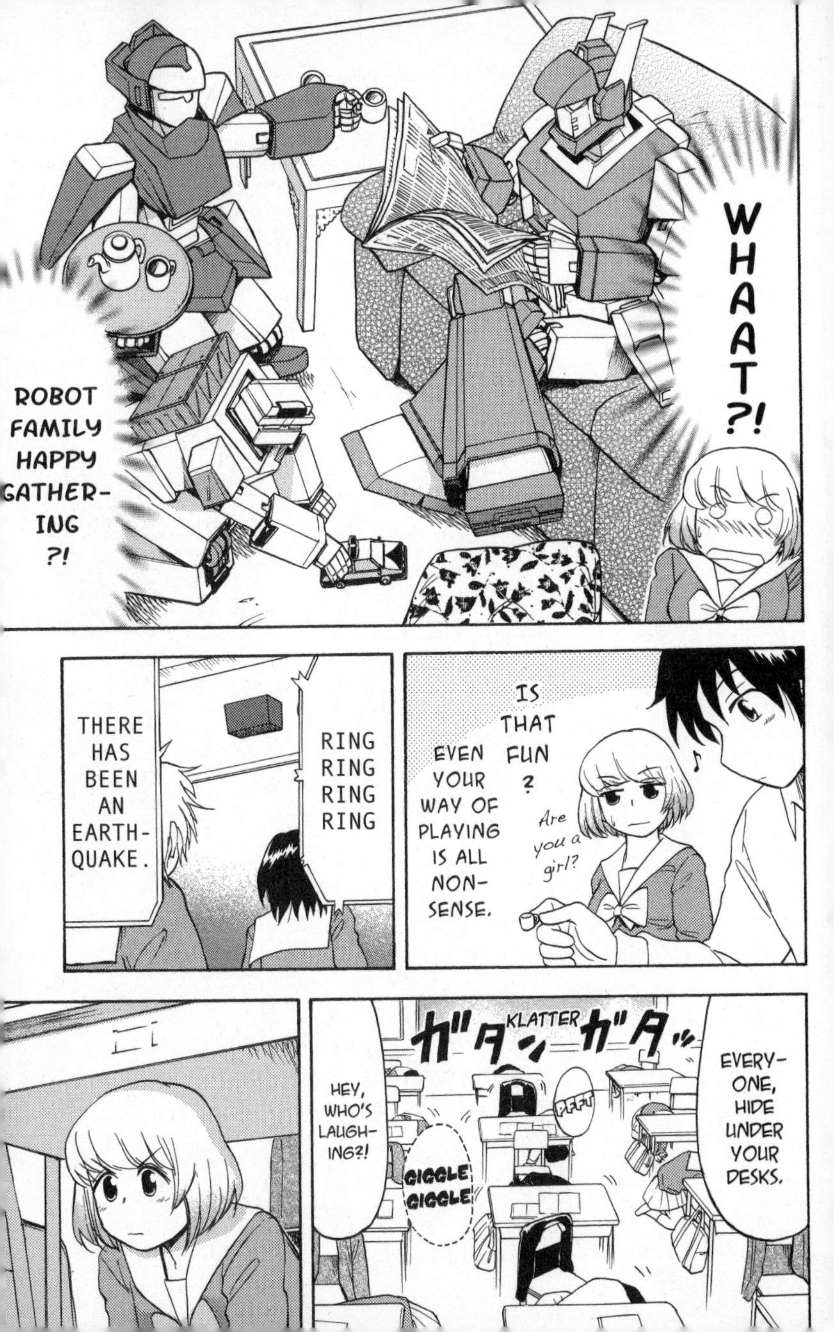
WHAAT?!
ROBOT FAMILY HAPPY GATHERING?!
IS THAT FUN?
EVEN YOUR WAY OF PLAYING IS ALL NONSENSE.
Are you a girl?
RING RING RING RING
THERE HAS BEEN AN EARTHQUAKE.
EVERYONE, HIDE UNDER YOUR DESKS.
ガタン ガタッ
KLATTER
PFFT
HEY, WHO'S LAUGHING?!
GIGGLE GIGGLE

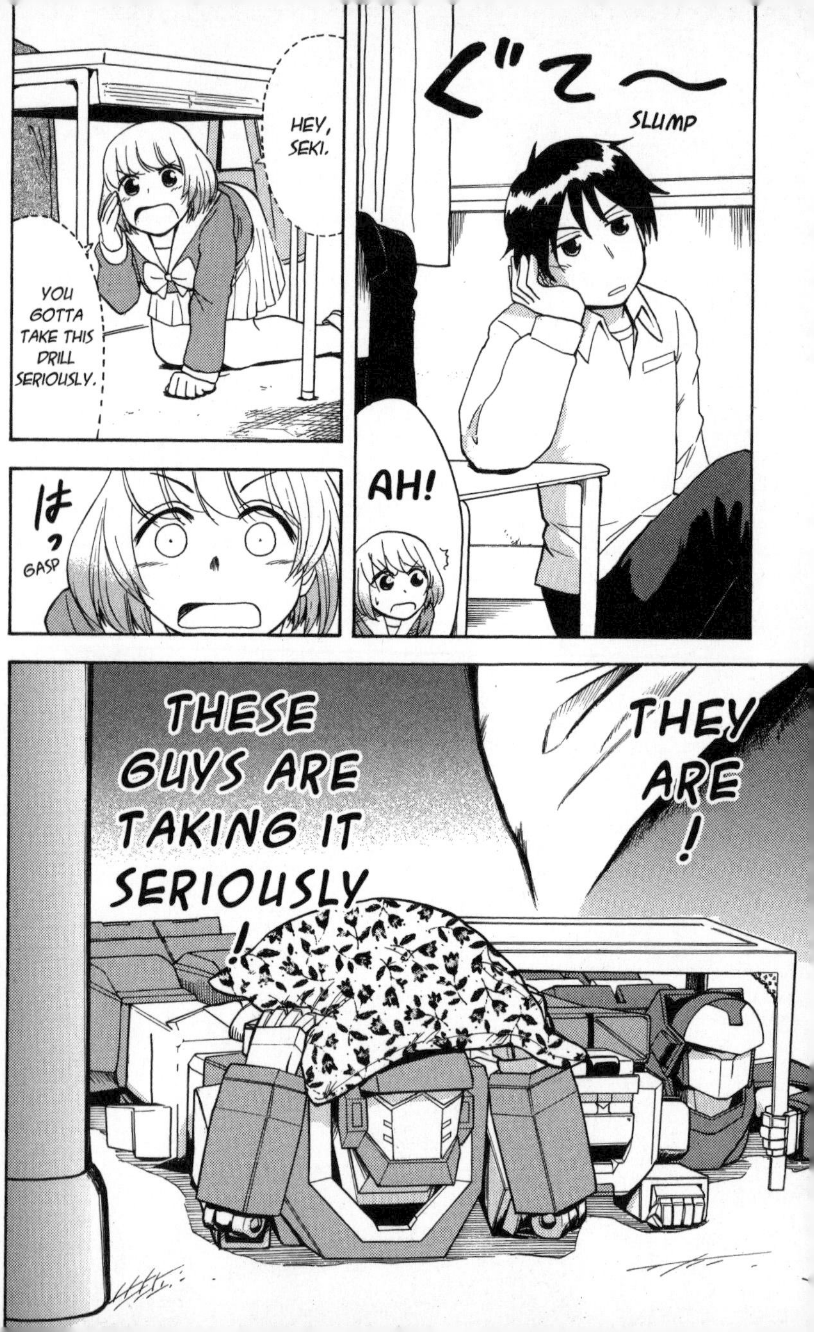
ぐてー
SLUMP
AH!
HEY, SEKI.
YOU GOTTA TAKE THIS DRILL SERIOUSLY.
はっ
GASP
THEY ARE!
THESE GUYS ARE TAKING IT SERIOUSLY!

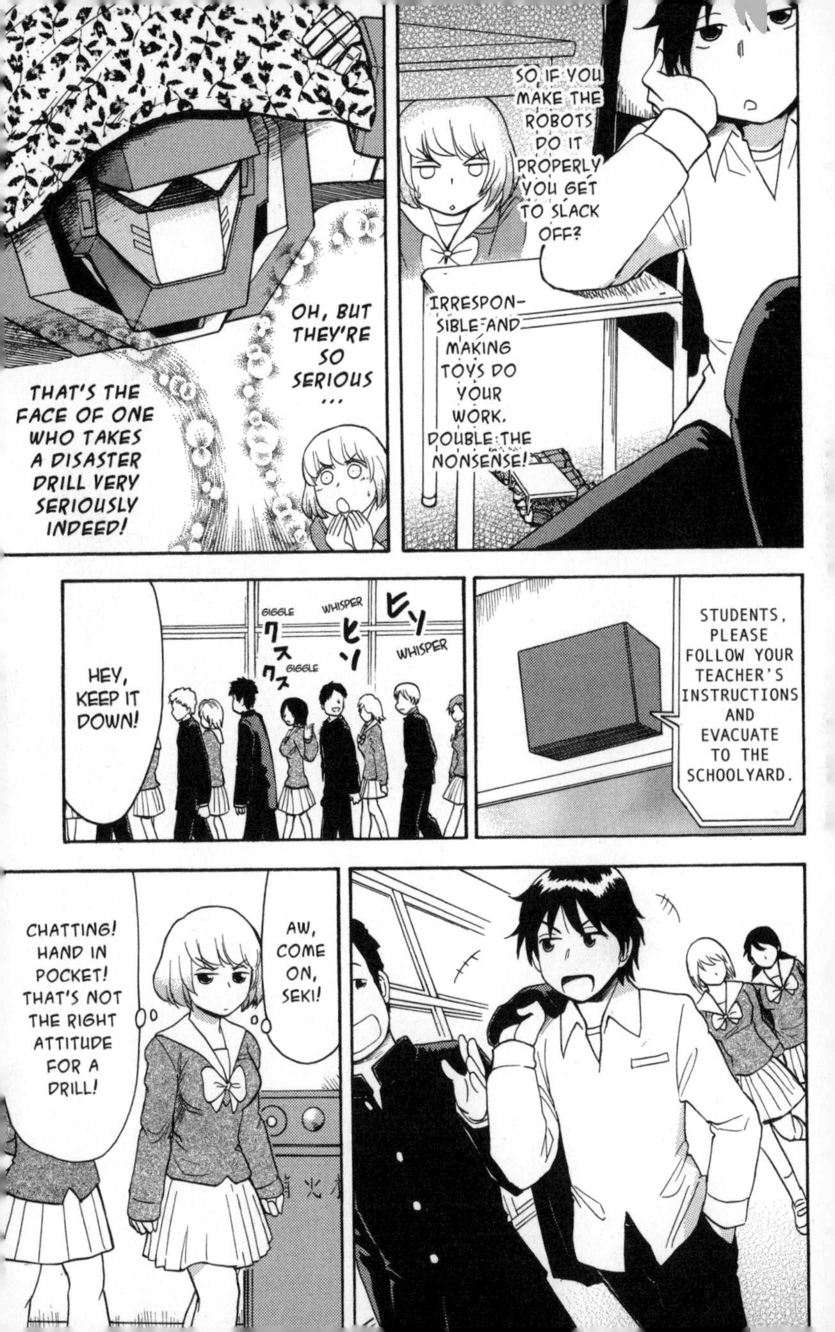
SO, IF YOU MAKE THE ROBOTS DO IT PROPERLY YOU GET TO SLACK OFF?
IRRESPON-SIBLE AND MAKING TOYS DO YOUR WORK. DOUBLE THE NONSENSE!
OH, BUT THEY'RE SO SERIOUS...
THAT'S THE FACE OF ONE WHO TAKES A DISASTER DRILL VERY SERIOUSLY INDEED!
STUDENTS, PLEASE FOLLOW YOUR TEACHER'S INSTRUCTIONS AND EVACUATE TO THE SCHOOLYARD.
ヒソ
WHISPER
ヒソ
WHISPER
クス
GIGGLE
クス
GIGGLE
HEY, KEEP IT DOWN!
AW, COME ON, SEKI!
CHATTING! HAND IN POCKET! THAT'S NOT THE RIGHT ATTITUDE FOR A DRILL!

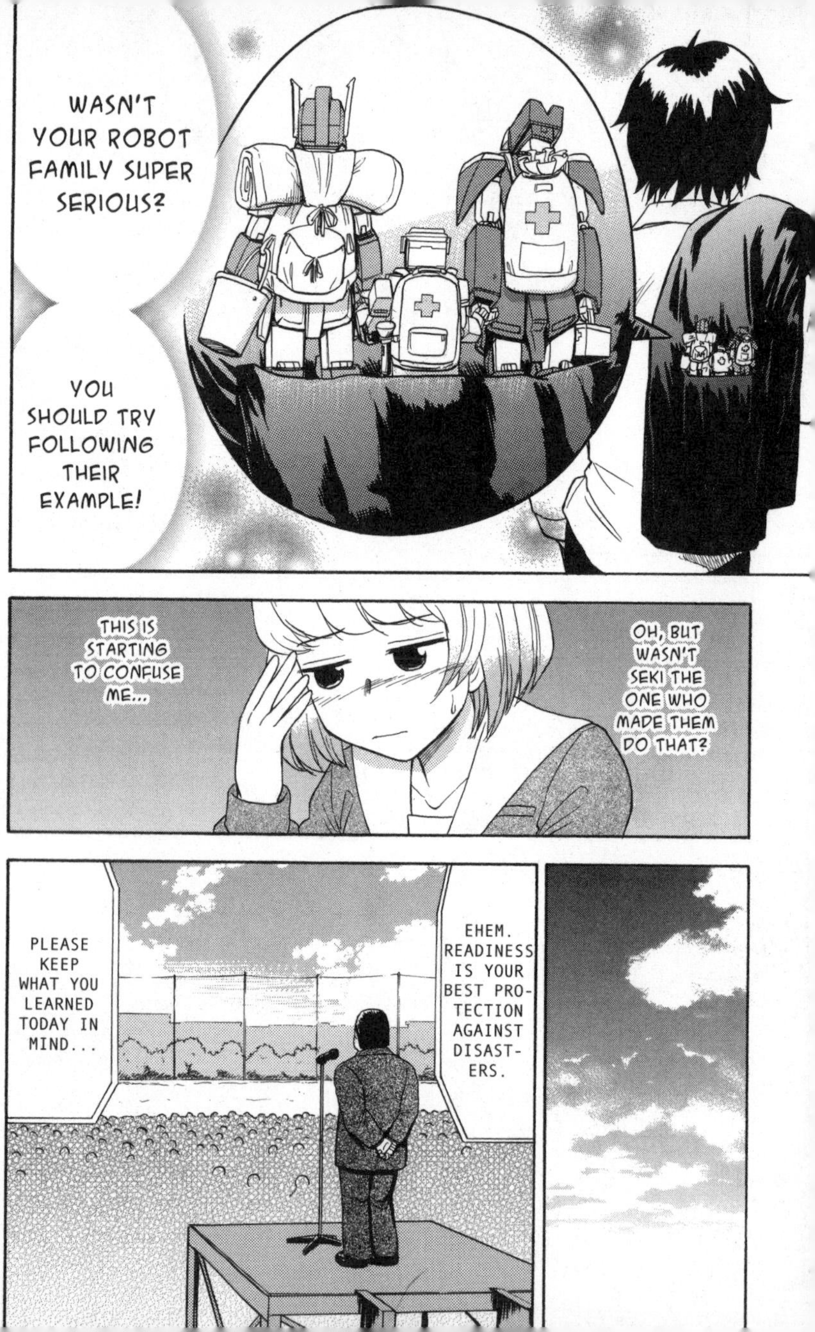
WASN'T YOUR ROBOT FAMILY SUPER SERIOUS?
YOU SHOULD TRY FOLLOWING THEIR EXAMPLE!
OH, BUT WASN'T SEKI THE ONE WHO MADE THEM DO THAT?
THIS IS STARTING TO CONFUSE ME...
EHEM. READINESS IS YOUR BEST PROTECTION AGAINST DISASTERS.
PLEASE KEEP WHAT YOU LEARNED TODAY IN MIND...

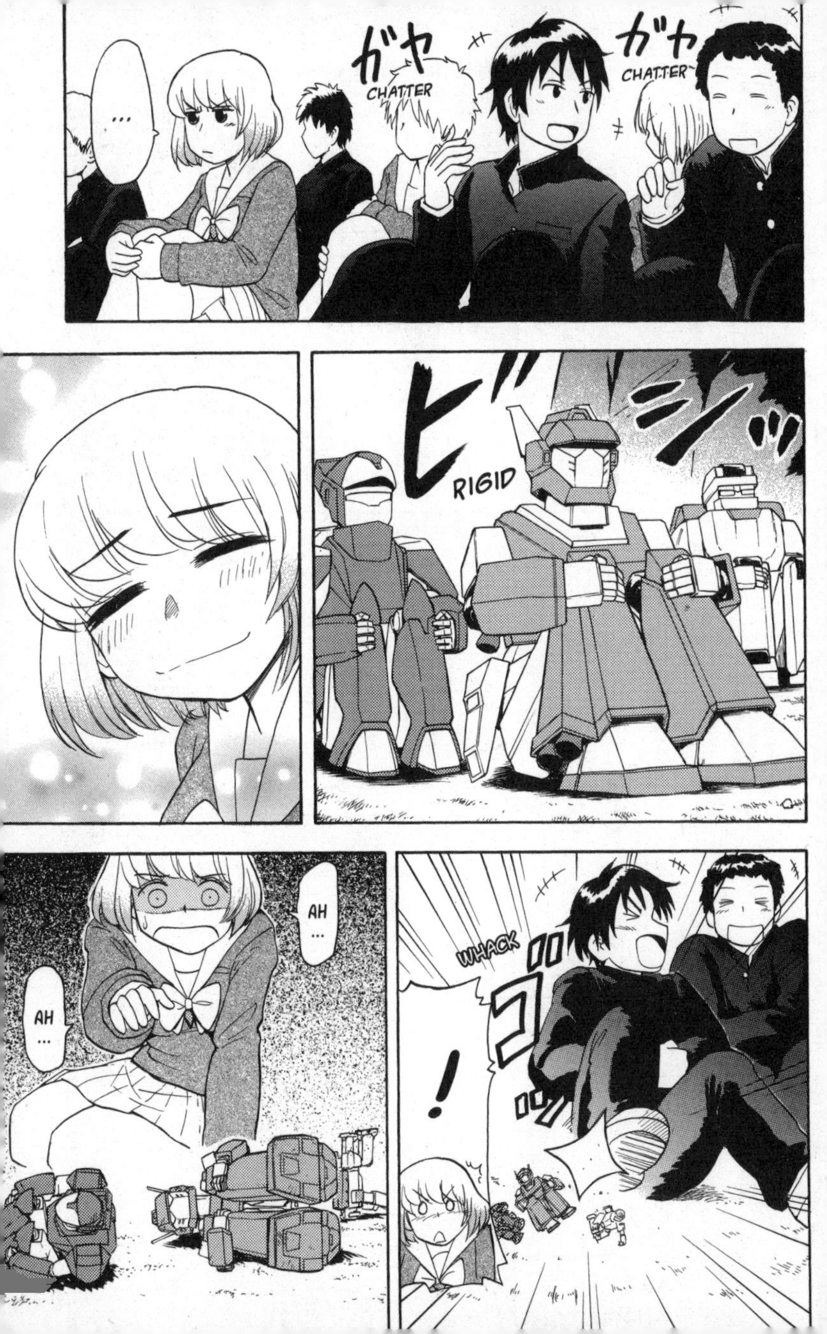

ガヤ
CHATTER
ガヤ
CHATTER
...
ビシッ
RIGID
WHACK
ゴッ
!
AH ...
AH ...

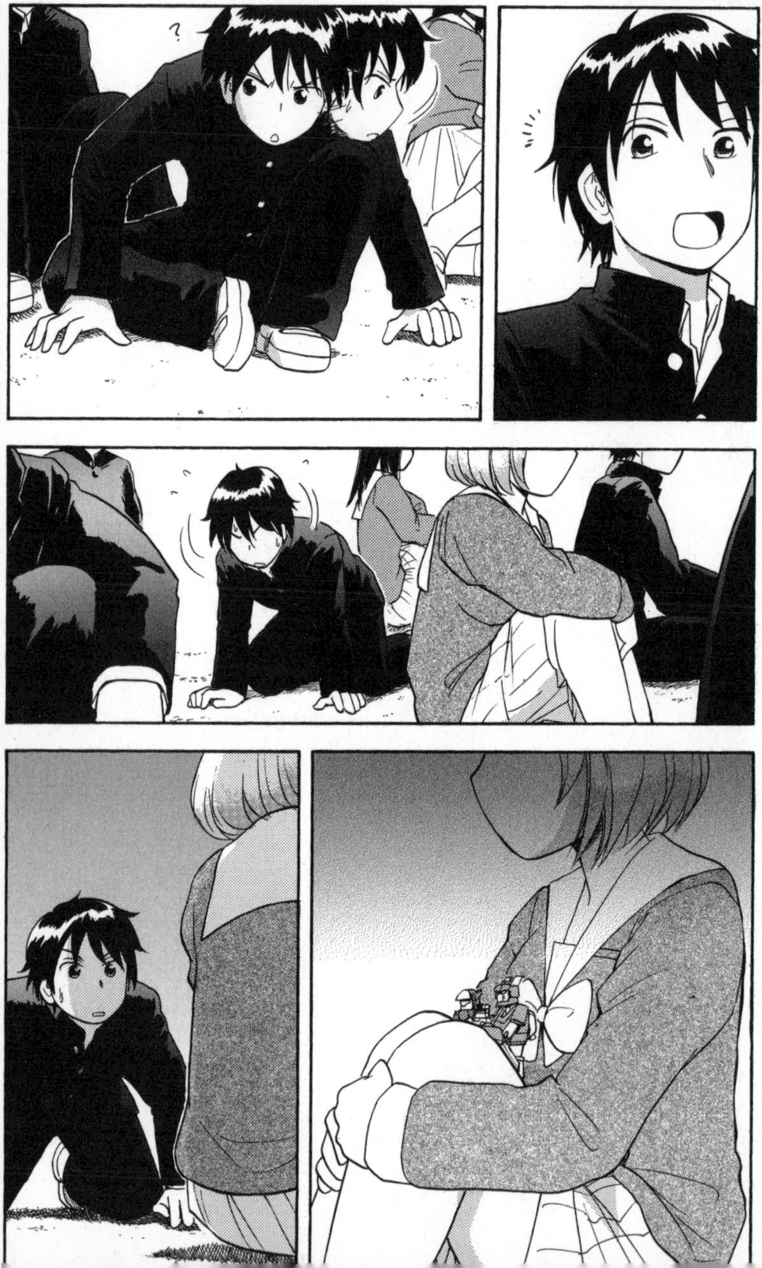

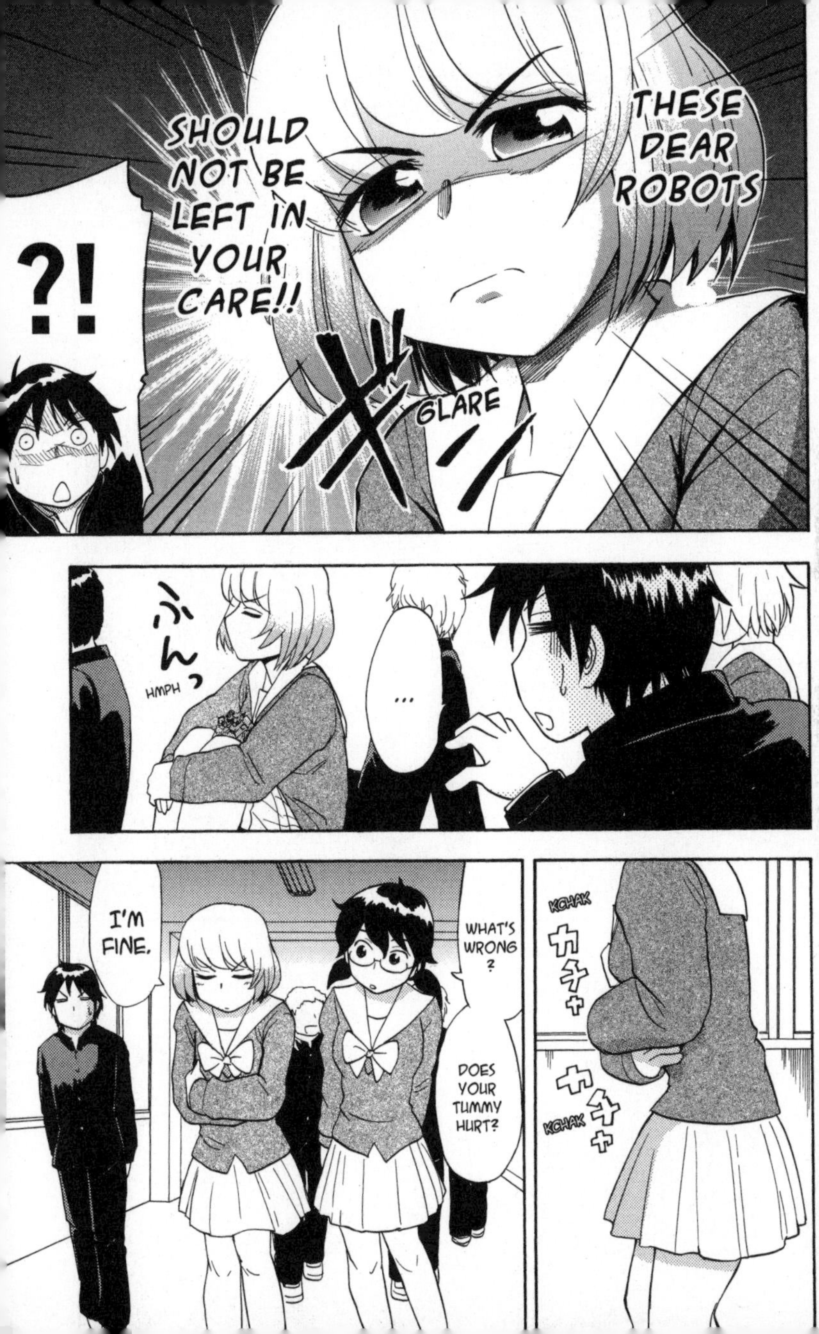
THESE DEAR ROBOTS
SHOULD NOT BE LEFT IN YOUR CARE!!
?!
GLARE
...
ふんっ
HMPH
KCHAK
カチャ
カチャ
KCHAK
WHAT'S WRONG?
DOES YOUR TUMMY HURT?
I'M FINE.

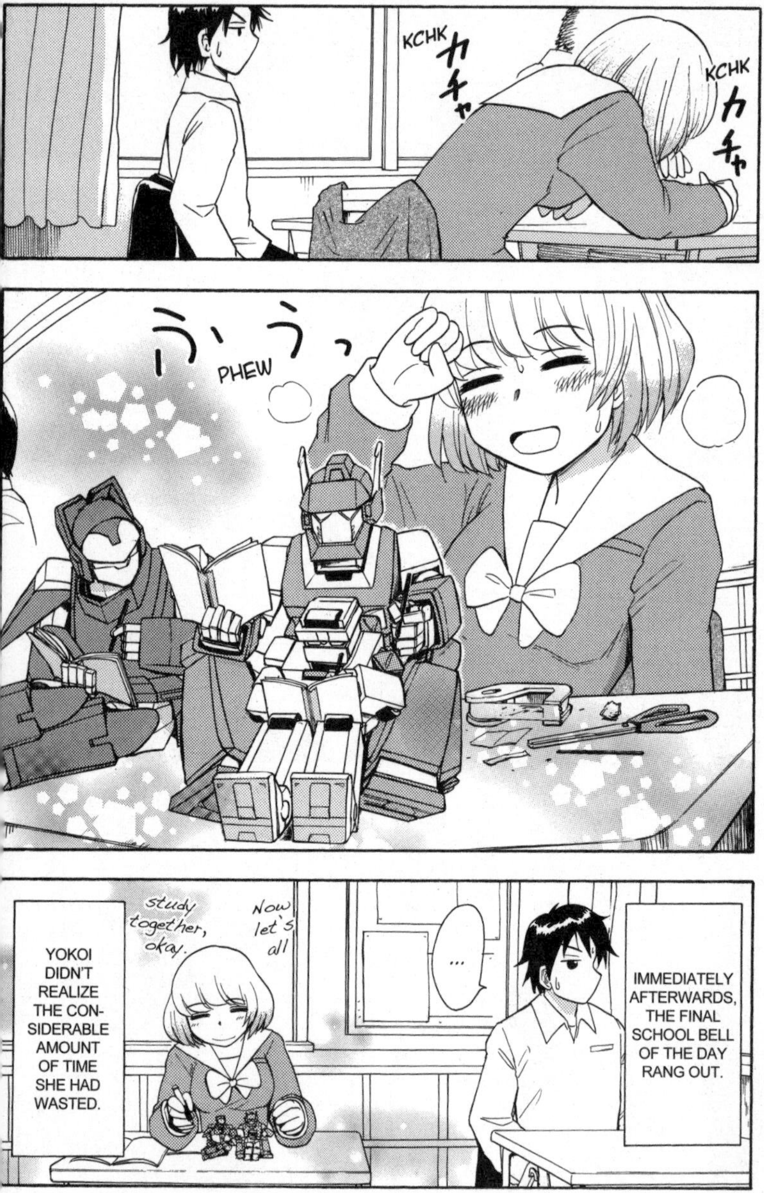
KCHK
カチャ
KCHK
カチャ
うぅっ
PHEW
IMMEDIATELY AFTERWARDS, THE FINAL SCHOOL BELL OF THE DAY RANG OUT.
...
Now let's all study together, okay.
YOKOI DIDN'T REALIZE THE CON-SIDERABLE AMOUNT OF TIME SHE HAD WASTED.

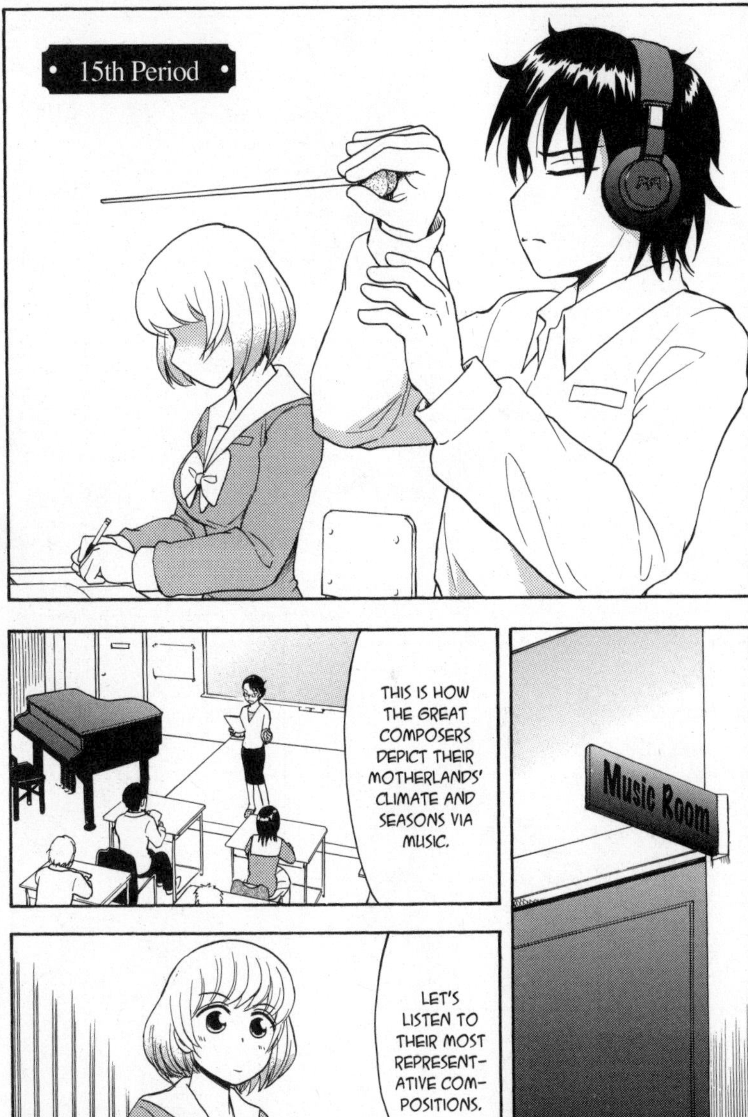
15th Period
Music Room
THIS IS HOW THE GREAT COMPOSERS DEPICT THEIR MOTHERLANDS' CLIMATE AND SEASONS VIA MUSIC.
LET'S LISTEN TO THEIR MOST REPRESENT-ATIVE COM-POSITIONS.

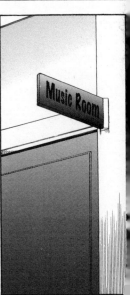

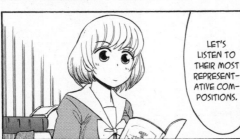

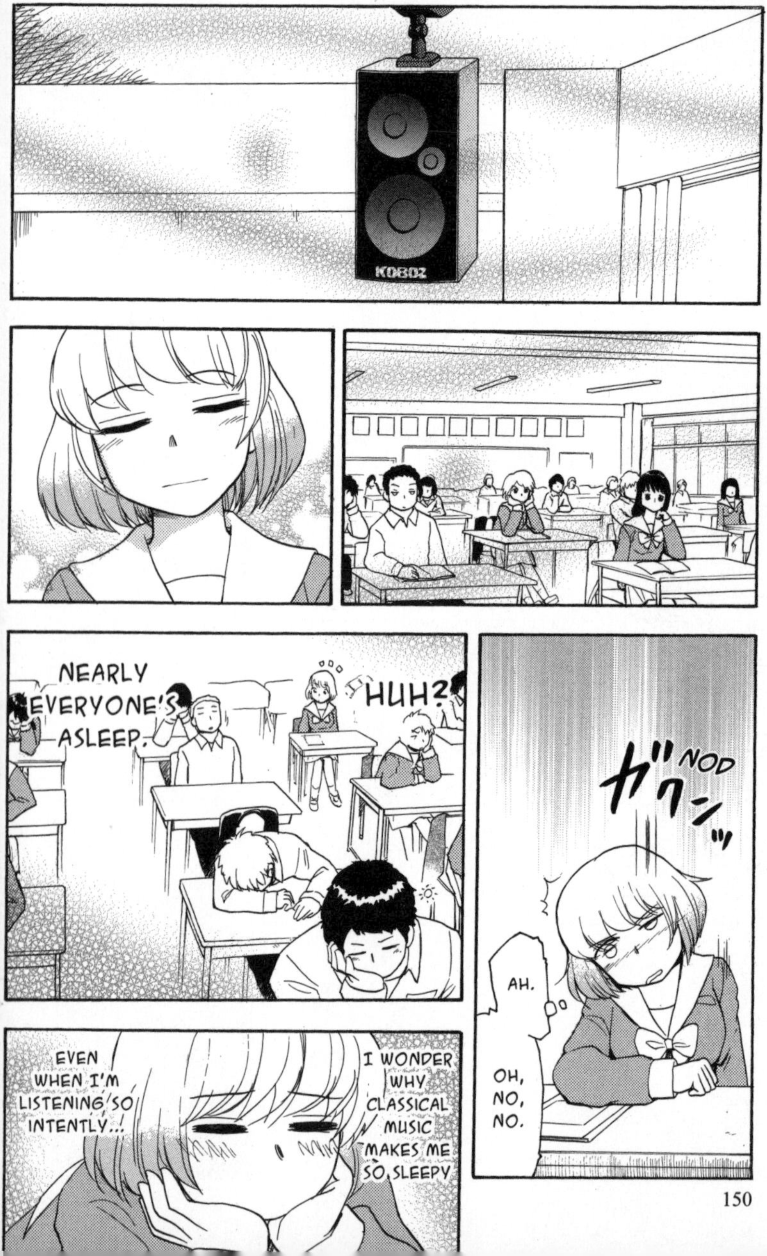

KOBOZ
ガクンッ
NOD
AH.
OH, NO, NO.
NEARLY EVERYONE'S ASLEEP.
HUH?
I WONDER WHY CLASSICAL MUSIC MAKES ME SO SLEEPY
EVEN WHEN I'M LISTENING SO INTENTLY..!

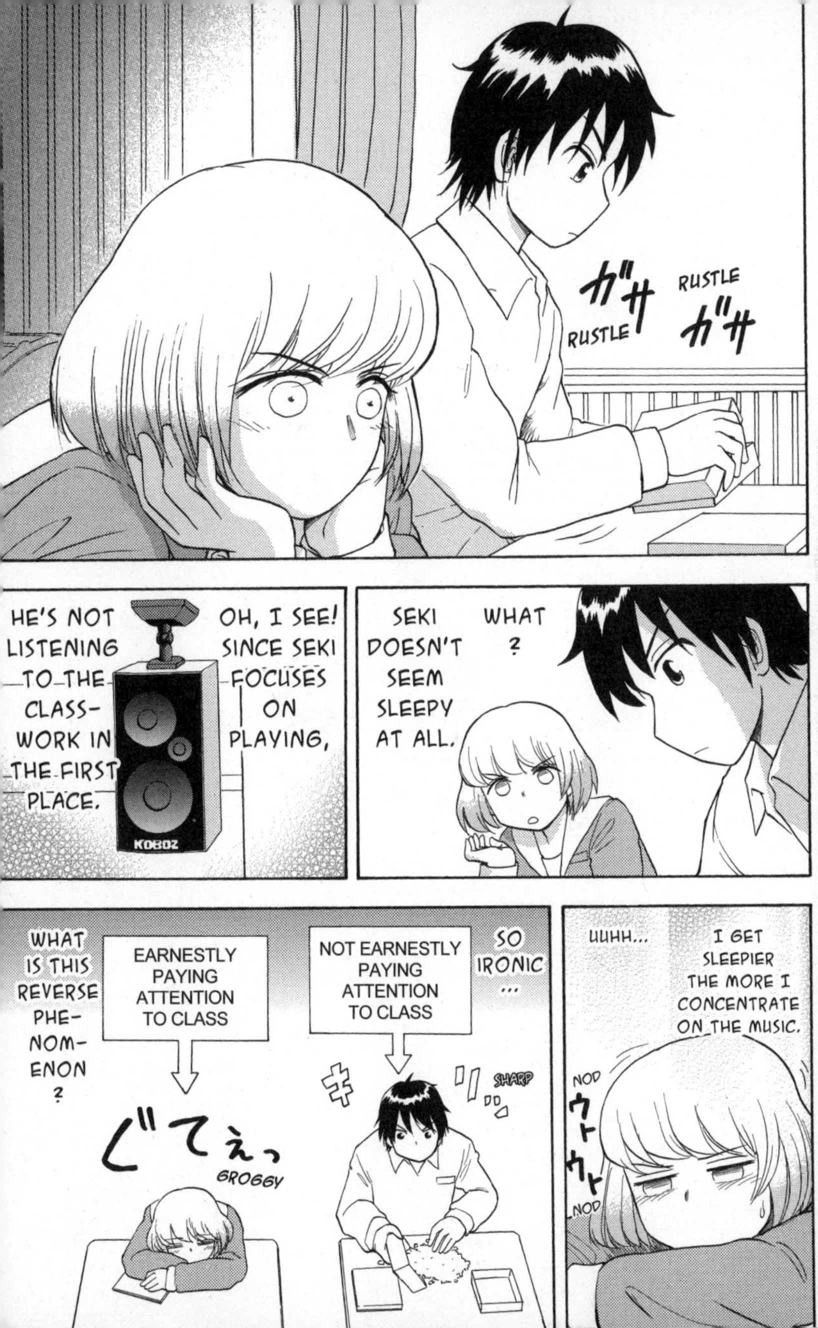
RUSTLE
ガサ
ガサ
RUSTLE
WHAT?
SEKI DOESN'T SEEM SLEEPY AT ALL.
OH, I SEE! SINCE SEKI FOCUSES ON PLAYING,
HE'S NOT LISTENING TO THE CLASSWORK IN THE FIRST PLACE.
KOBOZ
I GET SLEEPIER THE MORE I CONCENTRATE ON THE MUSIC.
UUHH...
NOD
ウトウト
NOD
SO IRONIC...
NOT EARNESTLY PAYING ATTENTION TO CLASS
キ
SHARP
EARNESTLY PAYING ATTENTION TO CLASS
ぐてぇっ
GROGGY
WHAT IS THIS REVERSE PHENOMENON?

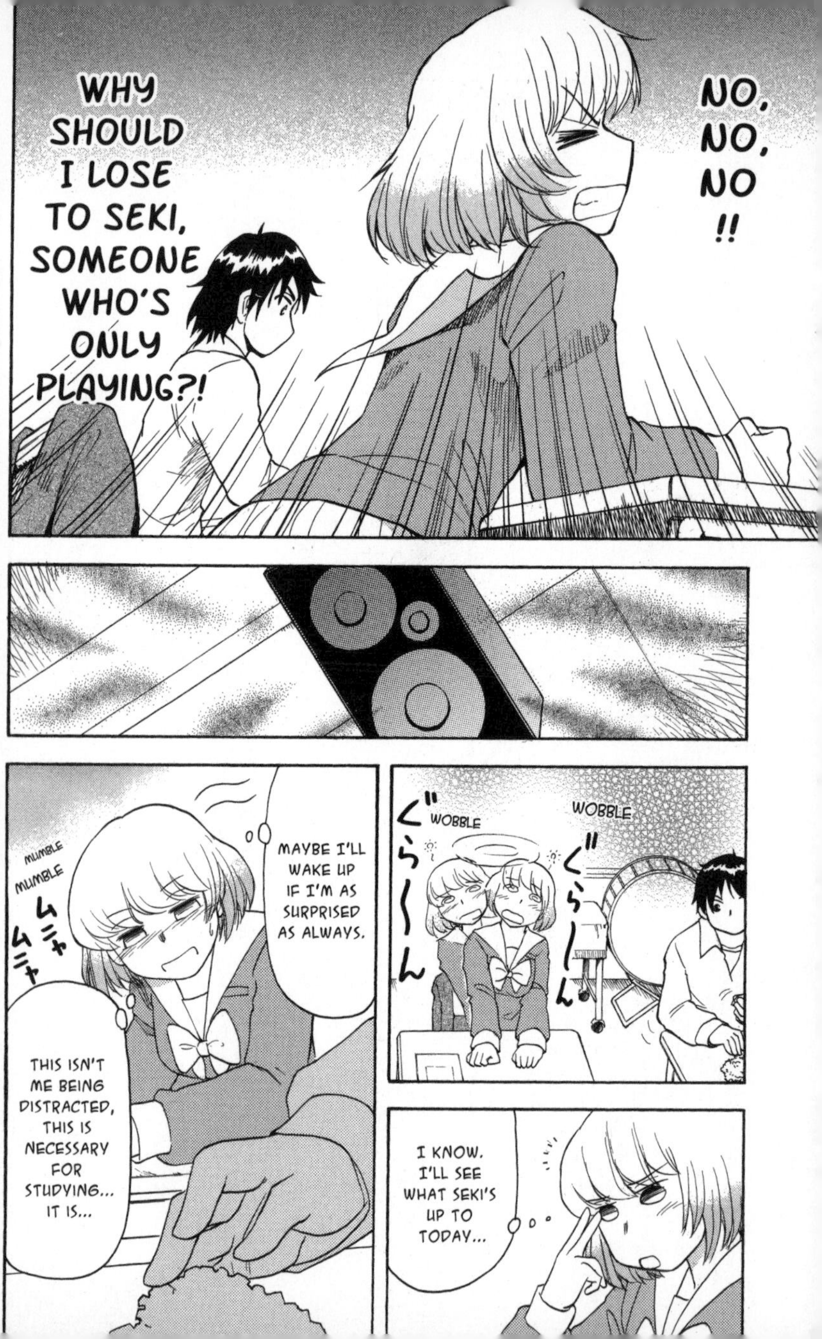
NO, NO, NO !!
WHY SHOULD I LOSE TO SEKI, SOMEONE WHO'S ONLY PLAYING?!
ぐら〜ん
WOBBLE
ぐら〜ん
WOBBLE
I KNOW. I'LL SEE WHAT SEKI'S UP TO TODAY...
MAYBE I'LL WAKE UP IF I'M AS SURPRISED AS ALWAYS.
MUMBLE MUMBLE
ムニャムニャ
THIS ISN'T ME BEING DISTRACTED, THIS IS NECESSARY FOR STUDYING... IT IS...

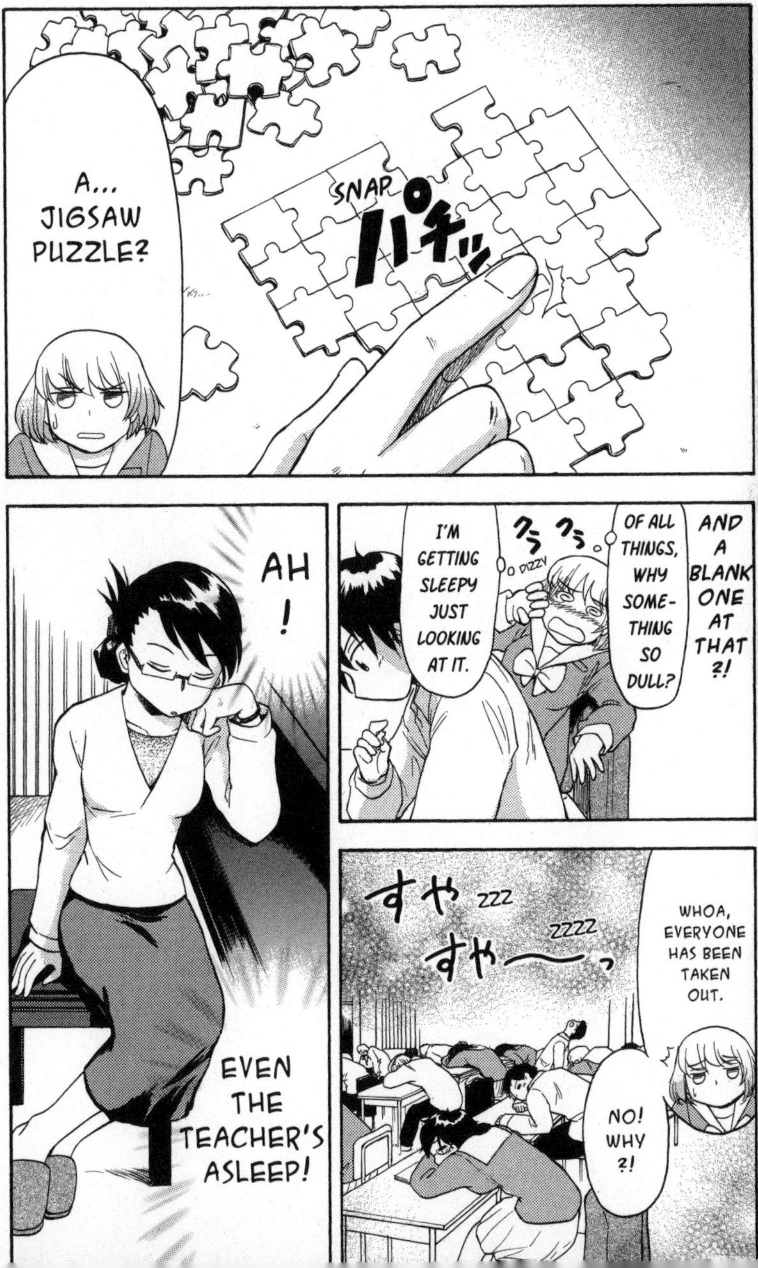
SNAP
パチッ
A... JIGSAW PUZZLE?
AND A BLANK ONE AT THAT?!
OF ALL THINGS, WHY SOME-THING SO DULL?
クラ クラ
DIZZY
I'M GETTING SLEEPY JUST LOOKING AT IT.
WHOA, EVERYONE HAS BEEN TAKEN OUT.
すや ZZZ
すや〜〜っ ZZZZ
NO! WHY?!
AH!
EVEN THE TEACHER'S ASLEEP!

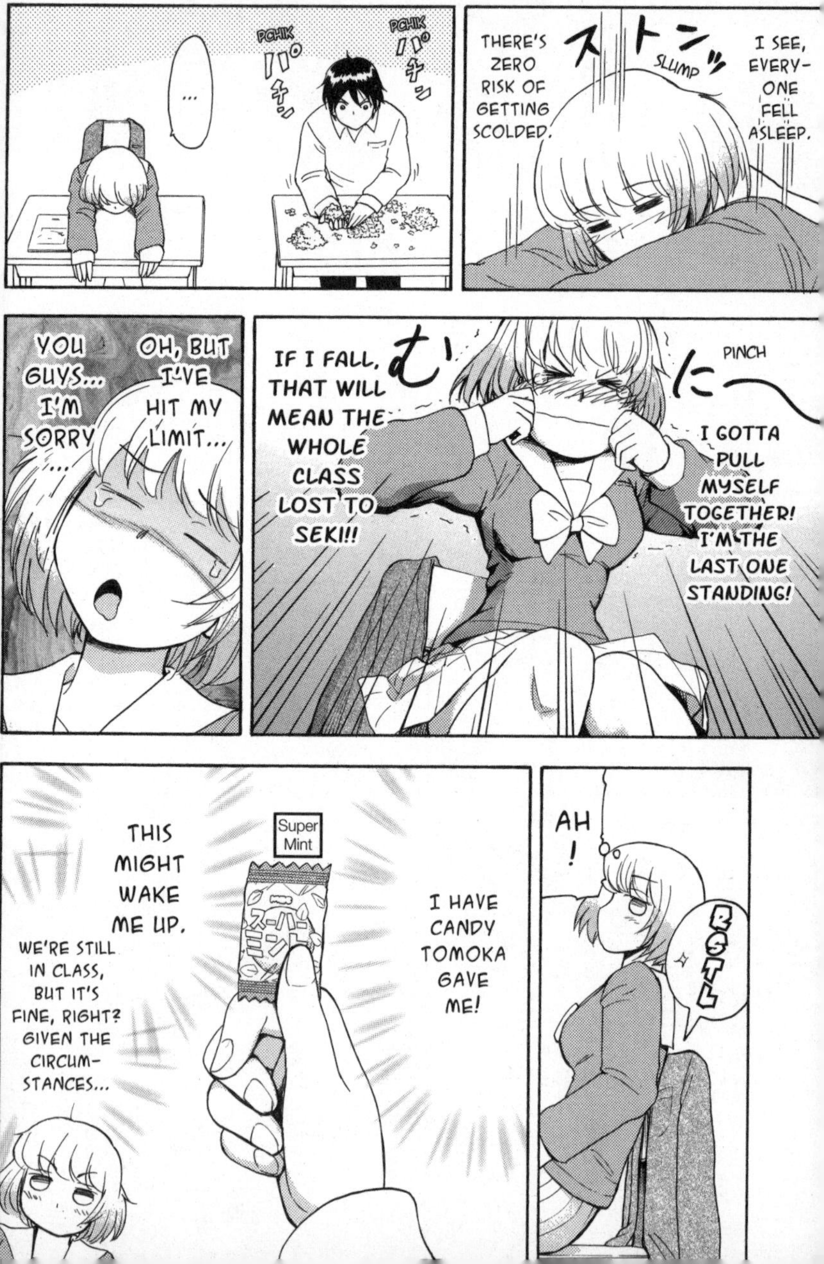
I SEE, EVERYONE FELL ASLEEP.
ストン
SLUMP
THERE'S ZERO RISK OF GETTING SCOLDED.
PCHIK
パチン
PCHIK
パチン
...
PINCH
むに
I GOTTA PULL MYSELF TOGETHER! I'M THE LAST ONE STANDING!
IF I FALL, THAT WILL MEAN THE WHOLE CLASS LOST TO SEKI!!
OH, BUT I'VE HIT MY LIMIT...
YOU GUYS... I'M SORRY...
AH!
RSTL
I HAVE CANDY TOMOKA GAVE ME!
Super Mint
THIS MIGHT WAKE ME UP.
WE'RE STILL IN CLASS, BUT IT'S FINE, RIGHT? GIVEN THE CIRCUMSTANCES...

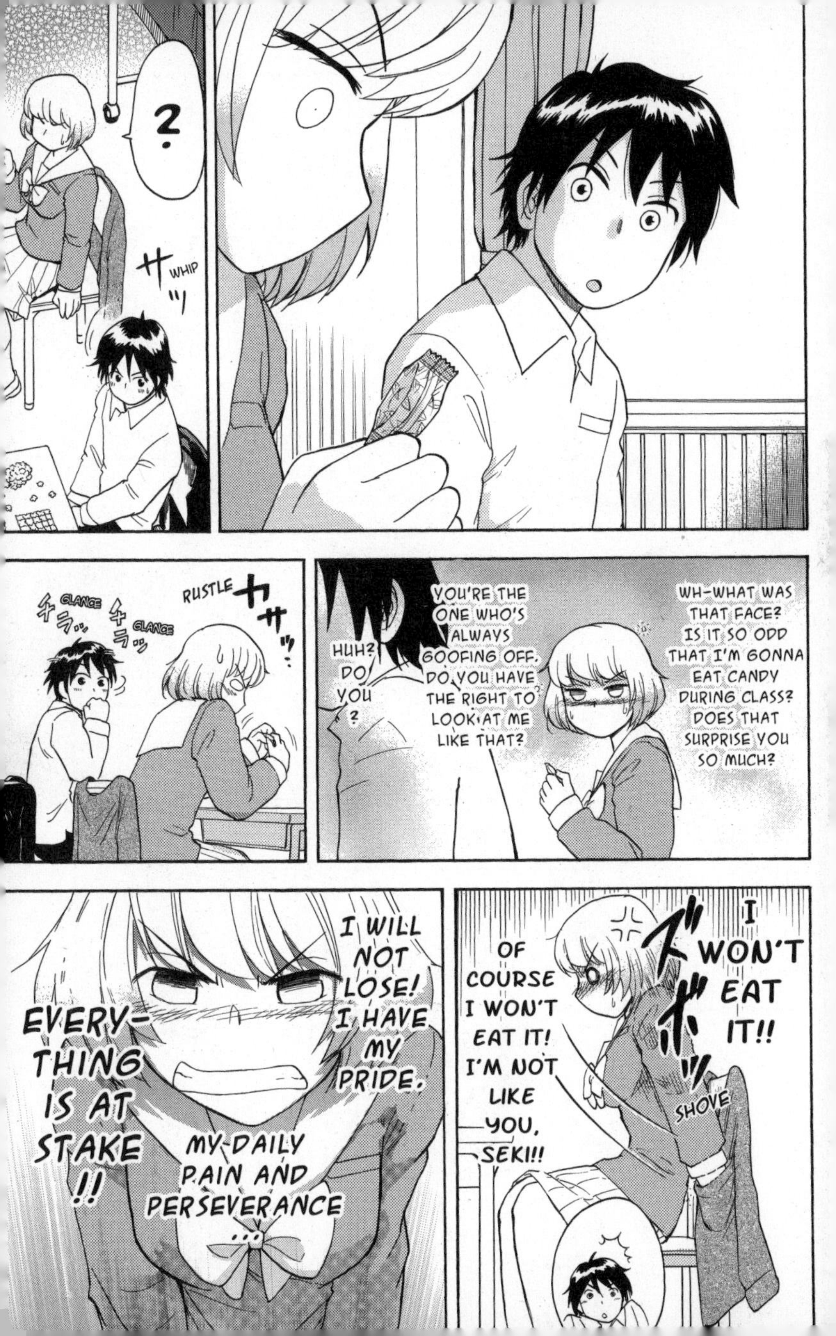
?
サッ WHIP
WH-WHAT WAS THAT FACE? IS IT SO ODD THAT I'M GONNA EAT CANDY DURING CLASS? DOES THAT SURPRISE YOU SO MUCH?
YOU'RE THE ONE WHO'S ALWAYS GOOFING OFF. DO YOU HAVE THE RIGHT TO LOOK AT ME LIKE THAT?
HUH? DO YOU?
カサッ RUSTLE
チラッ GLANCE
チラッ GLANCE
I WON'T EAT IT!!
ズボッ SHOVE
OF COURSE I WON'T EAT IT! I'M NOT LIKE YOU, SEKI!!
I WILL NOT LOSE! I HAVE MY PRIDE.
MY DAILY PAIN AND PERSEVERANCE...
EVERY-THING IS AT STAKE!!

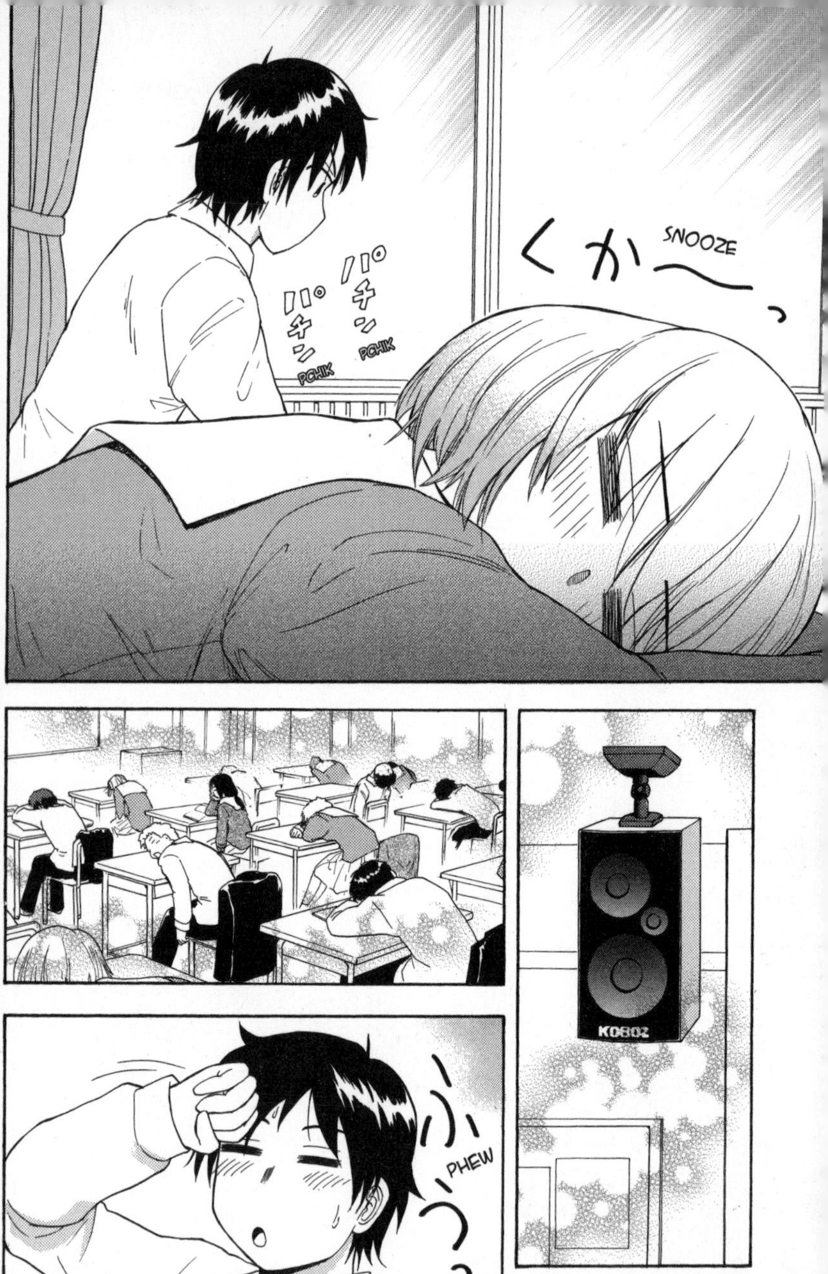
くか〜っ
SNOOZE
パチン
PCHIK
パチン
PCHIK
KOBOZ
PHEW

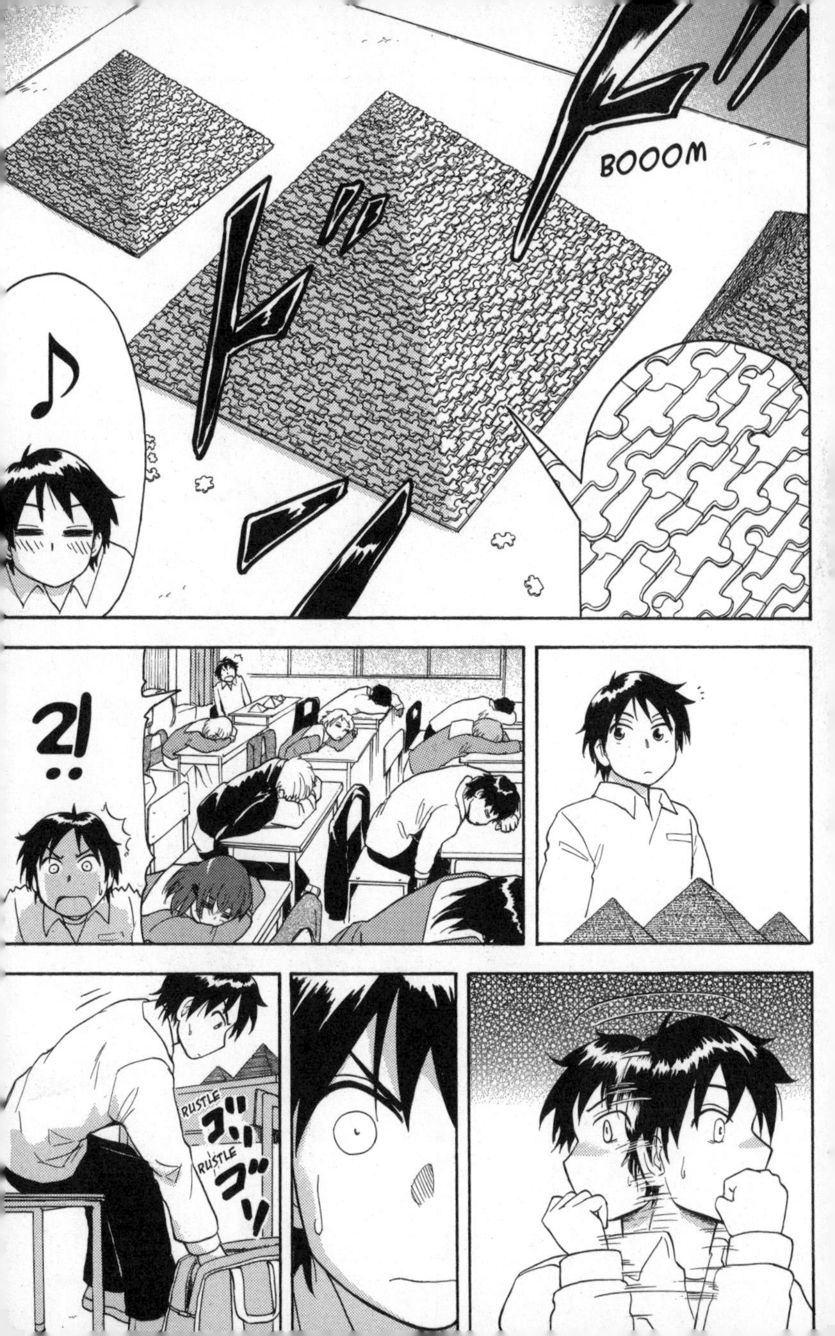
BOOOM
♪
?!
RUSTLE
RUSTLE

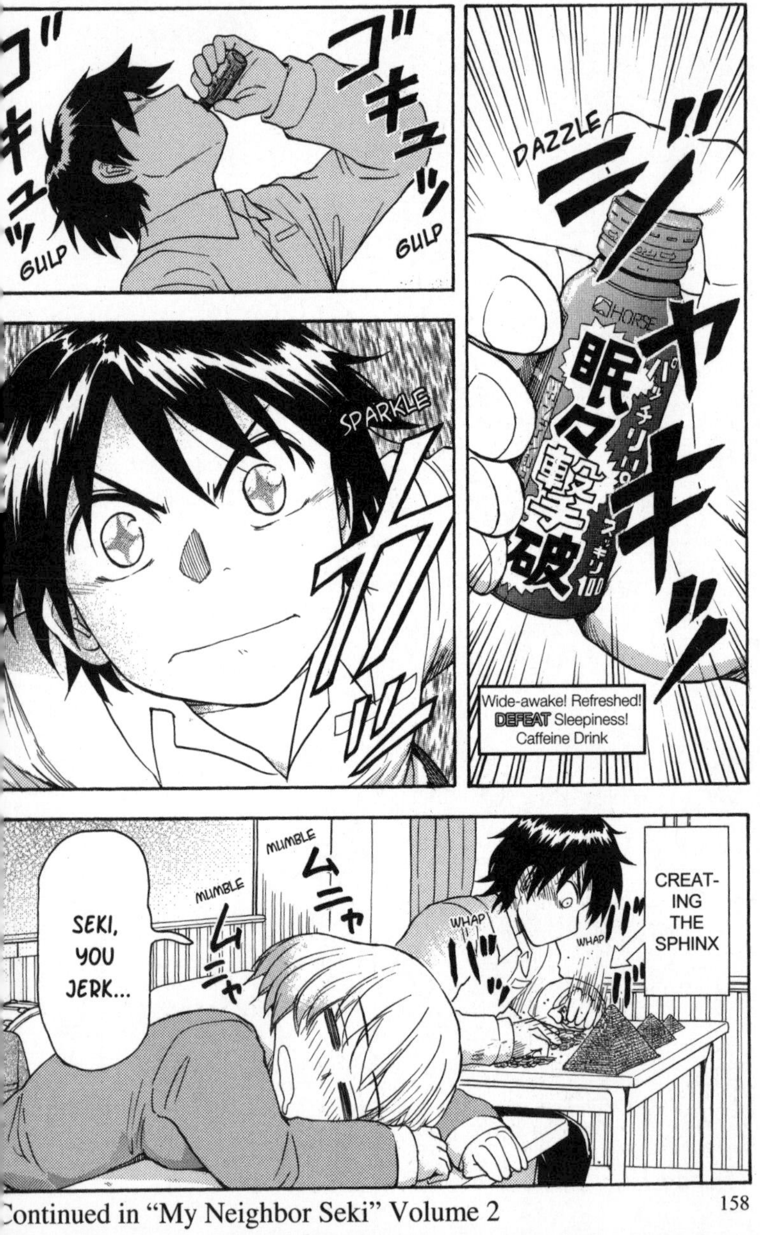
DAZZLE
HORSE
眠々撃破
Wide-awake! Refreshed!
DEFEAT Sleepiness!
Caffeine Drink
ゴキュッ
GULP
ゴキュッ
GULP
SPARKLE
CREAT-
ING
THE
SPHINX
WHAP
WHAP
MUMBLE
ムニャ
MUMBLE
ムニャ
SEKI,
YOU
JERK...

Continued in “My Neighbor Seki” Volume 2

Bonus ①

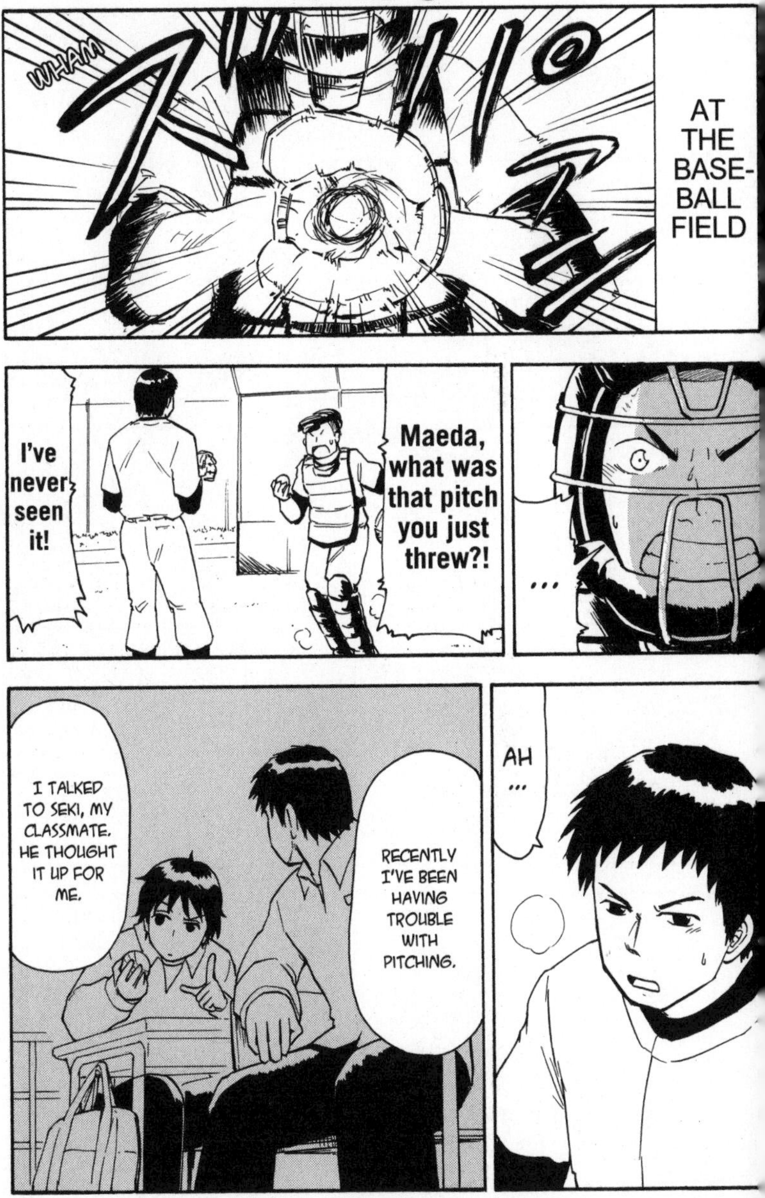
AT THE BASE-BALL FIELD
WHAM
...
Maeda, what was that pitch you just threw?!
I've never seen it!
AH ...
RECENTLY I'VE BEEN HAVING TROUBLE WITH PITCHING.
I TALKED TO SEKI, MY CLASSMATE. HE THOUGHT IT UP FOR ME.

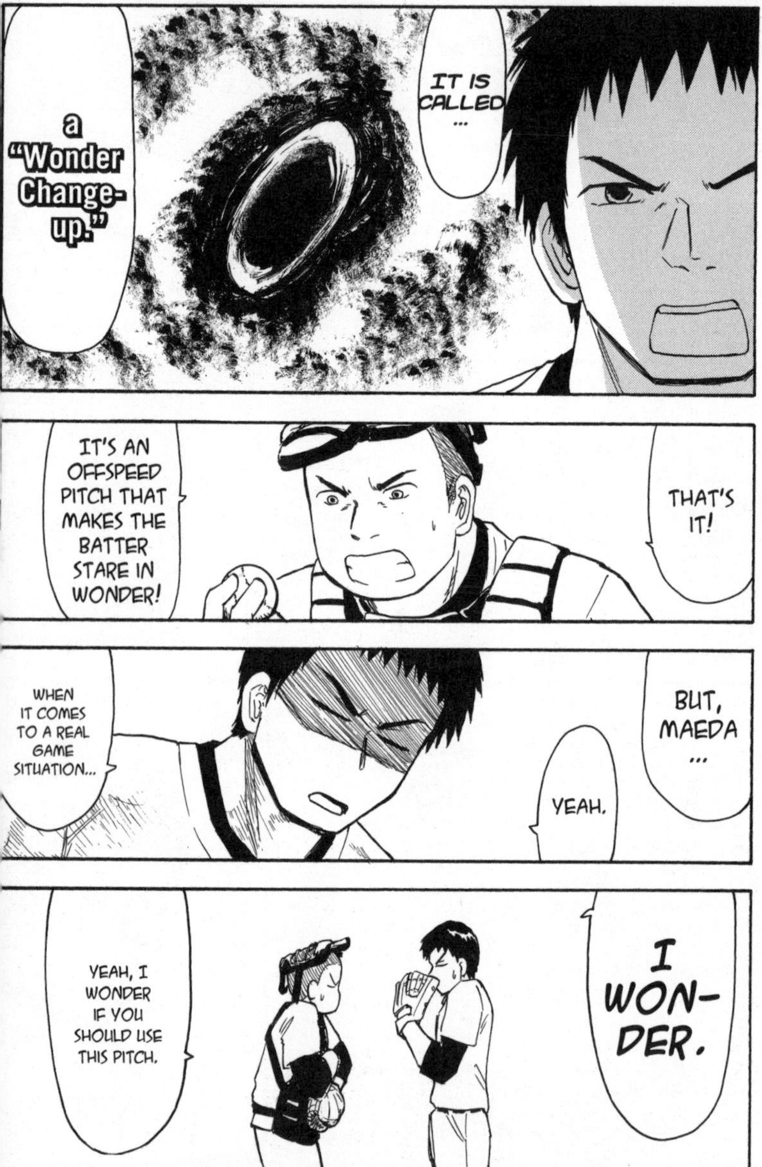
IT IS CALLED...
a "Wonder Change-up."
THAT'S IT!
IT'S AN OFFSPEED PITCH THAT MAKES THE BATTER STARE IN WONDER!
BUT, MAEDA...
YEAH.
WHEN IT COMES TO A REAL GAME SITUATION...
I WON-DER.
YEAH, I WONDER IF YOU SHOULD USE THIS PITCH.

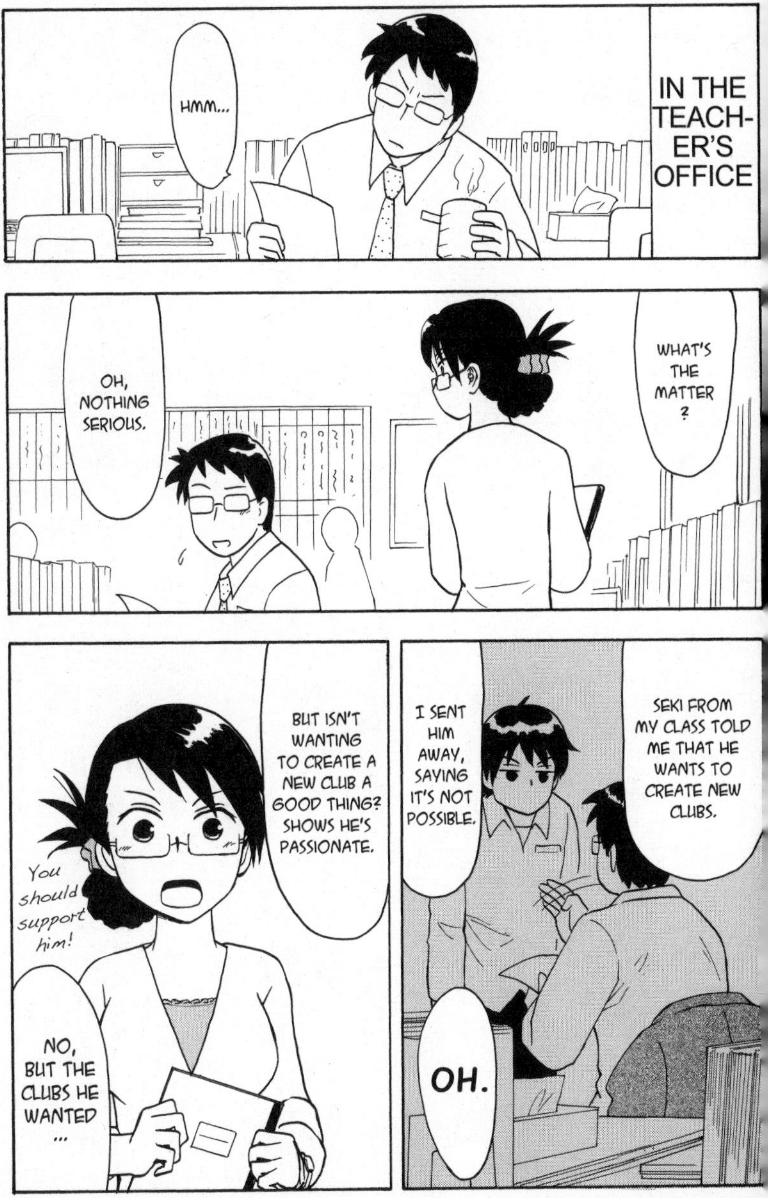
IN THE TEACHER'S OFFICE
HMM...
WHAT'S THE MATTER?
OH, NOTHING SERIOUS.
SEKI FROM MY CLASS TOLD ME THAT HE WANTS TO CREATE NEW CLUBS.
I SENT HIM AWAY, SAYING IT'S NOT POSSIBLE.
OH.
BUT ISN'T WANTING TO CREATE A NEW CLUB A GOOD THING? SHOWS HE'S PASSIONATE.
You should support him!
NO, BUT THE CLUBS HE WANTED...

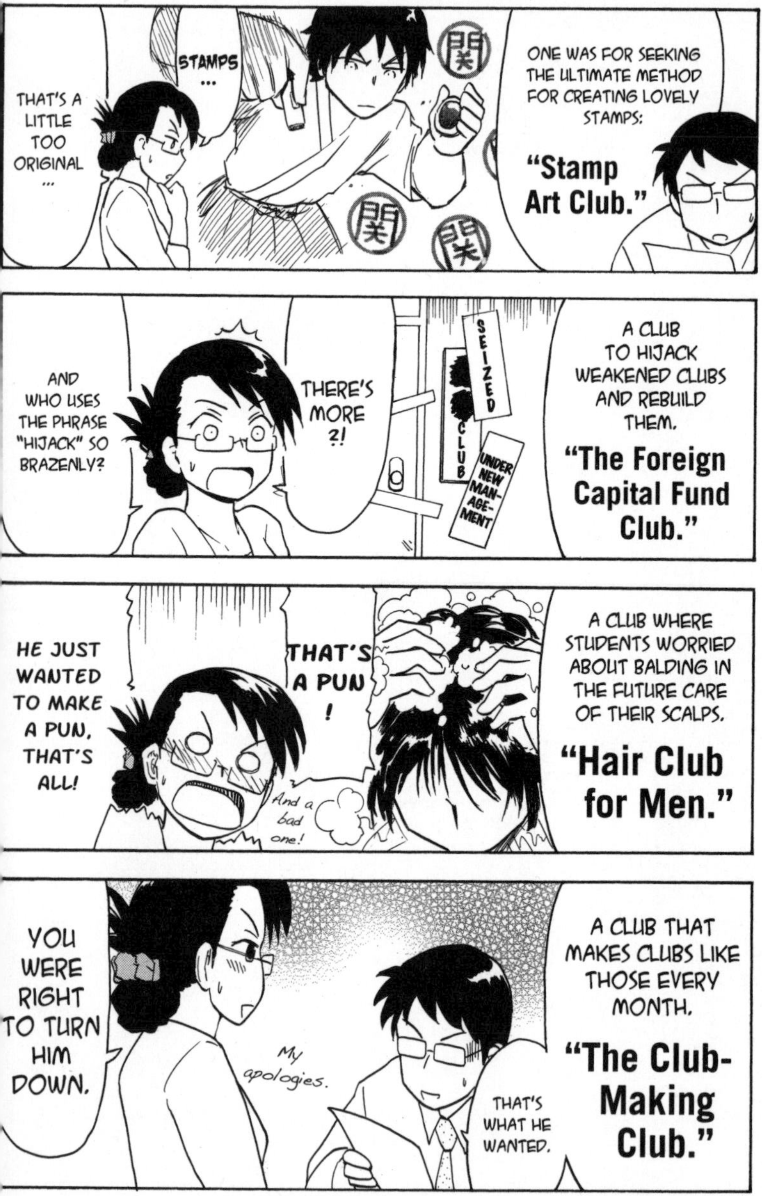
ONE WAS FOR SEEKING THE ULTIMATE METHOD FOR CREATING LOVELY STAMPS:
"Stamp Art Club."
STAMPS ...
THAT'S A LITTLE TOO ORIGINAL ...
A CLUB TO HIJACK WEAKENED CLUBS AND REBUILD THEM.
"The Foreign Capital Fund Club."
SEIZED
CLUB
UNDER NEW MAN-AGE-MENT
THERE'S MORE ?!
AND WHO USES THE PHRASE "HIJACK" SO BRAZENLY?
A CLUB WHERE STUDENTS WORRIED ABOUT BALDING IN THE FUTURE CARE OF THEIR SCALPS.
"Hair Club for Men."
THAT'S A PUN !
And a bad one!
HE JUST WANTED TO MAKE A PUN, THAT'S ALL!
A CLUB THAT MAKES CLUBS LIKE THOSE EVERY MONTH.
"The Club-Making Club."
THAT'S WHAT HE WANTED.
My apologies.
YOU WERE RIGHT TO TURN HIM DOWN.

Bonu
②

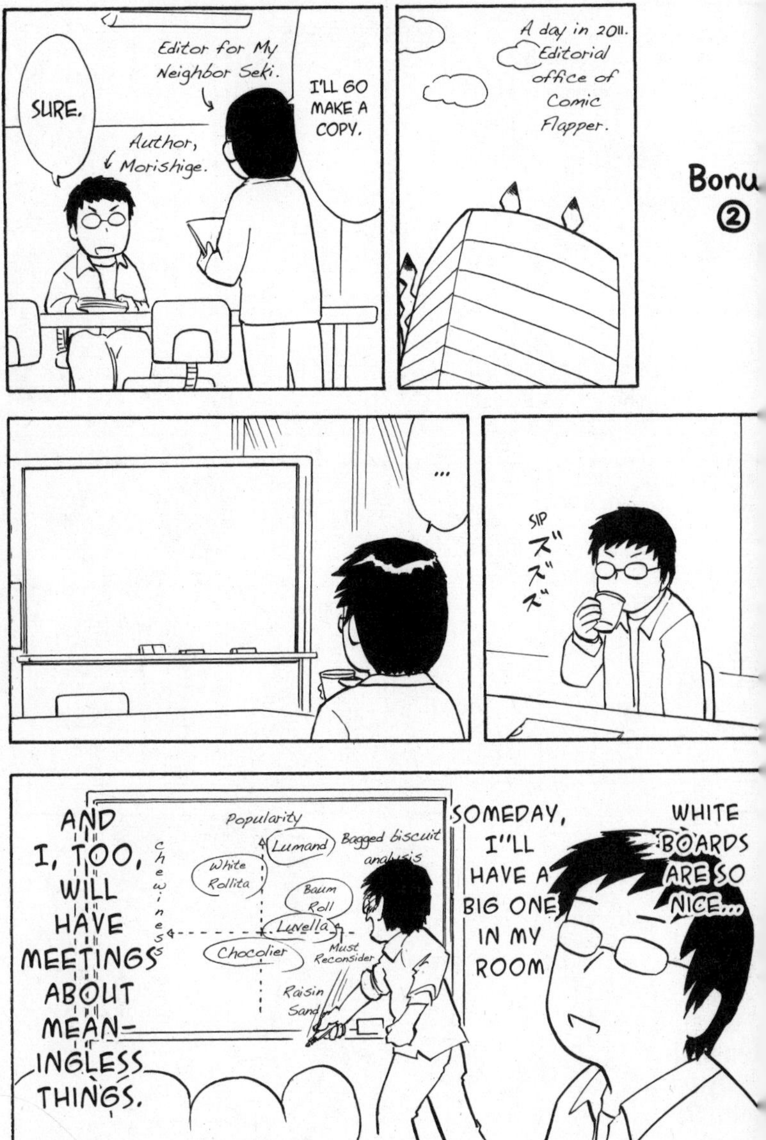

A day in 2011. Editorial office of Comic Flapper.
I'LL GO MAKE A COPY.
Editor for My Neighbor Seki.
SURE.
Author, Morishige.
SIP ズズズ
...
WHITE BOARDS ARE SO NICE...
SOMEDAY, I'LL HAVE A BIG ONE IN MY ROOM
Popularity
Bagged biscuit analysis
Lumand
White Rollita
Chewiness
Baum Roll
Luvella
Chocolier
Must Reconsider
Raisin Sand
AND I, TOO, WILL HAVE MEETINGS ABOUT MEAN-INGLESS THINGS.

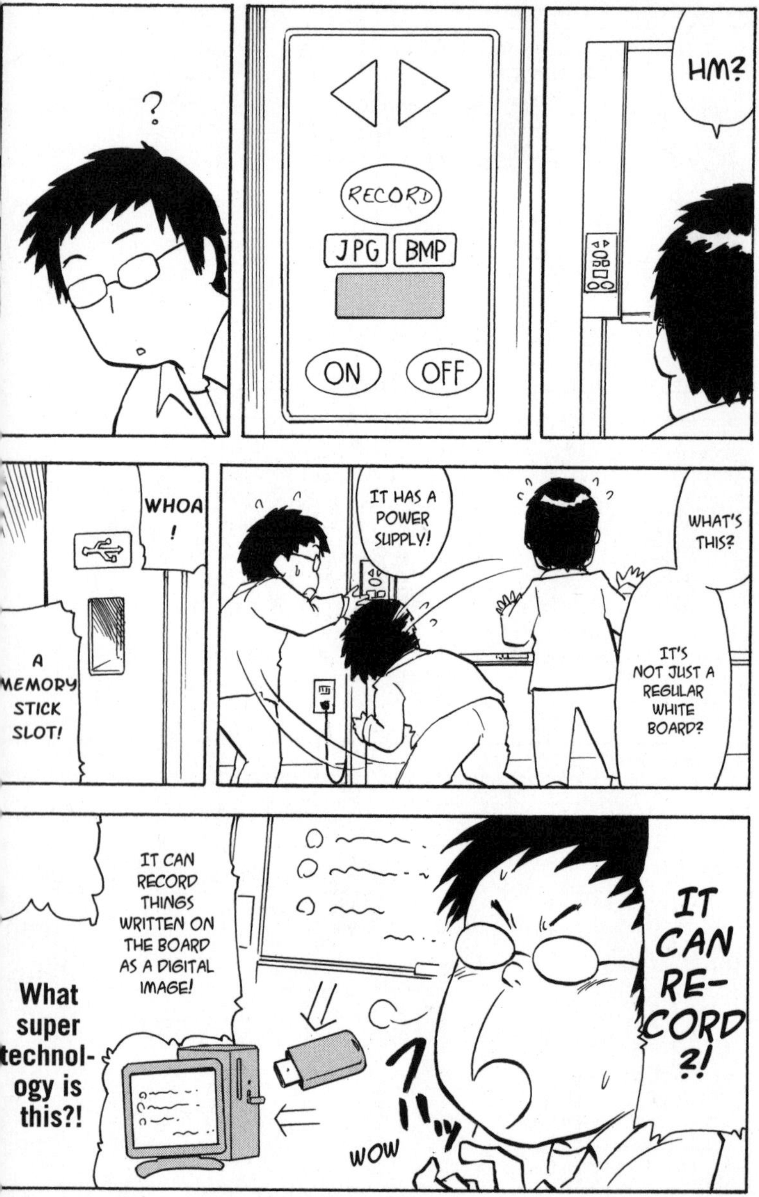
HM?
RECORD
JPG
BMP
ON
OFF
?
WHAT'S THIS?
IT'S NOT JUST A REGULAR WHITE BOARD?
IT HAS A POWER SUPPLY!
WHOA!
A MEMORY STICK SLOT!
IT CAN RE-CORD?!
WOW
IT CAN RECORD THINGS WRITTEN ON THE BOARD AS A DIGITAL IMAGE!
What super technol-ogy is this?!

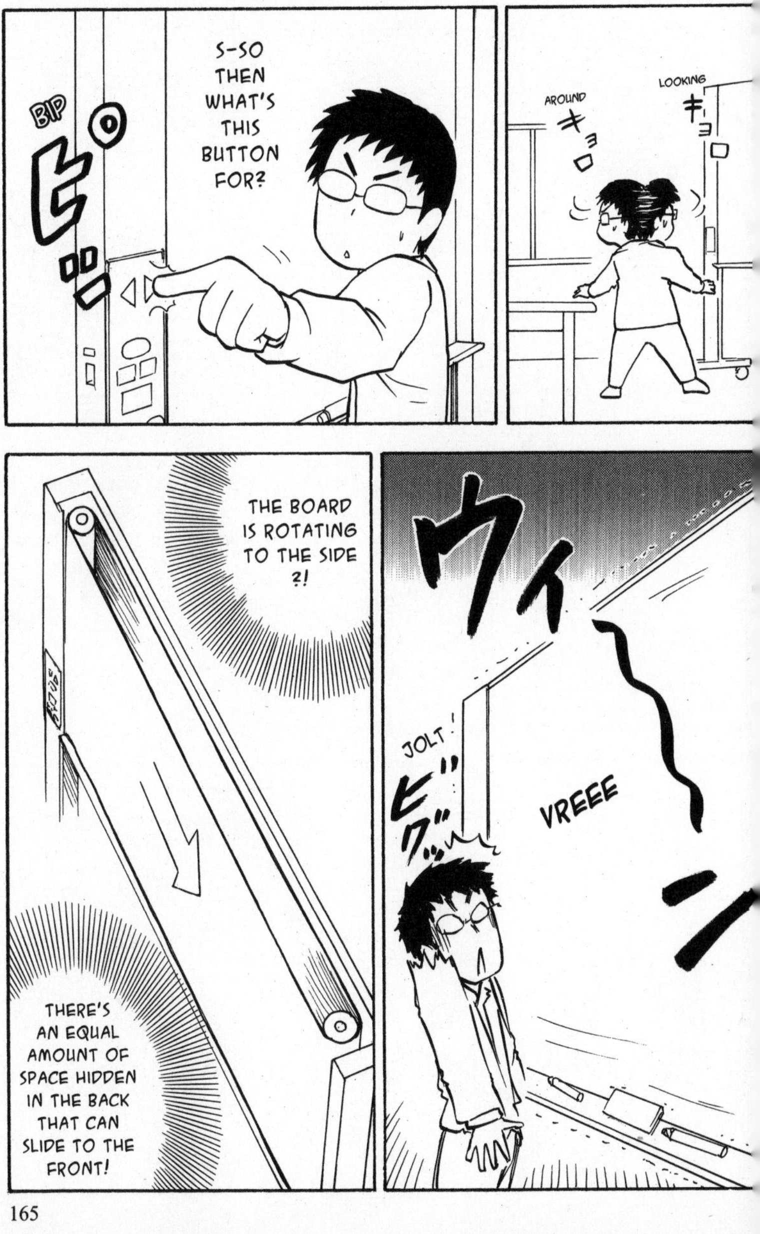
LOOKING
キョロ
AROUND
キョロ
S-SO THEN WHAT'S THIS BUTTON FOR?
BIP
ウイ〜ン
VREEE
JOLT!
ビクッ
THE BOARD IS ROTATING TO THE SIDE ?!
THERE'S AN EQUAL AMOUNT OF SPACE HIDDEN IN THE BACK THAT CAN SLIDE TO THE FRONT!

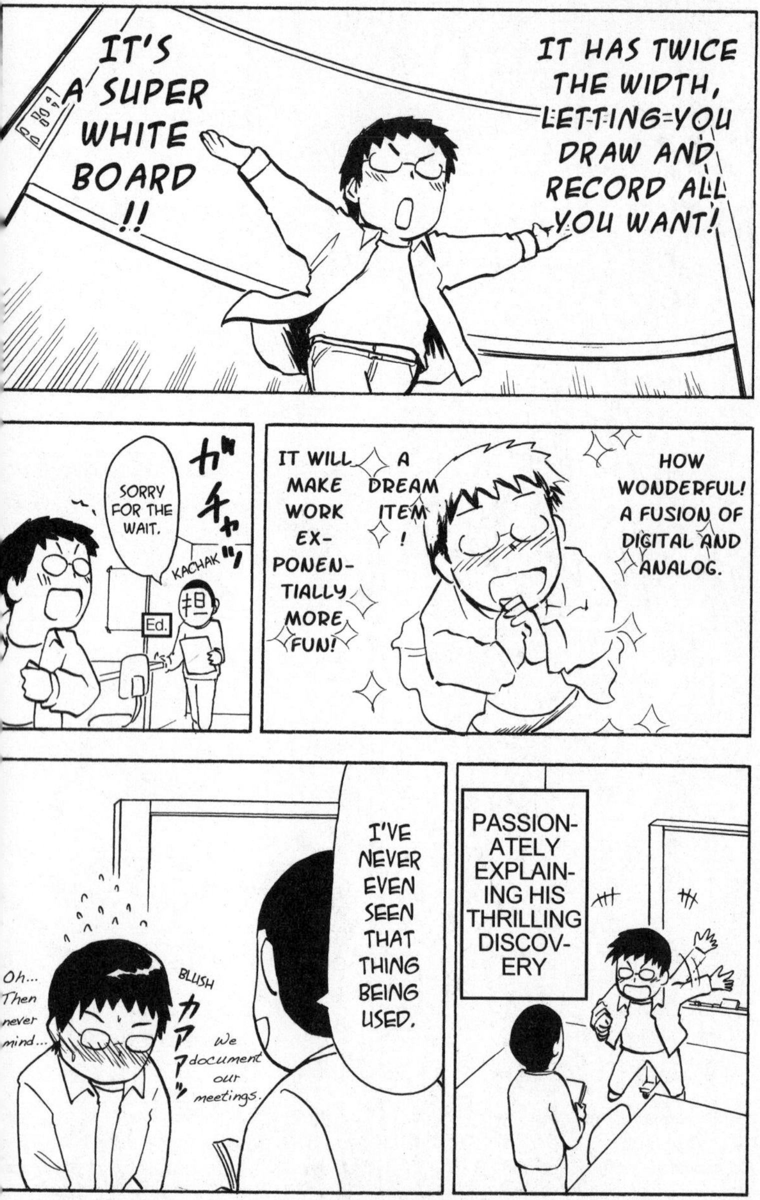
IT HAS TWICE THE WIDTH, LETTING YOU DRAW AND RECORD ALL YOU WANT!
IT'S A SUPER WHITE BOARD!!
HOW WONDERFUL! A FUSION OF DIGITAL AND ANALOG.
A DREAM ITEM!
IT WILL MAKE WORK EXPONENTIALLY MORE FUN!
ガチャッ
KACHAK
SORRY FOR THE WAIT.
Ed.
PASSIONATELY EXPLAINING HIS THRILLING DISCOVERY
I'VE NEVER EVEN SEEN THAT THING BEING USED.
We document our meetings.
BLUSH
カァァ
Oh... Then never mind...

My Neighbor Seki, volume 1
Tonari no Seki-kun

A Vertical Comics Edition

Translation: Yoshito Hinton
Production: Risa Cho
              Anthony Quintessenza

© Takuma Morishige 2011
Edited by MEDIA FACTORY
First published in Japan in 2011 by KADOKAWA CORPORATION, Tokyo.
English translation rights reserved by Vertical, Inc.
Under the license from KADOKAWA CORPORATION, Tokyo.

Translation provided by Vertical Comics, 2015
Published by Vertical Comics, an imprint of Vertical, Inc., New York

Originally published in Japanese as *Tonari no Seki-kun 1* by MEDIA FACTORY.
Tonari no Seki-kun first serialized in *Gekkan Comic Flapper*, MEDIA FACTORY, 2010-

This is a work of fiction.

ISBN: 978-1-939130-96-9

Manufactured in the United States of America

First Edition

Second Printing

Vertical, Inc.
451 Park Avenue South
7th Floor
New York, NY 10016
www.vertical-inc.com

Vertical books are distributed through Penguin-Random House Publisher Services.